Ascension

Ascension

The Story of a South Atlantic Island

DUFF HART-DAVIS

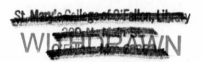
Doubleday & Company, Inc.
Garden City, New York
1973

ISBN: 0-385-00314-5
Library of Congress Catalog Card Number: 72-92218
Copyright © 1972 by Duff Hart-Davis
Printed in the United States of America
First Edition in the United States of America

In memory of
my mother

Ascension from the air. Devil's Riding School in the foreground, Dark Slope Crater behind, and (*top left*) part of the airfield runway

CONTENTS

ILLUSTRATIONS

ACKNOWLEDGEMENTS

My principal debt is to Cable and Wireless Ltd, who twice sent me to Ascension, and without whose help and encouragement this book could never have been written.

The company's association with the island is unique. Since 1922 Ascension has officially been a dependency of St Helena, which is a British colony. But for seventeen years before the Second World War, and for another ten after it, the Cable Company's staff, together with their St Helenian servants, were Ascension's sole inhabitants. To all intents and purposes the island belonged to the company: the staff ran all the services, including the farm, the hospital and the school, and the local manager acted as resident magistrate. AO (its Cable name) won – and still holds – a special place in the company's history and affections.

Many of the staff helped me with this book, but none more than John Packer. During three separate tours of duty on the island he has got to know it as well as anyone alive. In helping to build up the Ascension Historical Society and the museum in Fort Hayes, he performed a most valuable service. His handbook, *Ascension Island*, contains a mass of useful information, and as a guide to the local flora, fauna and geology he is unequalled, not least because his long legs take him up and down the volcanoes at a blistering pace.

I am also much indebted to Doug Rogers, the American founder of both the Ascension Historical Society and the Museum. His enthusiasm for the island is at least as great as that of any Cable man, and the tangible evidence of it which he created will be of enormous interest to everyone who works on Ascension in the future.

An equally generous donor of knowledge has been Peter Critchley, who for the past fifteen years has run the farm on Green Mountain, and together with his wife Grace has refreshed countless casual visitors (myself among them) with meals and drinks. If two nicer people exist, I do not know them; nor can I imagine anyone with a deeper interest in the island's history and development.

I should also like to thank the hundred-odd people who were kind enough to send me their memories of Ascension. Many wrote at length and entrusted me with precious documents and photographs. I am particularly grateful to Lt.-Col. W. R. P. Boultbee, H. Fowling, Miss Sybil Innes, Col. Dorothy Morgan (W.R.A.C. Rtd), Major C. B. Nichols, V. W. Oelrichs, E. E. Smith and Bernard Stonehouse. Gavin Fryer, an expert philatelist, put his own considerable research at my disposal, as did John Leonard, whose collection of Ascension stamps is unrivalled. George Campey, Head of Publicity at the British Broadcasting Corporation, and Maurice Turner, the B.B.C.'s Administrative Officer on Ascension in 1968, both went out of their way to help, as did Major A. J. Donald, R.M., The Royal Marines Historian. Skip Slape of Cable and Wireless showed immense skill and ingenuity in copying old photographs.

I am grateful to Major E. H. Ford for permission to include extracts from his book *The History and Postage Stamps of Ascension Island*, and to the British Ornithologists' Union for permission to reprint passages from *Ibis*.

Finally, I must record with keen regret the death of two people who were closely interested in the preparation of the book: George Joyce, who, as Public Relations Officer of Cable and Wireless, initiated the whole project; and Commander Jack Swayne, R.N. Rtd, who spent three years on the island as a boy and never lost his enthusiasm for it. It is sad that neither lived to see completed the task to which each gave such impetus.

DUFF HART-DAVIS
Henley-on-Thames,
February 1972

INTRODUCTION

Ascension is a small volcanic island that pokes up out of the South Atlantic almost exactly half-way between Africa and the bulge of South America. It lies just below the Equator – eight degrees south and longitude fourteen degrees west – and it would be intolerably hot were it not constantly swept by the trade winds that bluster across it from the south-east.

For me its fascination lies not in any great events that took place there, but in its physical strangeness. It has never played any major role in history, and probably never will; but the story of how the British struggled to make habitable what one writer called 'the abomination of desolation' is in many ways extraordinary.

Some people find Ascension hideous, and describe it accurately enough as a heap of clinker, slag and cinders on which the rakings from some gigantic boiler have recently been dumped. But for me, and for many of the people who have lived there, the island has a wonderful harsh beauty. Its landscape is fierce and exciting, almost surrealist in its starkness; and wherever you look you are instantly reminded that the place was created by fire.

The island is a peak on the Mid-Atlantic Ridge, a submarine chain of mountains running north-and-south down the middle of the ocean. The top of an exctinct volcano, it rises steeply some 10,000 feet from the surrounding ocean floor, and its highest point is 2817 feet above sea level. The part above the water is roughly the shape of an equilateral triangle, with sides about seven miles long, and the land area is only thirty-five square miles. For geologists it is a minor paradise, since to the eyes of an expert the extreme violence of the past is laid out with exceptional clarity. 'Ascension presents an ideal case of a complex volcanic island in its constructional stage,' wrote the American Reginald Daly:

> A half-dozen extensive lava-flows and a third or more of the sixty vents mapped look as if they had been formed not many centuries ago. So young are they that one cannot but be surprised when one learns that no hot spring or fumarole* is to be found. With marvellous directness most of the surface flows, cones and craters tell their story. . . .
>
> Green Mountain's base is a large basaltic cone truncated by a major explosion. Into the resulting caldera a trachyte dome arose, to a height of nearly 2400 feet above sea. . . . The eastern part of the dome and the trachyte flows alongside were blown away by a second explosion, forming a second caldera nearly a mile long and 1000 yards wide.

The final effect of these upheavals was to leave two quite different types of terrain. In the eastern half of the island the land rises steeply to the peak which for two hundred years at least has been called Green Mountain because, as you look from the sea, you can see that the summit and the slopes round it are the only parts of the island that support vegetation. The rock forming the Mountain is mainly white trachyte, and over thousands of years some of it has broken down to form rich soil.

But the western half of Ascension, which new arrivals always see first, is entirely different – a blackened, fire-blasted plain almost lunar in its desolation. From a wilderness of clinker, ash and tumbled lava rise nearly forty dead volcanic cones, grey, brown or bright rust-red. Their lee slopes are thickly coated with gritty black ash, and from their feet a wild jumble of rock stretches away to the sea. Even to the amateur, the different colours give clear indications of successive eruptions: the older rocks have weathered and oxidised to shades of ochre and rust, but the latest lava-flows

---

* Cavernous vent formed by hot gas escaping in the final stages of an eruption.

snake blackly round the flanks of the cinder hills looking as though they had only just solidified.

At close quarters the desolation of the low-ground is breathtaking, particularly in the north-west corner of the island. There the lava is piled high into petrified jungles, with black, basaltic rocks dumped in total confusion. Many are loose and tip when stood upon; many have razor edges that rip boots and shoes to shreds and lay your skin open if you stumble. No wheeled vehicle can move a yard through this chaos. Slow, careful scrambling – locally known as 'clinker-crawling' – is the only means of crossing it. There is no earth, no shade, no plant, no water. The sun blazes vertically down, and all that the rock gives back is a suffocating heat-haze.

Scattered about is an extraordinary variety of debris. Volcanic bombs lie everywhere, some weighing several hundredweight, some the size of peas, but all bearing in their shape and texture the marks of their violent passage through the air after they had been hurled from the throat of the Mountain. Sticks of lava, curled like the handles of enormous teapots or twisted like the branches of trees, ring with the hollow chime of porcelain when struck against other rock. These branch-like pieces gave rise to reports that the island had once been covered by a forest; now it is believed that the low ground is far too young ever to have supported any growth except a few shrubs and patches of grass.

Most of the island is thus still a lava desert, dusty, sterile, and baked by the equatorial sun; and it can scarcely have changed since the first settlers arrived in 1815. Up the Mountain, however, the story is entirely different.

So remote is Ascension – 800 miles from its nearest neighbour St Helena, 900 from the closest point of Africa, and 1400 from Brazil – that hardly any seeds reached it before men first settled there. James Cunninghame, who carried out the first botanical survey in the 1690s, found only four kinds of plant. The original fauna were equally scarce. Before the early sailors brought goats (and, inadvertently, rats), there were no animals at all except the sea turtles which came ashore to nest on the beaches, and the land crabs which at some stage in the distant past evolved from their sea-going relatives. Nor, with the possible exception of the rail, were there any land birds. The only other inhabitants were the sea birds, which nested in immense colonies among the rocks.

Into this natural vacuum the British Navy – principally the Royal Marines – brought a number of birds and animals and a huge variety of plants, as they wrestled from 1815 onwards to establish a farm round the upper slopes of Green Mountain. Most of the birds died, and so did many of the animals; but, in the absence of natural controls, those that did survive ran amok. Goats, rats, cats, pigs, oxen and donkeys all in turn got out of control and became a menace to agriculture.

The introduction of plants and trees was more successful, and the result today is astonishing. At all levels below 1000 feet, Ascension is still forbiddingly barren; throughout the year the temperature is in the high seventies and eighties, and the minute annual rainfall of five inches either evaporates instantly or disappears into the thirsty clinker and ash. But climb 2000 feet from sea level, up the western shoulder of the Mountain, and you enter another world. The air is ten degrees cooler; the gardens of the farm cottages blaze with exotic tropical flowers; Norfolk Island pines, eucalyptus, Cape yews, palms and evergreen oaks cast welcome shade; the huge flat fronds of banana trees sprout from the ravines; blackberries and wild raspberries ripen among thickets of ginger; cattle graze on the steep pastures, and a dense green mantle cloaks the precipitous sides of the Mountain.

All this is the legacy of the Marines. The creation of the farm, and the construction and maintenance of a reliable water-supply, absorbed an absurdly high proportion of the garrison's energies. The place was ostensibly an ordinary naval station, run like a ship under rigid discipline. Yet the official archives make it clear that the Royal Marines gave far more of their time to building and agriculture than to defence, and when one finds records of admirals sending home urgent requests for rooks, barn-owls and hedgehogs, one cannot help suspecting that some senior officers were seriously underemployed.

This is the real story of Ascension – how the Marines battled against a hostile environment and won a limited victory. 'Only the British would have bothered with such a place,' wrote the French naturalist Lesson in the early nineteenth century; and now, looking back with the hindsight of 150 years, one can hardly doubt that he was right.

Ascension is still extraordinary. Linked though it is with a global system of communications, it has no scheduled air services, no harbour, no hotel, no guest-house, no public transport. Nobody may land without permission, and in fact it is almost impossible for anyone to reach the island unless he or she has a job there.

The inhabitants pay no taxes, and the best Scotch whisky costs about 75 pence a bottle. No one – so far as I am aware – has ever challenged the island's claim to possess the worst golf course in the world. 'This is one of the strangest places on the face of the earth,' wrote a newly-arrived commandant in 1858, and he would say the same if he could go back and see Ascension today.

THE USELESS ISLAND

1501–1801

In the year 1501 King Manuel, wishing to send a fleet of four ships to India, entrusted the command of it to John da Nova, a noble from Galicia and a special magistrate of Lisbon, whose long experience of naval matters and honourable record with the ocean-going fleets had made him one of the most important men in the city.

As soon as the expedition was assembled, they sailed from the port of Belem on 5 March 1501. And on this voyage, as they passed eight degrees beyond the equator, towards the south, they found an island to which they gave the name Conception.

Thus, with tantalising brevity, the Portuguese historian Barros describes the discovery of the island now known as Ascension. Like all the other early authors who wrote about the period, his eyes were firmly focused on the distant lands in the East towards which the mariners were heading, and incidental discoveries made *en route* were evidently of little interest to him.

Nor, apparently, was the new-found island of much interest to Nova, for he sailed on and rounded the Cape of Good Hope early in July. A year later, as he returned towards home, he found another island which he named St Helena, and since this offered far better prospects for colonisation, he did not return to Ascension, which remained deserted.

It was not long, however, before another little armada found it. Having recently opened up the route to the East and established their empire in India, the Portuguese were mounting expeditions with astonishing energy: in the decade 1500–1509 no fewer than 138 ships set out to search for spices, gold and precious stones, and to do battle with the native rulers who were harassing the empire-builders.

Of these Indian princes, none was more perfidious than the Zamorin of Calicut. Nova was warned to look out for him in 1501, and by 1503 he had become so troublesome that King Manuel dispatched a special fleet to put him in his place. The commander of this punitive force was Alfonso d'Albuquerque, the great admiral who became Viceroy of India.

His fleet of four ships sailed from Lisbon in April 1503, and, fortunately, among the company was one Giovanni da Empoli, who went as agent for the Marchionni of Lisbon, and later described his voyage in some detail. His account gives a good idea of how uncertain an art navigation still was: Albuquerque evidently decided not to hug the coast of Africa all the way down, but to take the deep-sea route pioneered by Vasco da Gama in 1497; even so, he had only a vague idea of how to go about it:

> We left Lisbon on 6 April 1503, in the fleet of our commander-in-chief Señor Alfonso d'Albuquerque, made up of four ships – the *St James* of 600 tons, the *Holy Spirit* of 700 tons, the *St Christopher* of 300 tons and the *Catarina* of 200 tons.
>
> Having formed ourselves into a convoy, we began to navigate straight for Cape Verde. When we sighted the said Cape, the commander-in-chief consulted his pilots as to which course we should take to give ourselves the best run to the Cape of Good Hope. Normally, the direct route skirted the coast of Guinea, in Ethiopia, but since that land and coast were much affected by currents, reefs and shallows, as well as coinciding with the Equator, through the influence of which the wind cannot blow with any strength, we decided to avoid the coast and sail out into the open sea to a distance of 750 or 800 leagues.
>
> And so it was that, as we sailed in that direction, at the end of 28 days we sighted land – land which had already been dis-covered by others (according to unconfirmed claims) and called Ascension Island.
>
> We spent the whole night off shore in very stormy weather,

and came near to sinking because the wind was blowing across the island. The place was of no use as far as we could tell, and we left it behind us.

Sailing on, the ships crossed the South Atlantic twice, touching Brazil before heading south-eastwards again. At last on 6 July, ninety-one days out from Lisbon, and 'with the grace of God', they reached the Cape of Good Hope.

Tradition relates that it was Albuquerque who gave Ascension its name. Just as John da Nova first called the place Conception because he sighted it on the feast of the Annunciation, so Albuquerque is supposed to have renamed it Ascension because he reached it on Ascension day. Da Empoli's account, however, seems to scotch this view: the Italian text, though not entirely clear, definitely suggests that the island had already been named Ascension by someone else.

In any case, Albuquerque's ships sailed on without landing and it was left to some later Portuguese expedition to put goats ashore – a common move, made in order to provide fresh meat for any humans who might get stranded. There are brief records of visits in 1508 and 1512, and no doubt many others went unchronicled; but there is no mention or physical trace of the Portuguese ever having established a garrison, and the lack of fresh water within reach of the shore makes it most unlikely that they ever did so. The only permanent mark left by the earliest visitors was a track which they cleared from North East Bay – one of the few sheltered landing places – up over the shoulder of Green Mountain. Why they bothered to make the ascent is not clear: perhaps it was to fetch water from the spring 2400 feet up in Breakneck Valley, or perhaps simply to get a good view of the sea all round the island.

Yet the Portuguese by no means forgot their new possession, for on 25 August 1539 King John III gave Ascension its *foral*, or charter, thereby officially recognising it as part of the empire. But for nearly three hundred years the island remained uninhabited except by the goats, the land crabs, the myriad sea birds and the giant green turtles which came seasonally to lay their eggs in the hot sand of the beaches. At some stage black ships' rats got ashore – perhaps from the Portuguese vessels, perhaps from later wrecks; whatever their origin, they multiplied horribly, and by the early eighteenth century infested the island in swarms.

Human visitors were at first exceedingly rare. Among the earliest was the Dutch traveller Jan van Linschoten, who arrived in May 1589 on his way home from the East. One of the convoy's ships was in distress and leaking so badly that the men wanted the officers to:

... lay the goods on land, in the Iland of Ascension, and there leave it with good watch and necessaries, and so sayle with the emptie shippe to Portingall: and there procure some other shippe to fetch the goods, thinking it was sufficient to have it well watched and kept there, for that there commeth not a shippe in twentie yeares into that Iland, because there is nothing in it to be had.

The officers, however, said that it was too dangerous to take the stricken ship inshore; instead, they reinforced its pumps with more borrowed from the other ships, and the convoy limped home 'with great miserie and labour', the 'Admirall and all the Gentlemen that were in the shippe' taking turns to keep the pumps going day and night. Van Linschoten's account makes it clear that he did not go ashore: hearsay enabled him to write: 'There is not any fresh water in the Iland, nor one greene leaf or branch.' His pessimistic view is not surprising: if the clouds were down on the top of Green Mountain, he would have seen nothing but rock and cinders.

Even without landing, he could not miss the birds. 'By reason of the great quantitie of Fishes round the island,' he wrote,

ther are so many birds in it yt. it is strange, and they are of the bignesse of young Geese, & came by thousands flying about our ships, crying and making great noyse, and ranne up and down in the shippe, some leaping and sitting on our shoulders and armes, not once fearing us so that wee tooke many of them, and

wrung of their neckes, but they are not good to eate, because
they taste morish.* I thinke the cause they are so tame is,
because they see but few men. . . .

The shape and nature of the island ensured that almost all
visitors landed on its western side. Formidable ramparts of lava
guard the eastern and southern coasts, and the pounding waves,
driven day-in, day-out by the trade winds, make landing by boat
impossible anywhere but in a few tiny coves. The western shore,
however, is sheltered from the prevailing wind, and the lava fields
are broken by beaches of fine white sand.

In 1656 the Cornishman Peter Mundy, returning in the *Alleppo
Merchant* from his third voyage to India, echoed Van Linschoten
in describing the two features of Ascension which most struck all
who saw the island: the utter desolation of its surface, and the huge
population of sea birds. Landing on 8 June on the north-west
coast, Mundy saw:

a multitude of rarreg,† craggy, sharpe pointed hard rocks for
miles along the shoare and up toward the land, appearing
white with the dung of sea foule, of which there were innumerable of severall kinds. The most desolate barren [land] (and like a
land thatt God has cursed) thatt ever my eies beeheld. . . . I
conceave the whole world affoards nott such another peece of
ground; most partt of the collour of burnt bricke, reddish, the
substance stones, somewhatt like pumice stones; the rest like
cinders and burnt earth.

The birds Mundy found included 'big russett gannetts' which
would light on the ship's yards 'and suffer themselves to be taken
by hand like boobees'. Evidently the name 'booby', which has
clung to the *Sula* family ever since, originated in the birds' sadly
foolish habit of allowing themselves to be caught so easily.

* Morish = fishy
† Rarreg = ragged.

Remarking on Ascension's isolation, Mundy placed it 'aboutt 300 leagues from the coast of Guinnea and 169 leagues from the iland of St Matheo, the nearest land to itt'. This is one of several references to St Matthew, an imaginary island which appeared on maps early in the sixteenth century and obstinately remained on them until the nineteenth. For something that never existed, its life was remarkably long. Captain Cook was among those who hunted for it in vain: returning from his second voyage of discovery in 1775, he reached Ascension in May, spent five days there, and set off in search. 'I had a great desire to visit the island of St Matthew to settle the situation,' he later wrote in his journal. 'But as I found the winds would not allow me to fetch it, I sailed for the island of Fernando de Noronha on the coast of Brazil.'

St Matthew's situation remained permanently unsettled; but the island lived on until finally demolished by a withering note from Edward Heawood in the issue of *Nature* for 22 September 1928:

> The recurrence on a large number of maps, for at least two centuries, of the supposed island of St Matthew. . . . is a striking example of the vitality of error when once established.

By Mundy's day – the middle of the seventeenth century – Ascension was already famous among sailors for its turtles, which provided ships of all nations with the fresh meat essential for the prevention of scurvy. Mundy himself gave an accurate description of the sea monsters, recording how easy the female was to capture when she lumbered up on to the beach to lay her eggs: then as now, all a would-be captor had to do was to turn her on her back – '*situation*', as a later French traveller aptly remarked, '*qu'elle ne peut plus changer*'.

Mundy was much taken with the turtles' white, soft-shelled eggs:

> They will rebound half yard from the decke being throwne against itt (butt not to hard). Make butt a print with your

finger in one of them, itt is a pastime to gett itt outt againe, for you no sooner putt itt outt in one place butt itt appeares in another.

Although Mundy arrived in early June, at the end of the turtle season, his crew took five aboard, and he described them as 'good meatt, good refreshing'.

The early sailors credited turtle-meat with sweeping therapeutic powers – far more than the mere ability to cure scurvy. John Ovington, who visited Ascension in 1691, remarked that some turtles weighed as much as four or five hundredweight:

On these the hungry Mariners feed deliciously for the space of ten or 15 Days sometimes together. They esteem it no less nourishing and healthful than delightful, nor need they incur the danger of any Surfeit by the plenty of this dainty Food; but Chronical Distempers and inveterate Diseases have by this form of Diet been often abated; and those unwelcome Guests, by a constant use of the Food, have been forced to withdraw from their old accustomed Habitations. The Purgative quality in which it ends carries away the Disease with it, and repairs the Body to its former strength and Constitution.

Ovington was fascinated by the turtles, and not a little sorry for them: The sailors, he said,

... turn them by surprisal upon their Backs, which is a posture they are utterly unable to recover from, and are thereby frustrated of all Defence or Escape, and are a ready Prey to any that resolves to seize them. When the sensible Creatures find themselves in this desperate Posture, by which they know themselves to be in a lost and hopeless state, they then begin to lament their Condition in many heavy Sighs, and mournful Groans, and shed abundance of water from their Eyes, in hopes, if possible, to secure their Safety by their Tears, and Mollifie the cruel Assaults upon their Lives.

Ovington's observations and description were accurate enough, but his interpretation of the turtles' behaviour was entirely fanciful: they do indeed give heavy sighs, but this is merely their manner of breathing; and they do shed tears, but this again is a straightforward natural process, designed to clear their eyes of sand.

By 1673, according to the Dutch traveller John Struys, the English were visiting Ascension frequently, not only to stock up with turtle-meat, but also to use the island as a rendezvous and as an open prison for malefactors. He himself narrowly escaped being abandoned there with three hundred of his countrymen. Captured on St Helena by the English, who had just seized the island from the Dutch, he and his companions were put on northbound British ships. The Englishmen's idea, he says, was to dump the prisoners on Ascension, until one of their own ships should pass that way and rescue them; but when they could find no fresh water whatever on the island, they relented, and took the Dutchmen on to England where they set them free.

Others were not so lucky. In the 1930s a human skull was discovered near the Devil's Riding School, in the middle of the island; but it is impossible to tell how many more castaways met their end in the baking deserts of lava.

Well before the end of the seventeenth century, Ascension had become widely known as a sailors' post office. The Dominican missionary Friar Domingo Navarrete, who called in January 1673, recorded how three Frenchmen from his party had landed and

... found Letters ashore of French and English, who had pass'd by there the Year before; those that sail this way are so curious, as to write Letters, put them into Bottles of thick Glass, and leave them in a safe place but visible, by which the next Comers have intelligence who is gone by, and what Voyage, Weather and Delays they had.

Twenty years later, in 1693, Robert Everard reported a similar procedure:

When we anchored, our captain went ashore in the pinnace to see if there was a letter left in a bottle in a hole in a rock near the landing-place, which every ship that comes to that place leaves there, the island being uninhabited: We took the bottle out of the hole and found thereby that the *Kemthorne* was the last ship that was there.

Before they left, the captain sent ashore a letter of his own, also in a bottle, 'to be put in the same place where the other was taken out'.

Eighty years later, the practice was exactly the same. Louis de Bougainville, captain of *La Boudeuse*, called in February 1769:

In the afternoon the bottle was brought to me which contains the paper whereon the ships of every nation generally write their name, when they touch at Ascension Island. This bottle is deposited in a cavity of the rocks of this bay, where it is equally sheltered from rain and the spray of the sea. In it I found written the *Swallow*, that English ship which Captain Carteret commanded, and which I was desirous of joining. He arrived here on the 31st of January, and set sail again on the first of February; thus we had already gained six days upon him, after leaving the Cape of Good Hope. I inscribed the *Boudeuse*, and sent back the bottle.

These accounts, together with other similar ones, confirm what the physical nature of the island strongly suggests – that the traditional site of 'Letterbox', and the present Bottle Point, are both misplaced. They form the south-easternmost tip of the whole island: heavy seas pound ceaselessly on 400-foot lava cliffs, and to land anywhere in the area is out of the question. The real letter-box was clearly in one of the sheltered bays on the west coast.

In 1693, some men in Everard's party, finding dead turtles and signs of fire, supposed that there might be other sailors on the island.

Accordingly they took a survey from the top of a hill, where they found a cross, and named it Cross Hill; so looking, but seeing nothing like a ship or man, they returned on board again.

The original purpose of the cross remains obscure: it may have marked a grave, but more likely it was put up as a beacon. Either way, Cross Hill (or sometimes Crucifix Hill) – a symmetrical rust-red ash cone nearly 900 feet high – became the best-known landmark on the west coast, and has retained its name ever since.

Some eight years after Everard's visit, Captain William Dampier, a former pirate turned Royal Naval explorer and hydrographer, was on his way home from an official voyage of discovery to New Holland (Australia) when his ship the *Roebuck* sprang a leak just as he reached Ascension on 22 February 1701. A whole day's pumping failed to lower the water level, and at five in the morning of the 23rd they sailed into what Dampier called 'the Bay'. Since he does not mention Cross Hill (which would have been right in front of him if he had come to the usual anchorage), I believe it must have been South West Bay that he entered.

He entrusted the task of stopping the leak to the carpenter's mate – 'the only Person in the Ship that understood any Thing of Carpenters-work' – but not even this intrepid fellow could save the vessel. In order to reach the leak, he suggested the desperate step of cutting away the planks and timbers round it. Dampier, although alarmed by the proposal, told him to go ahead. 'I went down again to see it,' he wrote,

> ... and found the Water to come in very violently. I told him I had never known any such thing as cutting Timbers to stop Leaks; but if They who ought to be the best Judges in such Cases, thought they could do any Good, I bid them use their utmost Care and Diligence, promising the Carpenter's Mate that I would always be a Friend to him if he could and would stop it.

In an effort to staunch the flow, Dampier had a variety of bungs stuffed into the hole, including oakum, some pieces of beef, and his own bedclothes – but all to no avail. The water kept pouring in.

Still the Carpenter's Mate was not downhearted, and Dampier goes on:

> I asked the Carpenter's Mate what he thought of it; He said 'Fear not; for by 10 a clock at Night I'll engage to stop the Leak.' I went from him with a heavy Heart; but putting a good Countenence on the Matter, encouraged my Men, who pumped and bailed very briskly; and when I saw Occasion, I gave them some Drams to comfort them. About 11 a clock at Night, the Boatswain came to me, and told me, that the Leak still encreased; and that the Plank was so rotten it broke away like Dirt; and that now it was impossible to save the Ship.

They toiled all night, and the next day sailed in as close as they could; then they carried a small anchor ashore and warped the ship in until she was in only three and a half fathoms. 'Where having fastened her,' Dampier continued,

> ... I made a Raft to carry the Men's Chests and bedding ashore; and, before 8 at Night, most of them, were ashore. I had sent ashore a Puncheon, and a 36 Gallon Cask of Water, with one Bag of Rice for our common use: But great Part of it was stolen away, before I came ashore; and many of my Books and Papers lost.
>
> On the 26th following, we, to our great Comfort, found a Spring of Fresh Water, about 8 miles from our Tents, beyond a very high Mountain, which we must pass over: So that now we were, by God's Providence, in a Condition of subsisting some Time, having plenty of very good Turtle by our Tents, and Water for the fetching.

Tradition has it that they found water by following a goat. Perhaps they did; or perhaps they followed a goat track. Dampier himself makes no mention of it, but the place at which they are supposed to have found the water has been known ever since as Dampier's Springs, or Dampier's Drip, 'drip' being the more accurate description of the site in a precipitous ravine where water oozes from the rock walls.

For anyone who knows Ascension, it is fascinating to try and plot Dampier's movements about the island. Yet it is also futile, for his own account is full of obvious errors. To take only one: he cannot have walked eight miles from the beach to the spring. Eight miles is too big a distance for Ascension: from any of the beaches, it would bring you into the sea on the other side of the island.

Nevertheless, it is clear that Dampier's Drip is wrongly named, for the description he gave of the watering-place that saved them in no way fits it. Quite apart from the distance being wrong, he says that the spring was 'beyond a very high Mountain, which we must pass over'. Then he says that it was 'a very fine Spring on the South-East side of the high Mountain, about half a mile from its Top', and finally, that 'the continual Fogs make it so cold here that it is very unwholesome living by the Water'.

All these descriptions apply perfectly to the site of the spring in Breakneck Valley which later became the main source of the island's water supply. This does face south-east, and is much beset by fog (in fact low cloud gathering round the peak of Green Mountain). To reach it you do have to scale a 2400 foot ridge. Finally, there still exists what could reasonably be called a fine spring.

Dampier's, by contrast, faces west, is rarely if ever fog-bound, is not beyond any high hill to someone approaching from the west coast, and has never (as far as one can tell) had any more water than the celebrated drips.

In any case, Dampier himself survived, and a place on the island still bears his name. Living on turtles, land crabs, sea birds and goats, the castaways seem to have been quite comfortable. One day during their exploration of the Mountain they found a 'shrubby tree' with an anchor and cable and the date '1642' carved on it. Who the carver was, whether he lived or died, no one will ever know.

About a week after being wrecked, Dampier's party saw two

ships approaching in the evening, but by next morning they had disappeared over the horizon. On 2 April eleven sails appeared to windward, but these too went past.

Then on the 3rd three British men-of-war sailed up, together with the *Canterbury*, an East Indiaman, and anchored in the bay. Dampier and thirty-five of his men went on board H.M.S. *Anglesey*, and the rest of the party was split between the other ships. They loitered for four days (perhaps catching turtles), but then on 9 April they sailed for home.

Dampier was no doubt a rogue, but his narratives give the impression that he was an engaging one. Among the legends which he left behind on the island is one of buried treasure; needless to say, he mentioned no such thing himself, but this omission has not stopped hundreds of latter-day Ascensionites searching for it.

A generation after Dampier and his men had safely sailed away, a lone Dutch sailor was put ashore on the island as a punishment for sodomy. Repulsive as his crime was in the eyes of his shipmates, the suffering with which he paid for it was surely more terrible than even they could have intended. It is impossible to be sure exactly how many months passed before thirst and hunger killed him; but the diary he kept gives an appalling picture of the agony, both physical and mental, that he had to endure. The diary itself was found in January 1726 by sailors of the *Compton* in the author's tent on the beach, alongside his own remains. The extracts quoted here are from the translation first published in the *Harleian Miscellany* of 1746.

The first entry is dated 5 May (presumably of 1725). 'By order of the Commodore and captains of the Dutch fleet, I was set on shore of the Island of Ascension, which gave me a great deal of dissatisfaction.' The author listed his possessions as a cask of water, two buckets and 'an old frying pan etc'. Later references show he had a musket (but no powder or shot), a tea-kettle, a tinder-box, a razor, a bible and various seeds.

He pitched his tent by a rock on the beach and kept a constant lookout for passing ships. But by the next day he was already half wishing that an accident might put an end to him.

I walked very melancholy along the Strand, praying to God Almighty to put a period to my days, or help me out of this desolate island.

He killed three boobies, skinned and salted them, and put them to dry in the sun. His useless gun he used as a flagpole, tying a white cloth to it, and he spent most of his time collecting driftwood for his fire and exploring the island in an increasingly desperate search for water. On 12 May he wrote: 'I kept constantly walking about the island, that being all my hopes.'

That same day he planted onions, peas and calavances (chick peas) in the ground by his tent 'to see if they would produce any more, for as it was I could not afford water to boil them'. He lived on boiled rice, sea-birds' eggs and the fat of a turtle which he bludgeoned to death with the butt of his rifle.

The decline of his morale is clearly reflected in the diminishing size and frequency of the entries. At first he wrote several sentences every day, but by 16 May he could only manage: 'I looked out, as the day past; caught no boobies.' Then he began to lump several days together:

June 1st to 4th. It would be needless to write how often my eyes are cast on the sea, to look for ships; and every little atom in the sky I took for a sail.

By 8 June his water supply was down to two quarts, 'and that so thick as obliged me to strain it through a handkerchief'. He began digging wells and walked frantically all over the island until at last:

... God of his great bounty led me to a place where some water run out of a hollow place in a rock.

The immediate crisis resolved, he drank and drank until he thought he would burst, and then began a system of carrying water in his two wooden buckets from the spring to his tent. But guilt and fear, fostered by malnutrition, soon began to prey on him and induce delusions. On 12 June he wrote: 'I often think I am possessed with things I really want, but when I come to search find it only a shadow.' And then on the 16th:

> In the night I was surprised by a noise round my tent of cursing and swearing, and the most blasphemous conversations that I ever heard. I did nothing but offer my prayers to the Almighty to protect me in this miserable circumstance; but my fright rendered me in a very bad condition of praying, I trembling to that degree, that I could not compose my thoughts; and any body would have believed that the Devil himself had moved his quarters and was coming to keep Hell on Ascension. I was certain that there was no human creature on the island but myself; having not seen the footsteps of any man but my own; and so much libidinous talk was impossible to be expressed by any body but devils.

The wretched man prayed for forgiveness, but in the morning the air was still full of shrieks, and a voice crying 'Bouger'. Pathetic confessions for having used 'my fellow creature to satisfy my lust whom the Almighty Creator had ordained another sex for' failed to lay the ghosts. He began to dread the dark, and on the night of 20 June was 'prodigiously perplexed with spirits', being 'tumbled up and down' in his tent until his 'flesh was like a Mummy'.

By the 22nd he was so weak that it took him nearly all day to fetch water. His shoes, and feet, had been cut to ribbons by the lava, and on the 27th he moved his bedding and a few possessions to a hollow rock near the spring. But disaster soon followed, for two day later the water dried up.

On 2 July, searching for more still higher up the mountain, he sighted two herds of goats and pursued them, though he was far too slow to catch up. The next day he saw 'several hundred' goats, but again they easily eluded him. On the 9th the spirits returned to torment him:

> As I walked upon the strand, I heard again a very dismal noise

of cursing and swearing in my own language. During the time of this noise I never in my life saw so many fowls together, they looking like a cloud, and intercepting between me and the sky, deprived me of some of its light.

For this visitation at least there is a rational explanation. Clearly the birds were wideawake or sooty terns, which still frequent Ascension in enormous numbers, and do indeed darken the sky with their dense flocks. It is not hard to imagine how fiendish their shrill, raucous clamour must have sounded to someone half-deranged by fear, exhaustion and thirst.

The entries in the diary become more and more hopeless.

The 22nd, 23rd, 24th, 25th, 26th, 27th, 28th, 29th, 30th and 31st, my heart is so full that my pen cannot utter it. . . . August 1st, 2nd and 3rd, I walked out with my bucket in my hand. . . . 11th. Heard a terrible noise, as though there had been a hundred copper smiths at work.

On 18th August, during his perpetual search for water, dusk caught him on the wrong side of the island, and he was forced to spend the night between two rocks, where 'there was such a quantity of rats there that I thought they would have eat me'.

He never found water again. By 21 August he was 'so prodigious dry, that I was forced to make water in my scoop and drink it'. The next day he killed a turtle on the beach and drank nearly a gallon of its blood. This kept him alive, but by the 30th 'I was in such agony with thirst that it is impossible for any body to express it'.

At this point the dates become confused. After 30 August he reverts to 1 August, for which there is the most ghastly entry of all:

I was walking, or more properly speaking, crawling on the sand, for I could not walk three steps together. I saw a living turtle. I was not able to carry my bucket, but cut off his head with my razor, and lay all along and sucked his blood as it run out; and afterwards got my hand into him, and got out the bladder, which I carried home with me, and put the water into my kettle. . . .

7th September. I cannot live long; and I hope the Lord will have mercy on my soul.

The 8th, drank my own urine and ate raw flesh.

The 9th, 10th and 11th, I am so much decayed that I am a perfect skeleton; and cannot write the particulars, my hand shakes so.

The 12th, 13th, 14th, 15th, 16th and 17th, lived as before.

The 18th, 19th, 20th, 21st, 22nd, 23rd, 24th, 25th, 26th, 27th, 28th, 29th, 30th October the 1st, 2nd, 3rd, 4th, 5th and 6th, all as before.

The 7th, my wood is all gone, so that I am forced to eat raw flesh and salted fowls. I cannot live long; and I hope the Lord will have mercy on my soul. The 8th drank my own urine and ate raw flesh.

The 9th, 10th, 11th, 12th, 13th and 14th, all as before.

There the diary ends. The editors of the *Harleian Miscellany* remarked that 'it carries all the possible marks of sincerity'. I am not sure that I entirely agree. The story contains many horribly realistic details; but would a dying man have been able to write as much as that down? And what did he write *with*? One modern author claims to have seen the original diary in the British Museum, but I myself have been unable to find it. Is it altogether too sceptical to suppose that the castaway fabricated the entire journal and left it behind, when he was rescued, in the hope of eventually disconcerting the people who had marooned him? Certainly the journal contains one anomaly that is hard to explain: turtles frequent Ascension only during a definite season, from December to June, and it seems most unlikely that there could have been 'plenty' of them round the island, as the Dutchman says, during August and September. A possible explanation is that the dates of the diary are even more confused than they seem, and that the dying man (if he *was* dying) did not survive for nearly as many weeks as he thought.

Whatever eventually happened to him, one cannot help feeling that the Dutchman was exceedingly unfortunate in that no ship visited the island during the weeks that he survived. The British were already frequenting the island, and by 1754, when the Abbé de la Caille went there, it had become a normal port-of-call for the French on their way home from India – so much so that one of the bays in the north-west corner of the island was known as 'Frenchman's Bay'.

The Abbé was much struck by Ascension's colour and asperity. 'It is covered,' he wrote, 'with red earth resembling ground-up brick or burnt clay. ... The sight of the hill and the island as a whole presents the eyes with a hideous spectacle capable of inspiring horror.' He was fascinated by the birds, not least the boobies, which he called '*les fous*', and he concluded: 'Small and deserted though the Island of Ascension is, it could occupy a naturalist for a long time, and furnish a philosopher with much food for thought.'

Few of the early visitors can have been as energetic as Peter Osbeck, a Swedish priest who arrived in 1752 on his way home from China. Goaded, no doubt, by professional curiosity, and complaining vigorously about the heat, he scrambled to the top of Cross Hill to inspect the crucifixes:

As soon as we got on shore I went to a conic mountain a good way off the place where we landed. It was steep, and of difficult access, because with each step the sand and stones rolled down; the heat increased, and I was forced to rest several times. ... Neither on the sides, nor at the top, did I meet with one single plant; on the summit, where the air was very cool, stood a pole three fathoms long, which was provided with the necessary ropes for hoisting a flag. From the pole hung two crosses, the lower of which was wooden, and had the letters I.N.R.I. carved on it. Scarce a fathom above the wooden cross was a brazen one, at the bottom of which we could see 1748, the 15th of November; and higher up a *French* inscription, which could not be read, it being too high. On the pole and the wooden cross several dates of years, and several names, were carved.

Even though he remarked that he had never seen 'a more disagreeable place in all the world than this island', Osbeck seems to have explored it thoroughly, and he gained first-hand experience of the turtles (or 'tortoises', as he sometimes called them), the rats and the goats. His own crew turned thirty-one turtles the first night they were at anchor, and Osbeck described the procedure thus:

The sailors lurk at night on the shore; and when a tortoise is crept up they turn it upon its back with hooks (or, if they can, with their hands alone). In the latter case, they must take care of the animal's mouth, for it bites off a finger with ease; a misfortune which one of our sailors experienced this time.

The rats were as bold as ever:

Sailors that have been here before relate, that though they hung up their bags of meat on upright poles, they were by no means safe from these vermin; nay, that when people sat down to meals, they came out as if they demanded a share of the victuals with them.

The goats, he reported, had increased 'pretty well':

I saw a flock or two which were very shy, yet they might be caught by any one on foot, for they do not run very fast. One of them was taken and brought to our ship. It was of the least sort, and very lean. We observed immediately that it was not used to water; for tho' it drank some, it immediately ran through it, as if the water had been poured through an inclined tube. It was killed, but its flesh was liked but by few.

Together with all his facts, Osbeck reported one scrap of legend which perhaps was a distorted echo of the story of the marooned Dutchman. Near the landing place in Cross Bay, he wrote, were two grottoes, or natural caves:

> In that which was next the shore were several French and English letters, of last year, as advices to new-comers: the upper one is said to have been the habitation of an English supercargo, who some years ago was left here as a punishment for a detestable crime, with some victuals, and an ax, to kill tortoises, which he was forced to roast by the heat of the sun on the mountains. It is likewise related that another nation afterwards helped him away.

Twenty years after Osbeck's visit, Captain Cook and his companions found Ascension just as forbidding. Sated as they were with the wonders of the South Seas, they can hardly be blamed for their critical reaction. 'The dreariness of this island surpassed all the horrors of Easter Island and Tierra del Fuego, even without the assistance of snow,' wrote George Forster, Cook's naturalist and draughtsman, of their visit in 1775. 'It was a ruinous heap of rocks.'

A reputation for piracy has always been one of Ascension's more glamorous features, and Cook's own journal suggests that in his day it may have been partially justified; even if the island was not being exactly used as a pirates' lair, some nefarious activity was taking place there.

Cook, on board the *Resolution*, left St Helena in company with an East Indiaman, the *Dutton*, which

> ... was ordered to steer NWBW or NW by Compass, in order to avoid falling in with Ascension, at which isle it was said an illicit trade had been carried on between the officers of the Companies Ships and some Vessels from North America, who of late years have frequented the isle on pretence on fishing for Whales or Catching Turtle, when their real design was to await the coming of India Ships.

In order to put a stop to this trade, so pernicious to the

Company and commerce in general, the Company sent out orders to St Helena to order all their homeward bound ships to steer the Course above mentioned till they are to the northward of Ascension, thinking that this Course would carry them clear of these Smuglers.

We kept Company with the *Dutton* till Wednesday 24th, when having put a Packet on board her for the Admiralty containing some of the Officers Journals, we parted company, she continuing her Course to the west and we steered for Ascension, where it was necessary for me to touch to take in Turtle for the refreshment of my people, as the salt Provisions they had to eat was what had been in the Ship the voyage.

It was not long before Cook's suspicions were borne out:

While we lay in the road a Sloope of about 70 tons burdthen came to an Anchor by us, she belonged to new York, which place she left in Febry and had been to the coast of Guiney with a Cargo of goods and was come here to take in Turtle to carry to Barbadoes. This was the story the Master, whose name was Greves, was pleased to tell and which may in part be true, but I believe the Chief view of His coming here was the expectation of meeting with some of the India Ships.

Apart from the smugglers, Cook found a tremendous amount of fish all round the island, and on land an abundance of goats and 'Aquatick birds'. Ascension's surface he described as

... composed of barren Hills and Vallies, on the most of which not a shrub or plant is to be found for several miles, and where we see nothing but stones and Sand, or rather Slags and Ashes, an indupitable sign that the isle at some remote time has been destroyed by a Volcano, which has thrown up vast heaps of stones and even hills. Between these heaps of stones, we find a smooth even surface, composed of Ashes and sand and very good travelling upon it, but one may as easy walk over broken glass bottles as over the stones, if the foot deceives you you are sure to get cut or lamed, as happened to some of our people.

Cook's own explorations were limited, and he drew many of his details about the island from Captain Greves, 'who seemed to be a sencible intelligent man'. Among them was the fact that up on Green Mountain there were patches of good, cultivable land, and that some people had already 'been at the trouble of sowing Turnips and other useful vegetables'.

One of Cook's officers, sent to explore the north-east coast, discovered the wreck of a ship of about 150 tons, which had been partly burnt. Probably, wrote the naturalist Forster, it had been:

> . . . run on shore by the people, in order to save their lives. The distressful situation to which such a set of men must have been reduced, in this barren island, drew an expression of pity even from the sailors. But their misfortune was now become our advantage; for our provision of fuel being very low, Captain Cook sent his boats to take in sufficient quantity of timbers from this wreck.

Surprisingly few ships' bones litter Ascension today. Partly this is because the coast plunges steeply into the water, and the violent undertow sucks the rocks and beaches clean; and partly it is because generations of Marines, short of timber on a treeless island, scoured the coast time and again for anything that they could use. But beside the few ships that are recorded, many more must have foundered on the desolate volcanic shores.

One lucky man was Hugh Graham, an American whose ship was wrecked on Ascension in 1799. History does not tell how many of the crew were drowned, or how long the survivors spent on the island. But on 8 September Sir Thomas Williams, captain of H.M.S. *Endymion*, wrote in his log:

> At 3 came to in a bay on the SW side of the island. Sent the boats on shore. Found here 15 seamen, part of the crew of an

American ship that had been wrecked here – brought them on board.

But the success of the rescue was marred by another small tragedy. The log goes on:

John Ruby, a seaman that went in one of the boats, was missing. At daylight sent a boat on shore for the seamen left behind. Mustered the ship's company. At 11 the boat returned without having found the man. Filled and made all sail.

Evidently this story, or some similar one, spread among sailors generally, for between then and the time the island was occupied in 1815, it became common practice for passing ships to fire a cannon into the rocks to rouse up any castaway who might be languishing there. James Holman, who began his career in the Navy but went blind at the age of twenty-five and became an astonishingly adventurous traveller, saw this happen while he was still a professional sailor in 1801. 'We passed so near this island,' he wrote, 'that we sent a 24-pound shot among the hills, and saw it scatter the dust around the spot where it fell, but we did not send a boat on shore, for we knew it was then uninhabited.'

The peace of Ascension was soon to be shattered permanently. Far to the north in Europe Napoleon was already First Consul of France, and well launched down the long road that was to end with his exile on St Helena.

H.M.S. *ASCENSION*

1815–16

The decision to occupy Ascension was taken not by the Government in London but by Rear-Admiral Sir George Cockburn, who escorted Napoleon to St Helena in his flagship the *Northumberland* and arrived there with him on 13 October 1815. A brilliant and forceful officer, Cockburn had become an admiral at the age of forty-three; and now that he was in sole charge of the arrangements for Napoleon's security, he did not hesitate to carry out any measure that seemed necessary.

Reporting his safe arrival to the Admiralty on the 22nd, he hoped that the orders he had recently given for the occupation of Ascension would meet with their Lordships' approval. 'The taking possession of Ascension,' he wrote,

> ... is a measure which did not strike me while in England, but which has since appeared to me necessary, not only to give us a stronger right to examine any vessels arriving there, and to take from them any persons who may have escaped from hence, but more particularly to prevent America or any other nation from planting themselves there as upon a hitherto unoccupied and unowned island ... for the purpose of favouring sooner or later the escape from hence of General Buonaparte or any other persons unwillingly detained here.

Thus young Captain James White, Commander of H.M. Sloop *Peruvian*, found himself handed two sets of orders. One was marked 'Secret' and sealed; the other instructed him to sail away from St Helena to the north-east, taking with him the sloop *Zenobia*, commanded by Captain William Dobree, and, when he was 'perfectly out of sight of the island', to open the sealed package.

The secret orders were hand-written on foolscap vellum; but at the top of the first sheet the Rear-Admiral's full title was printed in all its far-ringing grandeur:

By Sir George Cockburn, Rear Admiral of the Red, and Commander-in-Chief of His Majesty's ships and vessels, employed and to be employed at the Cape of Good Hope, and in the seas adjacent, as far northward as the Equinoctial line, as far westward as the 15th degree of West Longitude, southward to the 60th degree of South Latitude, and Eastward to the 65th degree of East Longitude. . . .

'You are hereby required and directed,' the order told White,

to make the best of your way to the Island of Ascension, and in the event of your finding the said island (as is probable) unoccupied by people of any nation whatsoever, you are to take possession of it, hoisting upon it the English flag, and putting ashore upon it an officer, about ten men and a gun; and erecting upon it for these men (who are to remain constantly on shore) tents or other accommodation according to the means at your disposal and as the nature of the situation may require.

You will then take measures to ensure that every boat or vessel which may approach Ascension be minutely examined, and should there be discovered on board any such, either General Napoleon Buonaparte or any of the French persons who accompanied him to St Helena, he or they, as the case may be, must be immediately secured and taken (forcibly if necessary) on board one of His Majesty's sloops for the purpose of being brought back to this place if they do not produce a certificate from under my hand and *seal* setting forth that they have regular and full sanction for proceeding elsewhere.

Having landed, White was to prospect for water by digging

'deep wells', and then to return to St Helena in the *Peruvian*, leaving the *Zenobia* 'to retain possession of Ascension'. Captain Dobree was to keep his ship close inshore, unless he had to chase some other vessel off:

> The latter, however, Captain Dobree should never do, excepting some very particular behaviour in a vessel in sight of him give him reason to think it highly essential that he should examine her, and even in this case he is not, under any circumstance, to follow such vessel a greater distance than he is well assured he can regain within the period for which the shore party have provisions and water.

Should White find any other ship already at Ascension, his orders continued,

> You are not to take any steps with regard to establishing the party on shore until such vessel or vessels quit it, and during their stay you are to keep secret your intention on this head: but if contrary to every expectation you should find the island to be already taken possession of and occupied by any other nation, you are not to interfere therewith, but to return immediately to give me the information.

Furnished with these comprehensive instructions, the two captains set sail at eight o'clock on the morning 18 October, and for four days their ships travelled steadily before the trade winds. The fifth morning out was cloudy, but at 9.30 they spotted land to the north-west. The ships' log-books are brief and to the point, recording a minimum of factual information; but it is easy to imagine the men's curiosity and apprehension as they came up round the south-west point of the island during the afternoon and saw the nameless brick-red cinder-cones rising from deserts of lava, and the surf breaking on the jagged shore. The only named peaks were Green Mountain and Cross Hill: the rest of the island was completely uncharted.

At 5.10 p.m. they anchored in the big bay, in eight fathoms of water, with Cross Hill bearing south-south-east. The prospect cannot have been inviting. Even on that calm evening the swell must have been breaking heavily and sucking back down the steeply-shelving beach with a dangerous undertow. Immediately inland the ground, though level, was utterly barren – a wilderness of cindery dust strewn with lumps of clinker. Only on the heights of Green Mountain, five miles inland, can there have been the faintest sign of any vegetation.

The *Peruvian's* log records the moment of landing with a typical lack of emotion: '5.30 Captain White in company with Captain Dobree went on shore and took a formal possession of the Island in the name of His Britannic Majesty.' The *Zenobia's* log adds: 'At sunset hoisted the Union on shore.'

The crews spent the night on board, but next morning they went hard to work: 'Daylight manned all the boats and sent them away on different purposes, viz. Lt Hobson and party to dig near beach for water. Mr Miller, gunner, and party to haul the seine [fishing net]. Mr Mitchell carpenter to erect a flagstaff and build tents.' (The tents were clearly elaborate, as there are several references to 'building' them.)

The land party shot two goats, and the fishermen caught enough to feed both ships' companies. In the afternoon a twelve-pounder carronade was taken on shore. (A carronade, or 'smasher', was a short-barrelled, low-velocity gun which fired a relatively small charge and had an effective range of 200 or 300 yards. Its main advantage was its lightness, which made it easy to handle.)

The most serious disappointment came in the search for water. On the first day the diggers reached a depth of eleven feet, without reward. Next morning they gave up the original well and tried another nearer the sea, this time opening up a salt spring. Two further wells, one fourteen feet deep, also produced salt water, but not a drop of fresh.

Meanwhile more goats had been shot; stores and water had been landed, and three tents had been built on the small cinder hill which commanded the southern end of the long beach, and which they had already named Fort Cockburn. On the Wednesday Captain White had a field day in his gig, catching 110 fish with an average weight of three lbs each. Then on Friday, 27 October, he set sail for St Helena, leaving the *Zenobia* as guard-ship for the embryo settlement on shore.

For the next few months the *Peruvian* and *Zenobia* took turns at looking after the new base. Captain White returned to Ascension on 20 December with a garrison of eleven Marines, whom he landed on the 21st, and that afternoon Captain Dobree sailed for St Helena. During his passage the War Department in London caught up with accomplished fact and ordered the Admiralty to proceed with the occupation of the island. 'My Lords,' began a characteristically pompous minute to the Admiralty dated 26 December 1815:

It having been represented to His Royal Highness the Prince Regent that the Island of Ascension, situated in Latitude 7.20 south Longitude 14.18 west, had never been occupied by any nation, and is at present altogether uninhabited, and that its vicinity to the Island of St Helena might enable persons desirous of effecting the escape of Napoleon Bonaparte to attempt it from thence with greater prospects of success from the shelter which that Island would afford to the shipping employed on such an undertaking, His Royal Highness has been pleased to signify his Pleasure that Directions should be given to Sir George Cockburn for the occupation of the said Island, and I am commanded by the Prince Regent to desire Your Lordships would give the necessary directions accordingly.

Reporting back to Cockburn in St Helena, Dobree emphasised the problems caused by the lack of water. Ascension, he told the Admiral, was almost completely dry, and after a prolonged search they had found water in only two places. One was 'at the north-west base of Green Mountain', a quantity enough to keep fifty men going, 'constantly dripping from projections of slated rock'. (This was the present-day Dampier's.) The other he described as being at the mountain's 'southern base, four or five tuns collected in small reservoirs'. It is not clear where he meant, but perhaps the place later called Middleton's.

Cockburn evidently did not think Ascension had much future as a naval station. 'I do not agree in . . . supposing that Island at all likely to become a settlement of any value to us,' he wrote to the Admiralty on the 13 January 1816. Nevertheless, he already saw that it had possibilities as a victualling depot, and suggested that it should be stocked with basic supplies in case any vessel should call there in distress, having been turned away from St Helena, which was closed to all foreign shipping.

Some time in the next few weeks he decided to put the island on 'the establishment of a Sloop of War of the smaller class, of 65 men all included'. This, he said, would make for better discipline and be more effective than a company of soldiers, whom he could ill spare anyway. Thus Ascension officially became a ship.

The first regular crew were all volunteers. They included twenty Marines, and Cockburn put his own flag lieutenant, William Roberts, in command. In his orders, given on board the *Northumberland* on 14 March 1816, he reiterated that 'the primary object of ordering the occupation of Ascension' had been 'preventing persons of any Nation desirous of effecting the escape of Napoleon Bonaparte, from possessing themselves of that island'.

Roberts was to lose no time in building a battery to command the anchorage; he was to establish signal posts at the north and south ends of the island, as well as on Green Mountain; and in general he was to defend the island 'to the utmost extremity' against any attempt at capture.

'Another important object,' his orders continued, 'is the making of a depot for refreshment for the South Sea men, private Indian traders, foreigners and other vessels not permitted to touch here [St Helena].' To this end, Roberts was told to try and establish a garden.

The party sailed from St Helena in the *Ceylon*, taking with them six guns, six carronades, provisions for four months, cattle, potatoes and other seeds. They reached Ascension before the end of March, and found the *Raccoon* moored in the bay as guard-ship.

Almost at once a feud broke out over the relative responsibilities of the land and the sea contingents – the forerunner of innumerable rows on the same subject over the next hundred years. On 5 April Captain John Carpenter, commander of the *Raccoon*, sent a note complaining that his men had been harassed by Roberts' volunteers:

> Your men there abused them and have repeatedly done so, telling them that they had no right to go about the Island or to catch goats. . . . I have to desire that you will give instructions to the men under your Command that they will on no account interfere with any person I may think proper to send on shore.

Roberts replied with a placatory note saying that he would investigate the matter, but there is no record of how it was settled.

Already there was a party of men stationed at 'the Springs' – Dampier's – to carry out the vital task of collecting water. An ever-increasing system of gutters and pipes caught the water as it dripped from the rock-faces and ran it into barrels sunk in the ground. From there mules carried it nearly five miles across the baking lava to the settlement. The men at Dampier's became troglodytes, living in caves (which remain to this day) burrowed out of the soft black ash that forms the southern wall of the ravine.

The other distant centre of activity was 'the Garden'. Roberts' original orders had directed him to 'select the most promising piece of ground near the spot that you establish as Head Quarters and endeavour to cultivate it'; but this, as it turned out, was absurdly optimistic. Admiral Cockburn little realised that there was hardly a crumb of soil within miles of the landing-place, and scarcely a drop of rain to make anything grow. To find the right conditions, the pioneers had to walk four miles inland, almost to Dampier's, and then climb another 1500 feet up the western spur of Green Mountain. There, some 200 feet below the ridge across which the south-east trades hustled, they found a tiny sheltered plateau covered with rich soil, and in it they planted the carrots, turnips, and potatoes they had brought with them, as well as plants sent up from St Helena. For the first few months, fresh vegetables were out of the question, and to keep the garrison healthy lemon juice and sugar were issued at the usual allowance of one ounce per day per man.

Stores and equipment were scanty, but every single thing was held on somebody's charge, and it needed an order from the Commandant to change any item's status. 'You are hereby directed to convert the Iron Tar Barrel on your charge into a Roller,' said a note from Roberts to the carpenter, Robert Ward. 'Keep the same on your charge as such, for so doing this shall be your order.' When they ran short of buckets, Roberts issued a similar note directing the purser to make six new ones out of puncheons' staves.

Apart from the men's few private belongings, everything on the island was Government property – not merely the buildings, but food and animals too. ('I have to inform you,' said one report, 'that the Government horses in this island are very old.') And because everything was public property, it had of course to be described in suitably naval or bureaucratic language. Thus mules were never fit or unfit, but always serviceable or unserviceable.

In June 1816 Admiral Cockburn came to inspect the island, and as a result of his visit Roberts set about building a road to the springs and the garden; in September he reported:

By blowing up and removing a few rocks we now have a good carriage road to the first Spring – a distance of 4¾ miles from Head Quarters ; and I think with two carts (Artillery ones would answer best from their being light) that 70 or 80 gallons of water may easily be brought down daily if required.

A year later the carts had arrived and were in daily use. But until they came the transport of water across the lava, in sun temperatures over 100 degrees, must have been a murderous task.

The construction of the road to the mountain was in itself an astonishing feat. After rising gently to a height of about 600 feet, the hill suddenly takes off almost vertically; the road twists up it in a chain of serpentine convulsions known as 'the Ramps' on which gradients of one in three are common. More than twenty consecutive hairpin bends make this one of the steepest climbs in the world. The labour of building the road by hand under the equatorial sun must have been immense; the fact that it was completed so quickly, and that the Marines thought nothing of walking up it every time they had to visit the gardens, reminds one how extraordinarily tough men were before they had machines to do things for them.

Another major project which Roberts initiated was the construction of a pier. 'As the boats suffer much from the want of a good landing place,' he wrote in September, 'I have begun building a jetty and intend carrying it out about 30 yards to a rock which shows itself at low water.' This was the start of the pier on which people and stores have come ashore at Ascension ever since. The difficulty of landing without it is well described by the Rev. C. I. Latrobe, who arrived in November 1816 on his way home from a visit to missionaries at the Cape of Good Hope:

> To land on the sandy beach, even when the surf is least violent, would be attended with great danger. The only safe way is to back the boat into some cove between rocks, and as the swell heaves its stern towards the rock without touching, to leap on shore.

The leaping-ashore continues to this day. Ascension has never had a proper harbour – the land shelves away too steeply under water – and even with the pier finished, people coming off ships still have to wait their moment and jump the last foot or two from the boat on to the bottom of the steps.

In spite of a sore leg, Latrobe set off for a walk inland with Lieutenant Roberts and the Captain of the *Raccoon*,

> ... but the heat was so great, being 115 degrees Fahrenheit by

one, and 122 by another thermometer, and the sand, or rather powdered cinders, so troublesome to the feet, that after forcing ourselves forward for about two miles, we were forced to return. In all directions, nothing but the most barren and desolate region met our view.

Latrobe fully appreciated the discomfort of life on the island – 'the tents of the garrison are placed among heaps of volcanic matter, resembling cinder heaps in the neighbourhood of London' – but he was much taken with its extraordinary appearance:

The colours were inimitably beautiful, and as the sun began to decline, almost every shade of red, brown, purple, lilac, blueish-grey, yellow, orange, black and white was produced, in one or other part of the landscape.

One hazard which Latrobe escaped, but which plagued the islanders intermittently, was the 'Rollers' – immense waves which came in from the west, against the prevailing wind, often with devastating force. Since they came without warning even on the calmest days, and the cause of them was obscure, the garrison had to be constantly on its guard when working on the new pier.

A florid but accurate description of the freak waves was written by W. H. B. Webster, surgeon of the *Chanticleer*, who visited Ascension in the 1820s:

One of the most interesting phenomena that the island affords, is that of the rollers; in other words, a heavy swell producing a high surf on the leeward shores of the island, occurring without any apparent cause. All is tranquil in the distance, the sea-breeze scarcely ripples the surface of the water, when a high swelling wave is suddenly observed rolling towards the island. At first it appears to move slowly forward, till at length it breaks on the outer reefs. The swell then increases, wave urges on wave, until it reaches the beach, where it bursts with tremendous fury. The rollers now set in and augment in violence, until they attain a terrific and awful grandeur, affording a magnificent sight to the spectator, and one which I have witnessed with mingled emotion of terror and delight. A towering sea rolls forward on the island, like a vast ridge of waters, threatening as it were to envelope it; pile on pile succeeds with resistless force, until, meeting with the rushing off-set from the shore beneath, they rise like a wall, and are dashed with impetuous fury on the long line of the coast, producing a stunning noise. The beach is now mantled over with foam, the mighty waters sweep over the plain, and the very houses at George Town are shaken by the fury of the waves. But the principal beauty of the scene consists in the continuous ridge of water crested on its summit with foam and spray, for as the wind blows off the shore, the over-arching top of the wave meets resistance, and is carried, as it were, back against the curl of the swell; and thus it plays elegantly above it, as it rolls furiously onward graceful as a bending plume; while, to add still more to its beauty, the sun-beams are reflected from it in all the varied tints of the rainbow.

Stirring though they might be for a visitor, the rollers were a menace to the garrison, and soon a system of warning flags was devised to alert the captains of ships to the danger. One roller flag hoisted on the pierhead meant that only emergency landings should be attempted; two, that no landings whatever were possible.

By the autumn of 1816, Cockburn had been succeeded as commander-in-chief of the Cape of Good Hope Squadron by Rear-Admiral Sir Pulteney Malcolm. He, too, was nervous about possible attempts to rescue Napoleon, and sent Captain Festing in H.M.S. *Falmouth* to take possession of the even more remote island of Tristan d'Acunha (as it was then spelled) far to the south.

Unlike Ascension, Tristan turned out to be inhabited – by two men living on the foot of the wind-swept 7000-foot mountain. One was Thomas Currie (or Tommasso Corri), an Italian who had been there since 1810; the other was his 'apprentice', a Minorcan boy dropped by a passing ship. Currie told the British sailors that he had been taken to Tristan by an American called Jonathan Lambert, and employed as a gardener to work the small patch of cultivable ground and provide food for American whalers. Then, one day in 1812, 'under pretence of fishing and collecting wreckage', Lambert had taken the boat and sailed away, leaving Currie on his own without pay or clothes.

Lambert had already laid claim to the island: in the *Boston Gazette* of 18 July 1811 he had published a notice announcing that he, Jonathan Lambert, 'late of Salem', had taken possession of Tristan d'Acunha and had hoisted his flag upon it. Evidently the British knew this, for they quickly got Currie to sign a counter-claim:

I, Thomas Currie, resident on the Island of Tristan d'Acunha, do solemnly swear that I have never seen any colours hoisted or displayed on this Island, but those of His Britannic Majesty, from the time of my landing, the 27th Day of December, 1810.

Currie's signature, staggering across the bottom of the page, shows that he had almost forgotten how to write, if he had ever known. Nevertheless, the island became British, and seventeen men were left to defend it.

Meanwhile, the garrison on Ascension had been put on a new footing by an order from the Admiralty that reached the island in August 1816. Henceforth the men on shore were to be borne as supernumeraries on the books of the man-of-war stationed in the bay. The commandant was to have 'the conduct, command and superintendence' ashore, but the captain of the guard-ship also had a 'general responsibility and superintendence'. The reason for this curious arrangement was the impossibility of executing martial law on seamen on shore unless they were borne on the strength of some ship. Children born on the island were deemed to have been born at sea, and so were registered in the parish of Wapping.

The island's defences were precarious, to say the least. Guns protected the main anchorage, but the other beaches along the western and northern sides of the island lay unguarded, and security depended on the garrison getting advance warning of the approach of any foreign sail. The order to establish look-outs on the north and south extremities of the island proved unrealistic. The two best vantage points were Cross Hill, from the top of which there is a good view of the south-west, west and north-west coasts, and a round, flat-topped hill 2000 feet high which the seamen named Weather Mountain, near the eastern end of the island, from which the rest of the horizon is visible.

Look-outs were stationed on both these summits; news travelled up and down by semaphore, and on clear days the system was effective; but sometimes the top of Weather Mountain was hidden by passing clouds, and on several occasions ships hove in sight of the anchorage without previous warning. A twelve-pounder carronade was heaved to the top of Weather Mountain (no mean feat of strength and endurance), so that audible as well as visual warnings could be given.

Thus the British established a foothold on their unpromising new possession. It was hot, dry, dusty and unwelcoming; but at least it had the merit, unique among His Majesty's vessels, of not heaving about. As seamen of that generation and others remarked, serving on H.M.S. *Ascension* was a damned sight less dangerous and uncomfortable than being afloat.

THE MARINES TAKE OVER

1817–28

No order for the permanent occupation of Ascension has survived. Perhaps none was given. It seems likely that one commandant after another simply pressed ahead with the formidable task of trying to make the island habitable, without any clear idea of how long the Navy might remain there.

For the members of the garrison – or 'people', as the ship's company was called – this meant continuous hard labour: on the buildings, the defence batteries, the roads, the water supply, and the garden up the Mountain. An island log-book shows that stone buildings were already under construction by the autumn of 1817, and the daily entries give an impression of non-stop industry:

> Saturday 6th September AM moderate and cloudy. People employed at the garden and assisting the masons cutting stones. *Julia's* party at the battery, sawyers sawing plank, carpenter at the house at the garden. Arrived and sailed again the *Mary* merchant ship from Bombay bound to Cork.
>
> PM ditto. Scrubbed hammocks, washed clothes. Rd. 68 gallons of water from cart.

On Sundays the garrison was mustered for divine service, and the articles of war were read; but after this brief respite the men carried on with what official reports always described as 'the works' or 'the public works'.

A surprising number of ships either called or sailed past. British and American vessels came in for water, but a fierce welcome greeted anyone suspicious. Ships that could not be positively identified were assumed to be 'piratical', and were either shot at or pursued. 'At 5.30 saw a Brig passing to leeward,' says the log for 29 September 1817. 'Fired two guns shotted* to bring her to, without effect.' On 23 October the islanders fired six guns shotted at another strange brig and drove her off.

So numerous were the distractions, and so persistent the shortage of labour and materials, that progress with the buildings was extremely slow. A report by a naval officer, Captain Thomas Brown, who inspected the island on behalf of his Admiral in November 1821, shows that even after five years' occupation the settlement was in a thoroughly decrepit state.

A plan of the garrison shows nine buildings spread round 'Regent Square', the flat space a few yards inland from Fort Cockburn and the landing place. There was a Marine barracks, a forge, a carpenter's shed, a cookhouse and various stores, but the report said that the stone walls were all badly built 'by someone who had not grasped the principles of masonry', and that the roofs were made of tarpaulins nailed on rafters 'at a very great distance apart'. The galley in the cookhouse was 'an old Frigate's, entirely useless'. One defence battery was mounted on a stone platform but was completely unprotected; the other was on a mound of cinders and 'did not appear capable of being worked'.

The two houses up in the Mountain Settlement were also in bad repair, and parts of the gardens had been overrun by weeds and shrubs. The livestock included five serviceable mules, which lived at the Springs, and two unserviceable ones, which had been turned loose. The number of wild goats was unknown, but certainly over 150, and there were eight or nine oxen wild on the mountain.

The garrison was clearly too small to run the island efficiently. It consisted of only thirty-one officers and men of the Navy and Marines, two gardeners, a smith, a carpenter, a cooper, six Negroes, ten women and thirteen children. The women must have been tough, for some of them were sharing their husbands' troglodytic existence in the black cinder-caves at the Springs.

Captain Brown, author of the 1821 report, recommended that 'in the event of relieving these men [the garrison], care should be

* Loaded with small shot.

taken in selecting mechanics – viz., carpenters, masons, smiths and a cooper, for the purpose of keeping the buildings, drays, casks etc. in constant repair'. His advice was both sensible and prophetic: from then on most of the men who served on Ascension were chosen for their professional skills, and they spent the majority of their time exercising civilian talents rather than indulging in military pursuits.

That same year, 1821, Napoleon died, and so removed the original reason for the British occupation of Ascension. But by then the island had taken on another role, which increased in importance over the next twenty years – that of providing a sanatorium and victualling base for the ships engaged in suppressing the slave trade on the coast of West Africa.

From the first the Admiralty had realised that Ascension's climate was exceptionally healthy. In the steady, dry heat, moderated by the constant trade winds, and in what the *Africa Pilot* called the 'peculiar buoyancy and elasticity of the air', wounds healed well and men recovered quickly from the epidemics that frequently decimated ships' crews. There was a tremendous contrast between Ascension and the humid, fever-ridden coasts of Africa, where the British hunted the slavers both at sea and among the creeks and rivers that wound into the steaming jungle.

The Navy's brief was to patrol the whole of the African Coast from Cape Verde in the north to Benguela in the south; but in fact it concentrated its efforts on the 2000-mile stretch in the middle, from Conakry, in the modern republic of Guinea, to the island of San Thomé, off the mouth of the Gaboon river. The southern half of this sector – the Bights of Benin and Biafra, right in the crook of Africa – was the busiest theatre of all, and opposite it, some eight or ten days' sail out, lay the safe and salubrious refuge of Ascension.

Of the many ships that arrived at the island in distress, none did more damage than H.M.S. *Bann*, a twenty-gun sloop with a crew of 135 which came in during April 1823 with a virulent fever on board. Men were dying even before she reached Ascension: the stark phrase 'departed this life' dots the pages of the log-book during her run from the coast. So common was death that it was recorded quite without comment, among the other events of the day: 'Departed this life Henry Brown. Washed the lower deck.'

On 25 April the *Bann* anchored in the bay opposite Cross Hill and sent her sick on shore. One man died that day, another the next, two on the 27th, two on the 28th, and four on the 29th. Even worse, the plague spread to the garrison and took such a hold that it killed more than fifty of its members. For nearly six weeks the stricken ship rode at anchor, and even when she sailed again, on 2 June, she left the surgeon and the Master's mate behind to look after the invalids. Today a tomb on the beach, surmounted by a simple cross, records the disaster, the inscription ending: 'This tomb is said to contain the remains of 26 officers and men.'

After this tragedy, ships with fever on board were not allowed to come near the settlement, but were sent to a small, sheltered bay a mile and a half to the north. At first this was known as Sydney Cove; later it was called Comfort Cove, but as the irony of the name became intolerable it was changed again to Comfortless Cove. There, on a tiny beach hemmed in by some of the most terrifying lava on the island, the sufferers were put ashore. There was no question of any nursing; nor was there even any shelter, except what the sick themselves could arrange. Members of the garrison simply brought food and water overland and laid them on a rock or in a boat at a safe distance, firing a shot as a signal before retiring again.

The men who died on land were buried by their shipmates. Somehow they managed to scratch out graves in the ashy floors of the few narrow little gullies that can be found among the mountains of piled-up volcanic boulders.

Today Comfortless Cove has a strange and somehow oppressive air. Being one of the few safe bathing places on the island, it is heavily frequented: the sand is fine and clean, the sea warm, clear, and shark-free. But turn inland, and you are confronted by the menacing black lava, which has a sullen and brooding air even under the blaze of the midday sun, and seems, in its utter sterility, to redouble the loneliness of the pathetic little cemeteries that it guards.

No one knows how many men are buried there. In the Bonetta cemetery (the main one, named after a ship which was stricken in 1838) there are fourteen graves, most of them bearing names; five anonymous graves are tucked into another gulley, and there are three more in the Trident cemetery, on a flatter piece of ground to the north-west. But the records suggest that more people than this were buried in the area, and probably several lie utterly unremembered beneath the sterile ash.

Like Comfortless Cove, other places on the island had their names changed by successive generations of Marines. At some early stage 'Weather Mountain' became 'Weather Port Signal', and this in turn was shortened to 'Weather Post'. During the 1820s 'The Springs' became 'Dampier's'. A majestic ridge of cinder-cones in the middle of the island became first 'Zebra Hill' (because of its striped appearance) and then 'The Sisters'; another cone on the way to Dampier's and the Mountain became 'Travellers' Hill'; another with a spike of rock sticking up from the breached side of its crater was aptly christened 'Broken Tooth'. When ideas ran short, various forms of 'Red Hill' had to suffice – 'Mountain Red Hill', 'South West Bay Red Hill,' 'Sisters Red Hill' and so on. But – as was perhaps inevitable in a landscape so fire-scorched – the credit for the really fiendish natural features went to the Devil.

A huge circular bowl, four or five hundred yards across, and with sides over a hundred feet deep, became the Devil's Cauldron; a deep black cleft in beds of soft ash that plunges violently to the sea became the Devil's Ashpit; a stream of black lava laid over the sloping face of the South East Head plateau the Devil's Inkpot. Strangest of all is the Devil's Riding School – a shallow, oval crater some 400 yards across whose floor has been eroded into concentric rings of grey, white and pink that powerfully suggest the chariot-lanes in some diabolical hippodrome. A hundred years earlier, the marooned Dutchman had written in his diary: 'Any body would have believed that the Devil himself had moved his quarters and was coming to keep Hell on Ascension' – and now, in a fashion, the sailors had made his words come true.

Ascension's one substantial satellite – a flat-topped, steep-sided outcrop of rock lying some three hundred yards off the east coast – was christened Boatswain Bird Island, after the elegant, long-tailed Boatswain or Tropic Birds, whose name came from their shrill, piping whistle. Then, as now, the top of the islet was plastered with the guano of a huge colony of sea birds, and the place was useless to the settlers until much later on, when it became a source of fertiliser for the gardens.

Although the garrison at Ascension included some Marines from the start, it was commanded for the first few years by officers of the Royal Navy. Then, in 1823, there arrived the first Royal Marine commandant – and a formidable figure he was. Lt.-Col. Edward Nicolls was then at an early stage of his distinguished career (he later became known as 'Fighting Nicolls' and received a knighthood, numerous medals and a series of ghastly wounds); but already his combative instincts were well developed, as is shown by this extract from a letter which he sent to the Admiralty after the garrison had been forced to watch helplessly while a British ship was plundered by a pirate in sight of the island:

I do assure you, Sir, it was a bitter sight to British Marines who had been accustomed to insult the harbours of all nations but had never seen our own so treated, and had there been a shadow of a chance to have got a dozen of us on his decks, I feel sure no person on board of him would have ever been employed in piracy again.

Nicolls's energy boiled over into all his reports and plans. He had fifty-six liberated Africans brought to the island as extra labour, and asked the Admiralty if he could have some convicts for heavy work. 'I hear Government are sending all the convicts out of the country to the different Colonies,' he wrote, and suggested that he might have a few for roadmaking and work in the stone quarries.

Perhaps it was just as well that they never came, for he had difficulties enough without them. His most constant preoccupation was the food supply. Although the Mountain garden produced a steadily increasing amount of fresh vegetables, the bulk of the island's provisions came out in storeships from the Admiralty's victualling yard at Deptford. The passage took between six and ten weeks, and stores frequently went bad *en route* ('the potatoes during the voyage became quite unbearable from the stench that issued from the case'), but on the whole food seems to have survived the journey fairly well. Trouble began on Ascension, where, in the hot, dry atmosphere, the staves of the wooden store-casks shrank, letting in air and vermin, so that flour, for instance, was often 'sour-tasting and full of weevils' before the warranty on it had expired. Feats of endurance were rare enough to provoke individual comment: a letter to the Admiralty reported that a cask of bread opened after twelve months in store was 'as good as in the first week after its manufacture'.

Captain Dalrymple Hay, visiting the island in 1835, left this description:

The salt beef had been salted in 1809 and could only be eaten, after it was boiled, by grating it with a nutmeg grater. The pork was little better, but the biscuit was a caution.

The storehouses were dry, clean, and airy, but the biscuit, baked by a contractor at the Cape of Good Hope, had been long in store and positively swarmed with weevils and maggots. None was to be obtained to replace it, and in order to make it eatable, the bread bags filled with this biscuit were dragged out into the great square; on each bag was placed a fresh caught fish, the maggots came out of the bread and into the fish, and the fish was then thrown into the sea. A fresh fish was then produced until at last nothing came out of the biscuit, when it was pronounced fit for food and served out to the squadron.

A six-monthly demand for stores sent in during 1826 gives a good idea of what the islanders lived on. It included 16,353 lbs of bread,

10,000 lbs of flour, 5000 lbs of cocoa, 8226 lbs of sugar, 1023 lbs of currants, preserved beef and pork, besides rice, dried peas and 351 gallons of vinegar. Unlimited fresh eggs – pink-yolked and tasting slightly of fish – were available for much of the year from the immense colony of wideawake terns that nested on South West Plain, and during the season thousands were collected every week. The only fresh meat came from scrawny sheep and cattle sent up from St Helena and the Cape, or from the wild goats and turtles.

The turtles, as the garrison soon discovered, also had a definite season, from December to May, and during those months 'hands' were stationed on the beaches used for nesting – principally South West Bay, English Bay and North East Bay, as well as Clarence Bay, or Long Beach, next to the settlement. The outer bays were all a long, hard walk away through the pathless, clinker-strewn volcanic desert; so severe was the going that the men on turtle duty were issued with extra boots free.

Huts were built on the various beaches (a stone one still survives in South West Bay); since the turtles came ashore only in the dark, the men were on duty all night, and to keep them awake were paid 2s. 6d. for every captive. The rule was that the turtles must be allowed to finish laying their eggs before being turned.

The victims were left lying on their backs on the beach, with rocks under their heads for pillows. In the morning the men signalled the number turned back to the main semaphore station on Cross Hill, behind the garrison, and a boat would come round (the sea permitting) to collect the catch.

To load an inert or slightly struggling lump of 400, 500, or even 600 lbs into a small boat was impossible, so the turtles were re-launched with floats lashed to their flippers, and towed upside-down and backwards to the settlement. Later, when a larger boat became available, they were towed clear of the breakers off the beach on which they had been turned, and winched on board. Back at base, they were stored alive until needed in a pond built for the purpose at the south end of Long Beach – a walled-off enclosure about twenty yards in diameter, with gaps for sea-water to wash in and out.

Turtle meat was served regularly to the garrison, and also to the crews of visiting ships, in place of fresh beef. W. H. B. Webster, surgeon of H.M. Sloop *Chanticleer*, which called in 1828, described it as resembling good young beef or even veal. 'So little is it thought of here', he wrote, 'that many parts of it are thrown to the pigs, and sometimes even the flippers are so disposed of.' Many of the men did not like it, or became surfeited by its richness; and this superabundance of what in England was one of the rarest delicacies never failed to irritate the Lords of the Admiralty and other naval officers.

Later during the occupation an admiral commanding the West Coast of Africa Squadron made repeated attempts to have turtle soup struck off the rations of prisoners working on Ascension. They were getting it once a week, as an extra item on Tuesdays, and the island surgeon defended the practice energetically, saying that prisoners at hard labour in the tropics needed all the sustenance they could get. But not even his professional advice satisfied the Admiral, who ended a considerable exchange of letters by writing: 'I still think that prisoners at Ascension would not suffer in health if the Turtle soup were withheld.'

It was Nicolls, during the 1820s, who instituted the practice of selling or bartering surplus turtles to the captains of passing merchant ships. Money received was placed in the public account, and goods went into the public store, where the men could buy what they wanted at modest rates. When the Admiralty criticised the system in 1828, Nicolls put up a spirited defence, claiming that 'the privilege of bartering is a stimulus to men working under a tropical sun'.

Even with these occasional luxuries, the islanders' diet must have been one of extreme monotony, and the only regular spice was the ration of grog. No one understood the importance of rum better than Nicolls, and he was always ready to get his men their rights. 'From the nature of our service here, and the hardness of the work,' he wrote to the Admiralty in 1825, 'the men earnestly requested I would give them the old allowance of spirits.' He had his way; and the status of rum is clearly shown by this daily order of 1828:

G.O.

Parole – Honor   Ascension Island,
Countersign – Marine   January 1828

In consequence of the spirited and Soldierlike feelings manifested yesterday evening by Corporal Mark Elstol and the 12 privates, who volunteered their service after a hard day's work to march over in double quick time to S.W. Bay with a view to prevent that severe disgrace to a Soldier occurring, i.e., Suffering His Majesty's Island, or his or any property committed to their care, to be surprised, injured, or plundered.

Now, in order to show how much I approve of such good Conduct, and to Honor and compliment the above named Mark Elstol and his 12 Comrades, I hereby order the whole of the Detachment of Royal Marines, serving on this Island and the Artificers, two extra proportions of Rum. One this first day of the New Year of $\frac{1}{2}$ a pint, and one to-morrow of 1 Gill, to enable them to Drink up standing with 4 times 4 cheers an happy New Year, and many happy returns of them to our most Gracious Sovereign, King George the 4th, whose health and prosperity we ought always to be most proud and happy to hear named, with the gallant feelings and loyalty of his brave and most faithful Marines. It is hoped that Concord, good Comradeship, activity and strict attention to the duties we are here appointed to perform, will constantly pervade our Ranks and be made manifest in the Conduct of every individual which shall at all times and places command my best wishes and services for the good of every person under my Command.

On Wednesday the 2nd inst., the Detachment will drink their Gill to the health of His Royal Highness, the Lord High Admiral, &c., &c.

Some hands to go to the Out bays for Turtle to-night and to-morrow morning.

                         (Signed) Edward Nicolls,
                              Bt. Lt.-Colonel-Commandant.

The demand for stores quoted above included requests for 1005 gallons of rum and 2532 gallons of wine. Occasionally the garrison managed to get some beer as well: a note from the Admiralty in 1828 brought the good news that 'The Board have had about twelve Tuns of Beer brewed in their stores of a Superior Description, with a special view to its keeping good in a warm climate'.

Even with alcohol strictly rationed, there was inevitably a certain amount of drunkenness in the evenings; but it does not seem to have caused much trouble, and Nicolls had worse human problems to deal with. In October 1827 he wrote to the Admiralty complaining of

> ... the great trouble I have had with Mr. Smith the Surgeon ... the most quarrelsome troublesome man I ever had to deal with, not an Officer or Gentleman on the Island but what he has injured and insulted. ... The fact is, he is at times religiously mad, and was about to distribute tracts of a very dangerous tendency to our people. ... I was even obliged to order him not (as he termed it) to prepare a woman's soul for eternity, as I told him it was her bodily health he has to attend to.

Fortunately for Nicolls (and the woman, who recovered), the crazed Mr Smith was sent home.

In the constant heat and the close confines of the garrison, family feuds sometimes became vicious. Explaining why he had sent home Mrs King, wife of one of his private soldiers. Nicolls wrote that the couple

> ... were always fighting and quarrelling, that the woman cut the man so severely in the hand with a knife whilst he was beating her as to disable him from work for a month, and that in another quarrel they had he kicked her in the belly until the blood ran from her vagina, when she swore in my presence she would murder him.

A more persistent nuisance was the succession of pirate ships that kept appearing off the island. Although none dared make an

"FIGHTING NICOLLS."
GENERAL SIR EDWARD NICOLLS, K.C.B.

From a painting in the
Officers' Mess, R.M.L.I., Plymouth.

Vide page 248

Edward Nicolls, Royal Marines,
known as 'Fighting Nicolls',
commandant 1823–28

The house known variously as
Bate's Cottage, Captain's Cottage
and Governor's Lodge, in 1891.
Now demolished

Staff of the Eastern Telegraph Company on Wideawake Plain (site of the present airfield) in about 1910

The peak of Green Mountain from the air. The farm settlement is in the centre of the picture, with the highest of the Ramps below

Captain R. H. Morgan with Mr. G. O. Cannon, prospecting for phosphates, 1907

Royal Marine turtle-turners, 1907

attack, their presence kept the garrison on edge; in February 1828 Nicolls sent home this account of a typical marauder:

> I have also to report to you that we have had a very disagreeable visitor round the Island lately, a very fast Brig-rigged cruiser, evidently a pirate. He shows no colours, he was five hours overhauling a large ship on the 19th inst. and he came very near the batterys on the 22nd inst. after a large China ship chartered by the India Company. I had my boats all ready to carry him if he dared to attack her in the roads, but he sailed so fast and was so well handled that I should have had no chance to board him unless he got becalmed – a circumstance that rarely happens here – or that he came to anchor in any of the bays, when I should make certain of him.

Evidently pirate fever was rampant at the time, for that same year the fearless traveller Mrs Elwood, passing Ascension on her way home from India, recalled that the *Briton*, a fifty-gun vessel anchored in the bay, fired shots to bring her own ship to and warned it to watch out for suspicious-looking strangers. For the rest of the voyage home, she wrote, 'dreadful piratical stories were related, for the benefit of the nervous', but they reached England safely.

Another visitor at about this time was the budding author W. M. Thackeray. In Chapter III of his novel *The Newcomes*, published in 1854, he described little Clive Newcome's voyage home from India with his tutor:

> The passage was most favourable. They stayed a week at the Cape, and three days at St Helena, where they visited Bonaparte's tomb (another instance of the vanity of all things!) and their voyage was enlivened off Ascension by the taking of some delicious turtle!

The scene is laid in the 1820s, and since Thackeray himself had been born in India, the passage is clearly autobiographical.

Quite apart from supplying passers-by with turtles, the garrison on Ascension was extremely busy. Much of its energy was absorbed by the laborious process of supporting everyday life. Water had to be carted daily the four and a half miles from Dampier's to the Settlement; coal had to be carried from sea level up to the Mountain cottages, for the Africans working in the gardens complained of cold at night, when the temperature fell to about 65 degrees, and there was not a stick of wood to burn. Besides the Garrison, three outposts had to be victualled daily – the Mountain, Dampier's and Middleton Springs (another source of water almost in the middle of the island).

Apart from the Marines themselves, Nicolls' labour force consisted of a few Kroomen from the west coast of Africa, and a larger number of liberated slaves. His attitude towards the Africans was down-to-earth, but basically sympathetic. In January 1826 he wrote to his Commodore:

> The black men that Capt. Murray left with me in lieu of the Kroomen are clean and well conducted. They are getting very useful, but, poor fellows, they are continually asking me to get their wives over from Sierra Leone. I hope you will be so good as to have them sent. We are really in want of the fair sex, having only six on the island, which is far too few. . . . Those of them that have not wives in Sierra Leone request you will send them some. They wish them young, under 25.

Nicolls' passing reference to the shortage of 'the fair sex' is one of the very few mentions that occur in the official dispatches of what must have been a major problem throughout the occupation. From the earliest days a few of the officers and men had their wives with them, but the shortage of women was never less than acute. Apart from one or two female nurses in the hospitals (most of the staff were men), there were never any unattached women on the island. Even so, sexual problems hardly ever figure in the commandants' reports. Apart from a couple of incidents of homosexuality, and one occasion when a private soldier was sent home for trying to rape a bitch in the latrines, the Marines' frustration is utterly forgotten.

In spite of the demands of routine, several important projects were completed during Nicolls' five years on the island.

A road was cleared to South West Bay; a two-floored victualling store was built of stone, several water-tanks were finished, and a crane was mounted above the Tartar Stairs – the flight of stone steps let into the pierhead on which people landing from boats came ashore, the name having been taken from Admiral Sir George Collier's flagship. A lesser project, but one of lasting significance, was the placing in position of the original Two Boats – the two halves of a naval cutter were stood upright on either side of the road at the foot of the Ramps as shelters in which people might rest before tackling the climb. Today a whole village has sprung up beside the site, but two boats still flank the old mountain road, absurdly out of place so far inland, yet a vivid reminder of naval days.

Like many of the commandants who followed him, Nicolls was harassed by the need to keep Ascension's running costs as low as possible. He several times suggested to the Admiralty that the lime which Ascension produced should be traded in exchange for the African oak and other wood bought in Fernando Po and Sierra Leone for building. He even claimed that the local stone could, if quarried by convicts, be produced so cheaply that it would make a profit when sold in London.

None of these schemes came to fruition, not least because of the reactionary attitude of the Lords of the Admiralty, who, even then, always knew better than the man on the ground and had already elevated the art of bureaucracy to commanding heights. One case will illustrate the dispatch with which they conducted their affairs.

In Ascension's accounts for 1826 a discrepancy was discovered: in one place the proceeds of an auction of condemned stores were given as £5. 13. 11d., but in another the figure was £5. 15. 1d. The Admiralty opened up a long-range bombardment from London, and for months heavy salvoes rumbled back and forth.

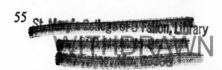

Dozens of letters and thousands of words – all carefully set out in long-hand on vellum – were exchanged, before Mr Sam Triscott, the Agent Victualler on the island, eventually established that the discrepancy had been caused by the fact that:

> 36 lbs of Bread condemned in store was put up for sale by Public Auction . . . and no person bidding for the same, he [a Marine officer], with the sanction of the Commandant, disposed of it by Private Contract for 1s 2d., which sum added to the £5. 13. 11 will agree with the £5. 15. 1, and he trusts that this Explanation will be satisfactory.

Handicapped though he was by this kind of niggling at home, Nicolls clearly felt, as the end of his command approached, that he had not entirely wasted his time. 'We are all in good health,' he wrote to the Admiralty, 'I am well supported by all present, and great progress has been made in all our works.' With the same letter he enclosed a note from the surgeon asking for a supply of 'Embden Grits' – a prospect of much advantage to the sick?

It is not clear what class of patient the Grits were supposed to benefit; but the garrison seems to have suffered no serious epidemic since the tragedy of the *Bann*.

One more of Ascension's memorials seems to date from Nicolls' day: the Redpole Monument, on the side of Cross Hill. The pillar is believed to commemorate the loss of H.M.S. *Redpole*, which was sunk by a pirate of Cape Frio (north of Buenos Aires) in 1828; and the white gravestones nearby are said to be those of members of the crew who died when the ship was at Ascension during 1820.

WILLIAM BATE

1828–38

Captain William Bate, who took over from Nicolls in the autumn of 1828, was one of the great figures of Ascension's modest history. So few of his private letters survive that it is difficult to know what sort of a man he was; but if his personal characteristics remain obscure, it is clear that he was an outstandingly efficient and conscientious soldier.

In the ten years during which he commanded the garrison he won the unfailing respect and admiration of his men. To the senior naval officers of the Cape of Good Hope he was the perfect commander of their curious outpost. 'I do not think the Marine Corps could produce an officer whom I could prefer as Commandant of this island,' wrote Rear Admiral Frederic Warren in 1832. 'Indeed,' he reported two years later, 'no praise that I can give of that officer is more than he deserves.'

Bate's extraordinary steadfastness is suggested by the fact that, before he came to Ascension, he had held the same post – Adjutant at the Royal Marine depot at Chatham – for twelve years; and it is confirmed by the fact that he never left the island during his ten years' command. He left solid evidence of his independent nature in the form of the two houses that he had built for his own use: one, known variously as Bate's Cottage, Commodore's Cottage and Governor's Lodge, on the side of Cross Hill behind the settlement; and the other, North East Cottage, a tiny shack nearly 2000 feet up on a spur of Green Mountain. Both were on wonderful sites – high, isolated and commanding tremendous views of the island and the Atlantic sunsets.

Hardly ever does a hint of personal problems or feelings appear in Bate's letters and reports to the Admiralty. He kept a daily

57

log-book of all the work in progress, which he sent home at the end of every month or second month, and he took advantage of any ship that called to post the latest news back to England. ('By the barke *Columbia* from the Cape to London I have the honour to acquaint you . . .'; 'I take advantage of the barke *Ceylon*, about to sail for England . . .'.)

But, from reading his voluminous official papers that have survived, you would never know that at the start of his tour of duty on Ascension he had a wife in England, or that in 1830 a ship arrived bearing news of her death. Yet every now and then his letters give a glimpse of his affection for the island in phrases like 'my little garrison' and 'my little island'. 'My little garrison I have pleasure in reporting in perfect health and everything going on as I could wish', is a common letter-ending.

A better source of hints about his character is a selection of daily orders preserved from the early years of his command:

14 Dec. 1828. The Commanding Officer has to express his surprise at the absence of so many of those belonging to the Garrison from Divine service this day, and trusts that he will not again have to make the same observation.

25 Dec. 1828. This being Xmas Day the Commanding Officer is pleased to forgive those men that are under the course of punishment.

20 April 1829. In consequence of Easter Week, the whole of the Garrison will have holiday tomorrow and Wednesday, the men will all dine together and the Commandant will grant them a double allowance of wine.

24 Dec. 1828. The Commanding Officer is pleased, in consideration of the general good conduct of the crew, to grant them a relaxation from their duties until Monday 4th January . . . and as it is his wish that they should enjoy themselves and be happy, everything shall be done to make them so, but at the same time he trusts there will be nothing in the shape of rioting or disorderly conduct.

Ascension certainly offered boundless scope for Bate's energy when he arrived in the autumn of 1828. One of his first actions was to order a report on the state of the island from a board consisting of two Royal Marine Officers, the two surgeons and the Agent-Victualler. Their survey painted a squalid picture. The men's quarters, it reported, were 'an assemblage of wretched low hovels', so uncomfortable that many of the inhabitants were in the habit of taking refuge at night under boats on the beach. The officers' accommodation was 'just one grade better' but the buildings formed 'complete nests of vermin and are in fact preserves for rats, mice, cockroaches, scorpions etc.'. The water-parties stationed at Dampier's were still 'bestowed in caves cut out of the cinder, very unsafe and damp'. The road to the Springs and the Mountain was in good order on the higher reaches, 'but from the ridge to the Garrison in a very bad state'.

Urgently as all these deficiencies called for improvement, the first priority was the creation of a reliable water system; for, as Bate immediately realised, the daily transport of water about the island was a crippling waste of labour and time. 'Immediately on my taking command,' he reported to the Admiralty in January 1829, 'I commenced an excavation for a tank to contain 500 tuns and I have great pleasure in stating to you that the first stone of it was laid on New Year's Day.' 'Tomorrow being the day appointed for laying the foundation stone of the new tank,' said the Daily Order for 31 December 1828, 'the Commanding Officer is pleased to give a double allowance of grog to the Establishment.' The site of the tank was in Dampier's ravine; Bate had had the spot watched since his arrival, and had found that 'after a moderate shower of half an hour it ran at the rate of a gallon in 40 seconds'.

Until the spring of 1829 the settlement had always been known as 'The Garrison', or just 'Garrison', and indeed the use of the name continued right into the twentieth century. But in the Daily Order of 3 April 1829, apparently on his own initiative, Bate christened the place with the name by which it has been officially known ever since:

3 April 1829. No name having hitherto been given to the settlement on this island, and this being the day on which the birth of our most gracious Sovereign is celebrated, the headquarters henceforth to be called George Town.

All through the summer of 1829 Bate pressed ahead with his master plan for the water supply, of which the tank at Dampier's was the first stage. His idea was to transfer water from the Mountain (where twenty or thirty inches of rain fell in a year) down through a system of pipes and reservoirs to Georgetown. Much of the scheme he could no doubt have completed on his own, but its lasting success owed a great deal to the help he received from a specialist – Lt. H. R. Brandreth of the Royal Engineers, who arrived on Ascension for the first of several visits in June 1829 after a slow passage of eighty days from England in the transport ship *Henry Porcher*.

Brandreth's career took him all over the world. He died suddenly in his forties, but he was clearly something of a genius, for the scheme which he devised for Ascension not only overcame the formidable natural difficulties but was so well executed that it kept the island going for more than a hundred years.

On his first visit he stayed a month, during which he made a complete hydrological survey of the island. After he had gone, Bate started on what he called his 'grand tank' – a 1200-tonner near the landing-place in Georgetown. He began excavations for it in August 1829, and laid the foundation stone on New Year's Day of 1830. Meanwhile he had sent home a request for iron pipes with which to connect the various reservoirs. Until they are laid, he said in a classic understatement, 'it must be all uphill work'.

So important were water and rain that even a moderate shower was worth writing home about. On 1 April 1830, for instance, he reported: 'I have the honor to report to you for the information of the Commissioners, that on Tuesday last we were favor'd with a few hours' rain that put into our tanks upwards of 80 tuns of water.'

The iron pipes were slow to arrive, so in May 1830 Bate obtained from a passing French ship one hundred bamboo canes of $1\frac{1}{2}$ inch bore and an average length of thirty feet, and used them to connect the mountain tank with the one down at Dampier's, letting a cask into the ground every 200 yards to take off the pressure. Whether or not this makeshift arrangement worked is not clear, but the proper pipes arrived soon afterwards, and the Garrison had the severe task of carrying them out and laying them ready on the clinker.

In the autumn of 1830 Brandreth (by then a captain) returned to supervise the work and to prospect further for a really reliable source of water. Until now this had eluded everybody, and in the frequent spells of drought all the known springs were inclined to dry up. But on the south-east side of Green Mountain, in a precipitous ravine known (with good reason) as Breakneck Valley, Brandreth found a seam of clay which he thought might prove the answer. He gave directions for a shaft to be sunk, and on 10 February 1831 the diggers struck water at a depth of thirty feet – a spring, flowing steadily at the rate of a gallon a minute. By Ascension's standards this was a miracle; the trouble was that the spring lay on the wrong side of the mountain – the far side of the ridge from the farm settlement and from the steep descent to Dampier's and the garrison.

Brandreth's solution of the problem was brilliant: to bore a 300-yard tunnel clean through the top of the ridge, and to pipe the water through it to the tanks at the farm. It was some time before this ambitious plan could be put into effect; but meanwhile the earlier pipelines were completed. Every dispatch sent home by Bate in the first half of 1831 refers to the progress of the work, and on 26 June he reported triumphantly: 'On Thursday last a trial was made of passing water from the Mountain to Dampier's tanks, and in 18 minutes 22 tuns of water was carried into the latter without the loss of a wineglass.'

When Brandreth departed later that month, Bate paid tribute to the great benefit he had done the island by means of his 'judicious suggestions'. Later that year Bate reported to the Admiralty: 'Having accomplished this great feat, it will relieve me of much severe work, both to man and beast.' And on New Year's Eve, he celebrated the achievement in the customary way:

31 Dec. 1831. Having accomplished the arduous undertaking of bringing the water down from the Mountain to the Garrison by pipes, the Commanding Officer is pleased to commemorate the same by giving the men an extra allowance of spirits.

The tunnel was started in May 1832. So accurately was the line for it laid that the parties working from either end met within a few inches of perfection, and the whole length of 930 feet was finished by 2 October. The spoil from the farm end was used to level the plot of land known as the Home Garden.

In the same year an octagonal tank was built in Breakneck Valley at a spot some distance below Brandreth's well where drips oozed from the rock. From there the collected water was pumped uphill 'by horse power' to the level of the tunnel mouth, and from that point onwards gravity carried it the whole way down to George-town.

At various later dates refinements were added to the system. In 1837 a second well was dug in Breakneck Valley; in 1863 the sweating horses were replaced by a wind-pump, and later catchments were built – sheets of asphalt or concrete laid on the slopes of the Mountain to shoot the rain into the wells. Also, from 1847, sea water was occasionally distilled in times of drought to augment natural supplies. But the basic system remained as conceived by Brandreth and Bate, and it is functioning to this day. Some of the original cast-iron pipes are still in use; if you put your ear to them, you can hear the pulse of the water as it is shoved uphill from the octagon tank. It is odd to reflect that this same sound was music in the ears of William Bate a hundred and forty years ago.

Besides being a first-class engineer, Brandreth was well travelled and educated, and he responded strongly to the stark beauty of Ascension. On approaching the island from the sea, he wrote in 1835:

Under a particular state of the atmosphere, when dark masses of clouds are congregated round the High Peak and bosom of the Green Mountain, and their black shadows are projected far down the plains, so that the only evidence of verdure – the solitary oasis amidst the surrounding desolation – is shut out from the view, it is scarcely possible that the imagination should conceive a picture more wildly sublime. It would assuredly have suggested to Milton a juster simile for his 'great arch-angel ruined' than Teneriffe.

By no means everybody who called found Ascension so stimulating. General G. C. Mundy, who paid a short visit in 1830, positively hated the place:

It would, I think, have gone far towards reconciling Napoleon to his island prison had they given him a glimpse of Ascension before they carried him to St Helena. Royal indeed must be the revenue that would tempt me to become 'monarch of all I survey' in this 'horrible place'.

Apart from planning the water supply, Brandreth helped Bate work out a general scheme for improving Georgetown, which, when he first arrived in 1829, 'consisted of a series of miserable tenements. ... The Africans occupied a congeries of wretched hovels, dark and filthy. A victualling store, a tank, and a small stone tenement for the officers, were the only buildings that redeemed the establishment from the appearance of an African village.'

At Dampier's, Brandreth reported:

The men had contrived to form habitations out of the extensive and compact bed of cinders and ashes in the neighbourhood. A little Devonshire woman inhabited one of these caves: her husband had scooped out a parlour and a bed-room, each about eight feet square, plastered the roof and sides, floored it with canvass, and given the whole a coat of whitewash; so that, while all in front and around the cave was black with ashes and other volcanic matter, all within was of unrivalled cleanliness and neatness. This little Devonshire dame was called Cinderella; and others, with more or less care and neatness, but with similar ingenuity, improved their accommodations in the same way.

In rebuilding Georgetown, Bate had one considerable advantage; all the stone he needed was available close at hand, and was quarried within a hundred yards of the pier. The quarries, eating slowly into the ledge on which the settlement was built, gradually widened the area originally known as Regent Square, but later called Bunghole Square, because it was there that the Marine coopers broke down into staves the casks in which all the stores arrived.

Georgetown's builders were much troubled by distractions, the most frequent and potentially dangerous being the arrival of fever-ridden ships from the coast. One such was the *Black Joke*, a well-known ex-slaver which came in during January 1830; she anchored in strict quarantine at Comfortless Cove, and her crew set up a temporary camp on shore. Bate followed the normal quarantine procedure:

I have directed one of her boats to be anchored at some distance from them, into which we put all they may want, and I will take care that they shall be supplied with everything that the island affords. We kill a sheep for them every other day, with plenty of vegetables, turtle and fish.

The quarantine rules needed to be enforced by the most explicit orders:

13 Jan 1832. The crew of the *Fair Rosamund* having been landed in Comfort Cove in consequence of the Small Pox, the Commandant strictly forbids any individual in the Garrison going within *2 miles* of the cove or holding any intercourse whatever with the said crew until further notice.

Occasionally verbal prohibition was not enough, and sentries were posted on Long Beach to guard the approaches to the quarantine area.

Most members of the Garrison seem to have dreaded the whole anti-slaving operation because it brought such dangers of disease; but a few men positively looked forward to it, among them Ronald Edwards, who wrote from Ascension to his brother John on 15 August 1833:

We are going for a cruise upon the coast of Africa for six or seven months and have all got our heads full of catching slavers and the quantum of prizemoney we are to get, but I am afraid we shall be disappointed, although they say there are plenty of slavers on the Coast. This ship is so large that they will see us a long way off, and the slave masters have such correct information of the cruising ground of the different men-of-war that they are always enabled to evade us by keeping between two stations.

Many ships called at Ascension, to land invalids, to collect water or to stock up with provisions. A minor disaster occurred when H.M.S. *Medina* brought in some wounded men during December 1830: the island's large boat was swamped and lost while taking out provisions. An apologetic letter from the ship's captain to Bate explained:

Every possible means has been used for the past 4 days, by sweeping and creeping, but it has been found impossible to recover either the boat or the provisions. Considerable rewards have been offered to divers to go down to the boat, but the sharks being very numerous round her nose, none could be prevailed upon to attempt it.

Often the garrison was called out to help ships in trouble. One such was the *Hall*, which was 'smashed into ten thousand pieces' by the rollers, but whose cargo was saved by the Marines' prodigious exertions. Another loss was the brig *Lady Durham*, which came in from Fernando Po during November 1834. She was supplied with provisions and was to have sailed again the next day; but at 3.30 a.m. she was found to be on fire, and she had to be set adrift and sunk at sea, taking with her her cargo of palm oil, ebony and four tons of ivory.

The barque *Premier* was no luckier. Calling in for water on her way from Madras to London, 'she was discovered to be on fire from stem to stern and must have been burning for many weeks'. Her cargo of cotton having ignited, all efforts to douse it failed: in twenty-four hours the ship was burnt out.

Pirates also continued to be a nuisance. In March 1829, for instance, a 'long low topsail schooner' skulked about off the island for several days, coming close inshore at night. Bate thought that she might have come to try and rescue six men taken out of a Brazilian privateer earlier in the year, and to forestall any attempt at landing he stationed small parties of armed men in all the bays at night, besides keeping an extra sharp lookout from the summit of Cross Hill and from Green Mountain.

Unauthorised turtle-hunters were another menace. Asking the Admiralty for 'two light field six-pounders and two Howitzers', Bate said he would take them by mule to the various bays

... in case of the appearance of pirates, or to keep ships from turtling. I was obliged to send a boat round to South West Bay last Monday, two whalers had hoisted out their boats and were busily employed, but from our getting early information by the semaphore on the Mountain they had only time to spear one turtle.

The turtles – mobile wealth delivering itself up nightly on the beaches – inspired Bate to a fever of activity. He converted the small boat harbour into a second storage-pond, and in a series of orders took every conceivable step to increase the harvest:

8 April 1829. The Boat Harbour having been converted to a Turtle pond, the Commanding Officer directs that in future no person bathes or scrubs their clothes in it.·

27 Dec. 1830. All persons belonging to the Garrison are forbid to go along the beaches frequented by Turtle during the season.

The captives he sold and bartered furiously. At first he charged £3 15s apiece, but when ships' captains complained that the price was extortionate, he had the meat of an average turtle weighed, and, finding it was 100 lbs, fixed the price at £2 10s, or sixpence a pound. In one terrific deal he sold the captain of the *Unity*, a passing barque, three-hundred turtles for:

55 Wether Sheep (which shall be kept for the African Squadron), 25 Chauldron of most excellent Coals, sixty Casks of Beef, ten of Tongues, One Dozen of Hams, twelve Barrels of Pitch and Tars, three Barrels of flour, eight Tons of Oat Straw with the grain in, One Cask of Wine, Fifty Bushels of Oats and Barley, Two Casks of Bread, five Bolts of Canvas, five Coil of Rope, One Hundred Deals, Nails, Paints, Oil, etc, etc.

Almost every dispatch that Bate sent home during his first season referred to the great abundance of 'Turtle' (he always used a capital letter and the collective plural), and to the number caught. On the night of February 14, 1822 they turned sixty-seven in one bay, which brought the total for the season to 300. By 21 March it had reached 800, and it ended at 1500 – the biggest ever recorded. At the height of the harvest no fewer than forty men were struck off on turtle-catching, and, as Bate admitted in one note to the Admiralty, 'it breaks in sadly upon our other work'.

From the earliest days a few of the turtles were shipped all the way back to England, some for the King and some for the Lords of the Admiralty. 'The transport has on board Turtle for His Majesty and for the different Heads of Departments', wrote Bate of one vessel that called in 1829.

The captives travelled upside-down on deck, with no maintenance other than an occasional bucket of water thrown over them. In a paper presented to the Royal Geographical Society on 8

June 1835 Captain Brandreth gave a spirited account of the voyage home:

On my return from my first visit to the island, the commandant freighted the transport with sixty of the finest flappers that the season had produced. They were destined for some of the most distinguished individuals in England; and the largest and finest was set apart for his late Majesty, with instructions, that if but one survived it should be considered as so appropriated – the commandant acting, as nearly as possible, upon the principle that the king never dies. And the precaution was by no means unnecessary, as in fact only one did survive.

To prevent intrigues in favour of particular patrons or friends, each turtle was marked on his fair white belly-shell with the name of the owner; and the sailor in charge of the party duly reported each morning their state and condition, as thus: 'Please your honour, the Duke of Wellington died last night'; or, 'I don't like the looks of Lord Melville this morning, sir'. Then followed certain interesting questions – 'How is the Lord Chancellor?' 'Why, he looks pretty lively, sir;' and so forth.

On Ascension itself, the contempt with which the Garrison treated turtle meat irritated Brandreth as much as it had Surgeon Webster of the *Chanticleer* a few years before 'The supply in general is so abundant as to be issued to the ships and troops as fresh meat,' wrote Brandreth; 'and this transcendent delicacy is cooked after the ordinary fashion of beef or mutton. I have witnessed, indeed, the fins of a splendid turtle cast away as offal: let me add, however, that the offence was commited by a Negro, and not by a more civilised being.'

Even without the distraction of the turtle season, Bate had his hands full. Besides being in military command, he was also in charge of the moral and spiritual welfare of the 200-odd people on the island. He was legally empowered to hold divine service, to conduct marriages and christenings, and to bury the dead.

Divine service, which consisted mainly of prayers, was held

every Sunday under a verandah or, later, under the colonnade of the barracks. It was never popular, and Daily Orders recommending attendance had to be reinforced by more positive ones definitely instructing everyone to be present.

In July 1830 Bate started the island's first school,

> ... under the superintendence of Lance-Corporal Barber and his wife, to be conducted on the Rev. Dr Bell's system as laid down for Regimental schools. ... The Commanding Officer trusts there will be no occasion to call the attention of parents to this essential part of their duty towards their children.

The fees were threepence a week for each child of three and over, and twopence a week for those of two or less.

Bate would never have been able to maintain the building programme without the help of a considerable African labour force. The Navy's operations on the coast, and the ships' frequent visits to Ascension, ensured a regular supply of both Kroomen from the Gold Coast and liberated slaves from other parts. Whatever their proper names, they were soon re-christened by the sailors: James Flea, Tom Coal and Jam Tart were names that anybody could understand. The Kroomen were considered to be much superior ('three of them are worth five Africans', said one scornful note); they 'volunteered' to serve two-year spells on the island and were paid sevenpence a day. The liberated slaves got between fourpence a day for a third-class man and sixpence for a first-class one. Some brought their wives and children with them; the island's establishment in 1830 included forty-six African men, fourteen boys (in the naval sense of juniors), twelve women and fourteen children.

The Marines' attitude towards them varied considerably. Some regarded them as useful animals. ('The officer in charge of the mountain applied for six of these women to be sent up for the purpose of breeding with a view to secure the agricultural labour.') Others looked after them surprisingly well: when Jack Fryingpan had his hat, which contained all his pay, knocked overboard in a scuffle with a seaman, the Englishman was ordered to pay him back the whole of the £12. 11. 1. Bate himself, as one would expect, was scrupulously fair:

> *20 August 1831.* It is the Commanding Officer's most positive order that no soldier or African is struck by any officer or N.C.O. on any pretence.

With his combined African and English work-force, Bate made good progress on many fronts – not merely with the water supply, but also with several large buildings. Fort Cockburn was reconstructed, and a start made on a new hospital in the Garrison, and a new Marine barracks on the Mountain. Then, in February 1832, a bombshell arrived: a letter written and sent nearly five months before by Admiral Warren, Commander-in-Chief of the Cape of Good Hope Squadron, ordering Bate to suspend 'all outlay' until he himself arrived at Ascension. Evidently the cost of running the island had alarmed the Admiralty in London, and the Lords Commissioners had ordered an inquiry.

Bate immediately stopped work on the public buildings and waited for the Admiral. When Warren finally arrived in the middle of March, he was delighted with the state of the island; he gave orders for the hospital and barracks to be completed, and told Bate to proceed also with Fort Cockburn and with 'Tower No. 1', a defence outpost designed to cover Comfortless Cove.

In an optimistic assessment of the island's defences he wrote:

> Long possession of this island by an enemy is impossible, for the Garrison has a safe retreat in the Mountain and by cutting off the supply of water and frequently attacking the enemy, would soon make them glad to leave.

Warren's optimism extended to the state of Ascension's finances, which he felt could be subtantially improved by increasing the export of turtles; and if he was inclined to be over-enthusiastic, he was quite practical enough to see ways of cutting through the bureaucratic knots which were pushing up expenses needlessly. He found it 'inexplicable', for instance, that African oak should be shipped to England, sawn in dockyards there, and then sent all the way back to Ascension, when it could come straight and free of charge from Fernando Po to the island, where 'we have Marines who saw without any additional pay'. Equally absurd was the arrangement whereby fodder for the animals came all the way from England: it could, Warren rightly said, be sent from the Cape far more quickly and cheaply.

It is hard to tell what favour his proposals found in Whitehall; but for the moment Bate had got the go-ahead and in the next two years he finished the Mountain Barracks and the Hospital. The Mountain Barracks was his one big mistake: it was badly sited at nearly 2500 feet just on the lee side of the ridge behind the farm, and was made thoroughly damp and uncomfortable by the fog, or low cloud, which frequently envelops the summit of Green Mountain. So unpleasant was it that in the 1860s a new barracks was built lower down the slope, beneath the fog-line, and the old one became first a cowshed and then a dairy – probably the only one in the world to bear a stone-carved crest of the Royal Marines.

The Garrison hospital was far more successful, and it survives to this day, a graceful, single-storey building with an arched colonnade, standing on the level plateau some fifty feet above the sea just inland from Regent Square, the site of the original camp.

Medical knowledge was limited and diagnosis erratic, to say the least. Whenever someone fell ill, a 'survey' of his health was made by a panel of at least two surgeons and two Marine or naval officers all of whom signed the appropriate form. Scurvy was well-known, and could be dealt with by the issue of fresh meat, lime juice or green vegetables, whenever they were available; but far more sinister complaints make regular appearances in the records, among them 'phthisis incipiens', which seems to have described any state of general debility. Although the island's climate was, and is, extremely healthy, some men could not stand the heat: in 1837, for instance, three surgeons took 'a strict and careful survey' of the health of John Pratt, the Agent Victualler, concluded that he was 'labouring under dyspepsia', and recommended a change of climate.

The new hospital was the first of the stone buildings with which Bate dignified Georgetown, and it was soon followed by the Royal Marine Barracks, which was originally a similar shape and also survives, although with a second storey added later.

Before this could be finished, however, in the middle of 1834 Bate suddenly received an order instructing him to make drastic reductions in the strength of the garrison. Seventy out of two hundred non-commissioned officers and privates were to be sent home as soon as possible.

To Bate, half-way through his grand design, this must have been a shattering blow. But on paper there is not a syllable of protest or appeal. Besides getting rid of the humans, he told the Admiralty,

> I will avail myself of every opportunity of disposing to the best advantage of the surplus cattle, and in the event of my not being able to do so, shall as the works are completed turn them out to feed on the resources of the island, so that there shall be no expense to the Government.

Bate was by no means the last commandant of Ascension to be crippled by changes in – or rather the lack of – any proper policy in London. The Lords of the Admiralty seem never to have made up their minds about what they wanted Ascension to be. Time and again, after repeated requests for more men from the officer in charge, the island's strength built up to a pitch at which real progress could be made with the work in hand. Time and again the axe fell just as everything seemed to be going well. It must have been heartbreaking, especially on the farm, where land brought into cultivation with enormous labour inevitably reverted to its former state of uselessness.

Bate carried on as best he could. One Sunday in March 1835 Captain Brandreth dropped in on his way home; he stayed only one day, but professed himself 'highly gratified' with the way the various works had been accomplished. That same summer the

Marine barracks was finished, and the depleted garrison turned its attention to completing the blockhouse in Fort Cockburn.

From occasional scraps of information one can catch glimpses of their routine. Reveille was at 5 a.m. or 5.30 a.m. and work began at 5.30 or 6. There was a pause for breakfast, a long lunch-break from eleven to three, avoiding the worst heat of the day, and then another session of work until sunset at 6.30. On one day each week two drill parades were held, one at dawn and the other just before dusk.

The main interest and excitement must have been the arrival of ships bringing news from England, from the coast of Africa, or from even more outlandish places. ('The brig *Unity* brought intelligence of an insurrection in China.') And occasionally – though, from the point of view of the Marines, not nearly often enough – the pattern was broken by some slight novelty.

In 1836, for instance, a small schooner from the Cape and St Helena anchored in the bay, the skipper wishing to open a market with the islanders. Among the luxuries he offered were 'wine, beer, fruits etc.'. Now Bate, as other references show, took great trouble to keep the demon alcohol within bounds; and on this occasion he reported in his journal:

I desired the Master to give me a list of his prices, with the exception of the wines – and if they were reasonable I would submit them to the garrison; that the men should put down what they wished, and if approved of, he might land them, but that if he allowed one single article to come on shore clandestinely, I would immediately order him to sea.

Needless to say, trouble set in at once:

The second day after his arrival, I found several men intoxicated, and on searching their barracks in one man's chest were seven bottles of Cape Wine. Immediately had him before me and promised forgiveness if he would tell the truth . . . he acknowledged that whilst sentry on the beach, he with two other men launched the jolly boat a little after 12 o'clock at night went off to the schooner and purchased from the crew 7 gallons of wine.

The culprits were sentenced to extra labour, and, when they refused to do it, to corporal punishment. Normally the maximum was forty-eight lashes, but on one occasion Bate sentenced a man to 250 lashes (of which he got 200) for 'irregular conduct in endeavouring to impose on his Commanding Officer'. Other penalties included temporary loss of rank and something known as 'the Black Hole' – presumably a form of solitary confinement, which in Ascension's heat cannot have been very pleasant. The severity of the punishments reminds one of the rigours of naval life in the early nineteenth century; Bate was clearly an officer of exceptional humanity, yet even he saw nothing extraordinary in sentencing a man to 200 lashes.

In spite of the strictness of discipline, occasional fatalities occurred among the members of the garrison or ships' crews. In 1831 one Marine killed another with a blow during a fight over cards in the Mountain settlement, and in March 1835 John Taylor, gunner of H.M.S. *Lynx* was drowned. 'This poor man,' Bate wrote, 'fell a sacrifice to his own imprudence, by venturing into the sea contrary to the wishes and advice of those who were with him.' It was left to someone else to record that Taylor had been swept away 'in the attempt to obtain a Man-of-War bird shot by Corporal Wilson'.

By then – 1835 – a new commanding officer had taken over the Cape of Good Hope Squadron: Rear-Admiral Patrick Campbell, who became obsessed with the slave trade to a degree that Admiral Warren had never been. Already, by the end of 1834, he had reported to the Admiralty that his ships were 'placed in what are considered to be the most favourable positions for suppressing the slave traffic', and for the next four years he harassed the slavers with a zeal that was ultimately to prove fatal to Bate and many of his men. To blame him for doing his duty assiduously would be ridiculous; yet it is certainly true that, by calling frequently at Ascension in his own flagship the *Thalia*, and by generally stepping up the pursuit, Admiral Campbell ensured that almost every disease known on the coast was brought to the island.

His own dispatches resound with successful anti-slave operations, and many of his ships' captains composed their individual reports from the safety of Ascension, to which they often brought the captured vessels, with or without their wretched human cargo. This account, from Lieutenant Puget, acting commander of H.M. Sloop *Trinculo* in October 1835, is typical:

> I am happy to be able to inform you that the *Charybdis* has added another vessel to the list of captures, having taken the *Argos* brig with 429 slaves on board. He sailed from the Bonny with 500, but, that river being very sickly, he says they died; but being chased three days, he acknowledges having hove overboard 10 slaves the last day, who were likely to die, together with the other Lumber he got clear of. The crew said the major part of the rest went the same way. . . .
>
> When at Port Antonio, the Master of a slave brig in that harbour gave me much information – he says that, knowing at Havannah that the slave trade will soon be put a stop to, every vessel they can get hold of is sent for slaves. . . .
>
> To the southward they are literally swarming, and one a very fine brig called the *Christina*, well armed and carries a thousand.

Writing to the Admiralty from Ascension in December that year, Admiral Campbell called for more ships and said: 'The traffic in slaves appears to be carrying on to a most extraordinary extent, both to the northward and southward of the Line, by Spanish and Portuguese vessels.' One of the ships' commanders added: 'The whole coast is in such a stew, they know not what to do.'

In the next two years Campbell's cruisers scored one success after another. Between October 1836 and March 1837 alone they captured eleven Portuguese and two Spanish vessels with a total of 3983 slaves on board. But the victories, in the end, were dearly bought. After the rains of 1837 many of the ships were hit by fever: the *Dolphin*, for instance, lost her captain, her second master, the assistant surgeon, three seamen and two boys during the run from the coast to Ascension; and the *Curlew* lost six seamen, three Marines and five boys. In May H.M.S. *Scout* reached the island with her captain, Lieutenant Charles Baldwin Acland, 'lying a corpse', according to Bate's report. He was buried in the main graveyard behind Comfortless Cove.

Meanwhile Bate was carrying on steadily with the public works – principally quarters for officers, and a water-pipe that ran right out to the pier-head so that ships could load directly from it. The first to do so was the *Atholl*, and Bate reported that she took on 'about a tun in 12 minutes, which saves an immensity of labour and the wear of the casks'.

Some idea of the isolation in which the captain and his garrison had to operate, and of the iron routine by which they were bound, is given by the fact that news of the death of King William IV, which occurred on 20 June 1837, took nine weeks to reach them, and yet they reacted to it with total formality. Bate wrote in his journal:

The lamented death of his most gracious Majesty reached this island on the 25th August and on the Sunday following at daylight minute guns commenced firing from the fort, taken up by *Columbine* and *Curlew* at anchor in the bay, until 73 had been fired, with the flags at half-mast until sunset, the next at daylight the colours were hoisted on the fort and a Royal salute fired in honour of our most gracious Queen Victoria.

More to the point for the Marines than such out-of-date ceremony,

At noon an extra glass of grog was given to drink the health of Queen Victoria and wish her a happy reign.

Considering how many sickly ships called, it seems astonishing that the health of the garrison remained intact for so long. Crews with diseases known to be contagious like cholera and small-pox were still banished to Comfortless Cove, but seamen suffering from other complaints were taken into the new hospital. Diagnosis was extremely haphazard, and it was only a matter of time before some serious epidemic took hold among the people on shore.

The year 1838 opened on a bad note when the *Aetna* arrived in a low state, having lost twenty-five men on the passage from the Coast. The *Forester* lost five men on the way from Sierra Leone, the *Raven* four officers and eleven men. All these ships anchored off Ascension while the survivors recovered.

None, however, had a worse time than the *Bonetta*, which reached Ascension on 29 January. The lethal progress of the fever is recorded in the staccato entries in the ship's log: '8.30 communicated with the health boat in consequence of having several sickly on board of yellow fever. Hoisted quarantine flag, furled sails.' One man died that day, and at least one on most of the days in February. 'Departed this life ... departed this life': the phrase recurs in almost every entry.

The ship anchored in Comfortless Cove and put the invalids ashore. Those who died on board were buried at sea, those on land in the graveyard in the lava, all (because of the heat) within an hour or two of their expiring. On 8 February came the grimmest entry of all: 'Departed this life H. P. Deschamps (Lieutenant and Commander).' Beneath this some other hand repeated in stark emphasis: 'Lieutenant and Commander dead,' and for the next nine days, while the fever raged at its worst, the log was left empty. Marines from the garrison brought the crew bread, turtle meat, mutton and water, dumping them at a safe distance; but otherwise there was no help that anyone could give.

Not until 13 March, after six weeks at anchor, was the *Bonetta* in a sound enough state to sail for the Cape, and even then she left an assortment of invalids in the garrison hospital. Her stay is remembered to this day by a little cemetery named after her in the rocky wilderness behind Comfortless Cove, although not all its fourteen graves belong to members of her crew.

Whether it was the *Bonetta* or the *Thalia* which caused the disaster that followed, one cannot now tell; but towards the end of March a vicious epidemic broke out in the garrison and killed at least twenty-five men, including Bate himself. The Commandant's death was a stunning blow, made all the worse by the fact that no one had realised, until the last moment, that he was seriously ill. The shock it caused reverberated through the doom-laden dispatch sent home by the second-in-command, Captain Evans:

> Ascension Island,
> 1st May 1838.

Sir

It is my melancholy duty to acquaint you for the information of the Lords Commissioners of the Admiralty that this once healthy island has been and is I regret to say still suffering under a visitation of most malignant fever which made its appearance amongst us towards the latter end of March.

I have no doubt Sir before this can reach you, you will have heard the melancholy news from Rear Admiral Sir F. B. Capel who touched here in the *Winchester* on the morning of Sunday the 15th at the moment we were making preparations for the interment of our beloved and revered Commandant who was then lying dead in the garrison. . . .

On the day after the departure of the *Thalia* symptoms of the disease manifested themselves in the garrison. On Monday the 9th the Commandant left the garrison and walked to the Mountain in apparent health to give charge of the Mountain to Lieutenant/Adjutant Barnes, who accompanied him. On Tuesday he complained of having caught cold, and feeling indisposed, but we were not aware of his illness being serious until Saturday morning.

In the meantime the fever had broken out with violence in the Square, a great portion of the garrison were seized with it, and nine persons including the Commandant were buried between the 9th and the 15th, five funerals having taken place on Saturday 14th, and our beloved Commandant made the sixth death on that fatal day.

He breathed his last at the North East Cottage in the Mountain at half past seven that night to the inexpressible sorrow and deepest regret of every individual on the island, more particularly of myself, who thus lost an old friend of 23 years' standing, ten of which we had served together on this island.

We committed his remains to the grave with every mark of military respect that our distressed means in the garrison would admit of.

So the little island, which Bate had looked after and loved for ten years, was suddenly left without him. The sturdy Captain Evans automatically assumed command:

15 April 1838. It having pleased the Almighty Dispenser of Events to remove from this life our late revered and Esteemed Commandant – I in conformity with the rules and regulations of Her Majesty's Service do now take command of this Island and Garrison.

As soon as the fever had died down, Evans ordered the survivors to church:

5 May 1838. It having pleased Almighty God to visit this island with great affliction and sickness, Divine service has of necessity been suspended for two successive Sundays. It will therefore be performed tomorrow and all persons able to attend will do so to offer up their thanksgiving for their preservation during the heavy calamity that has befallen us.

Evans was a thoroughly competent officer: visiting commodores and admirals spoke highly of the state in which he maintained the garrison and the public works. But I feel that neither he nor any of the Marine and naval commandants who succeeded him ever tackled Ascension with quite the same combination of enthusiasm and imagination as Bate. None of them fell so completely under the island's spell or responded to it so strongly.

It is a cruel irony that, while officers who did far less for Ascension are effusively remembered on the walls of the island's church,

Bate has only a small plaque which, inexplicably, has both his Christian name and surname wrong, calling him 'Edward Bates'. Yet if the title is awry, at least the message is very much to the point:

> This tablet was erected on the reduction of the island in 1882 as a token of admiration for his energy and skill in carrying out so many valuable works to which the island still owes much of its comfort.

GARRISON LIFE

1839-50

Bate's official successor, Captain Roger Tinklar, did not last long. An irritable officer, whose temper was doubtless not improved by an 'angry wound' in his leg, he took over from Captain Evans in January 1839 and was soon complaining of the many 'vexatious practices' which he found he had inherited. One was the Marines' habit of using many different types of currency – among them doubloons, two kinds of rupees and 'cut-money', or quarter dollars roughly chopped up with a chisel. British currency, Tinklar reported, was being hoarded, and whenever condemned stores were auctioned, the men brought out their foreign coins with which to pay. Altogether, Tinklar estimated that there was some £100,000 of currency on the island.

His popularity can hardly have been increased when he abolished 'the long continued practice (pregnant with danger to good order and discipline) of issuing spirits to the men unmixed'. Even so, he seems occasionally to have become quite jovial; once, for instance, he féted the officers of a French barque and made so bold as to give them a turtle. Writing to the Admiralty soon afterwards, he hoped that their Lordships would approve of such actions, 'which show an undeniable evidence of the liberality of such a nation as Great Britain'.

Liberal or not, in the autumn of 1840 Tinklar fell ill and died, apparently from some liver-complaint. Two lieutenants held the fort in succession until his appointed successor, Captain Henry Bennett, arrived in April 1841, but in December he too died, after only seven months in office. Fortunately the sudden mortality among commandants was not matched in the garrison, and there was no general epidemic.

Thanks to an account written by General Simon Fraser, R.M., who in 1843 was a lieutenant and acting adjutant on the island, one can get a graphic picture of Ascension at that time:

Georgetown [wrote Fraser] is built in the form of a square, and here are the quarters of the married soldiers, the single men occupying the barracks, a large building encircled with a wide verandah. There are small cottages for the Officers' quarters, and two hospitals, one of the latter being exclusively for fever patients. . . . The black men's quarters were all built near the shore, and were called Krootown. Every house was surrounded by a wide verandah, which was an absolute necessity in that climate, being the only means of making any dwelling habitable. the houses themselves were built of stone from the shore. . . . Our cottage had neither fireplace nor window-glass in any of the rooms, but the latter was scarcely required – there was no change of season at Ascension, the heat was intense all the year round; so that the window places were always open during the day, and closed at night by venetian shutters, kept as open as possible to admit the air. Our walls were whitewashed, instead of being papered, or painted, so that such venomous insects and scorpions might be easily seen on them. . . .

The black men employed on the island as cooks and servants were, for the most part, liberated Africans. Only the Marine Officers had a white man for personal attendance in addition to the cook.

Life must have been thoroughly uncomfortable. In spite of Bate's elaborate system of pipes and tanks for making the most of rain, water was frequently scarce, and the tanks in Georgetown were kept locked, a small amount being doled out daily to each family, according to its numbers. Clothes had to be washed in sea water. On one occasion supplies of fresh water failed altogether, and emergency shipments were brought up from St Helena. Fraser records how, 'whenever a dark cloud was seen, every piece of crockery about the house was brought out and ranged along in front of the verandah, so that we might catch any rain that fell, but none came'.

The food must have been monotonous in the extreme. Officers could occasionally buy luxuries from passing ships ('Champagne could sometimes be procured from the French ships, and also brandy,' wrote Fraser); but the rank-and-file Marines had little to supplement their rations except the usual extras – scraggy meat from the goats, sheep and cattle and, at certain seasons, turtles and the eggs of the wideawake terns. The gardens on Green Mountain produced a considerable quantity of fresh vegetables, but most of them, and much of the meat, seem to have been given to British men-of-war, or sold to passing strangers, rather than issued to the garrison.

Apart from the constant heat, there were many irritations, not least the insects. Only the scorpions were positively dangerous, but Georgetown was also infested with cockroaches, which, though harmless, had a strong smell. 'Streams of ants, too,' wrote Fraser,

... used to pay us regular and repeated visits, entering by the front door, marching through the dining room, and finally wending their way to one or other of the bed-rooms, and at last making their exit through the window-place. ... At first we attempted to get rid of them, but found it quite impossible. ...

Mosquitos were furious, and unwearied in their attacks. ... Sleep was impossible unless when quite surrounded by mosquito curtains. But one of the greatest and most trying pests of all was the common house-fly: they were round us at all times in myriads. Neither breakfast nor dinner service could be set down until the very moment of use, and every glass or tumbler had a cover which was only removed for a moment and then replaced: reading or writing was a most difficult task, as the fly-switcher was in constant use.

None of these aggravations, minor in themselves, can have been made any more bearable by the rigid naval routine that prevailed. The garrison was up at five, to take advantage of the cool of the morning, and from about 6.30 onwards the day was one of steady work. This entry in the commandant's journal of 1844 is typical of dozens:

Monday 15 January. A.M. Light breezes and fine weather. Wind SE. Rollers setting in from the Westward. Carpenters employed making shower bath, handling tools and fitting up Brigantine *Independancia* for a coal depot. Masons, labourers and Africans building Coal Shed, cutting stone, and clearing Freight Vessel. Saddler repairing harness. Smiths shoeing and making iron work for cart.

Wheelwright repairing Turtle Waggon and Cart, Sawyers cutting plank. One painter on board H.M.S. *Madagascar* and fitting cisterns to shower bath.

P.M. Strong breezes. At 12.15 arrived and anchored in the bay the brig *Rambler*, P. Hutchinson master, from St Helena bound to London. Hands employed as in the morning . . . water expended 700 gallons.

Working uniform, for officers and men alike, was a suit of white duck and a Panama hat to keep off the sun. Saturday afternoons were generally free, but on Sundays, although they had no work to do, the Marines were made to parade for inspection at 10 o'clock in the morning, and then again at 2 p.m. for divine service, which was conducted by the chaplain of the ship in the bay, or, if none was available, by the Commandant, who was still legally empowered to bury the dead, to marry and to christen.

Divine service was no more popular then than it had been in Bate's day, and although no one seems to have been punished for shirking, frequent sharp notices from the Commandant, Captain Thomas Dwyer, were needed to keep attendance up to strength:

The Commandant is sorry to be called upon to remark that several persons belonging to this Establishment are in the habit of absenting themselves on Sundays from Divine Service. He hopes it will not be necessary for him again to remind these

The Naval Canteen, 1907

One of the goats brought to bag, 1907

E.T.C. staff at the Dewpond on the Peak. The Superintendent, H. R. G. Elms, is fourth from the right in the tattered shorts, about 1910

Grass being harvested on the plains after the great rain of 1924

Rollers, with wall of turtle pond in foreground

St. Mary's Church, with Cross Hill behind

persons that a more regular attendance at Divine Service as enjoined in 'the articles of War' will in future be expected.

Services were held under the arched colonnade of the Marine Barracks. On 6 September 1843 the cornerstone of a church was laid by Mrs Dwyer, wife of the Commandant, but labour was so short and progress so slow that the building was not completed for nearly twenty years. The builders were not helped by the long-range attempts of the Admiralty in London to influence the church's shape and appearance: official ideas and plans invariably arrived so late as to be a menace, as this note from the Commandant to the Director of Works makes clear:

> Ascension,
> March 13 1844.
>
> Sir, I have the honor to be in receipt of your letter of 5 December 1843 enclosing a sketch of the proposed Chapel at Ascension, and in reply state that, your instructions to conform to this design shall be diligently followed.
>
> I regret that greater progress should not have been made with this building, but the interruptions here are so numerous and so unceasing that I see little hope of its ever being completed unless other measures and greater power than I have been able to exercise be put in play.
>
> I have the honor to be,
> etc. etc.
> sgd. Thos. P. Dwyer, Captain, R.M., Commandant.

No 'greater powers' were forthcoming, and the design kept being changed. In 1845 the Commandant was ordered 'to cause the church now in progress at Ascension to be enlarged by advancing the walls 8 or 10 feet at the entrance end'.

Visiting the island in July 1845, Commodore William Jones, Commander of the West Coast of Africa Squadron, found the church only half built. Artificers had started the walls, he reported to the admiralty, but they could go no further until materials for the roof were sent out from England, the original materials 'having long since been converted by Commodore Finlaison and the Chaplain into a roof for the present church, which under the name of "school house" had been erected without my being consulted'.

This building, sixty feet by thirty feet, was already being used for divine service. An attractive contemporary pencil and water-colour sketch shows that it had four windows and five buttresses on each side; and to Commodore Jones it seemed perfectly adequate. 'Its appearance and accommodation,' he wrote, 'appear to me quite as good as in many a country church in England.'

His representations made no impression on their Lordships in London, who ordered the proper church to be finished as soon as possible. Somebody – possibly Sir David Acland, whose son was buried in Comfortless Cove – had given a considerable amount of money towards the building, so that its completion was essential on moral if not on religious grounds.

After further long delays it was eventually finished – the spire at first, it is said being clad with beaten-out biscuit-tins – and on 9 May 1861 it was dedicated as St Mary's by the Bishop of St Helena. It was restored in 1879–80, and again in 1912; but its basic shape is the same today as it was a hundred and thirty years ago.

The strict formality visible in Dwyer's letters and orders permeated the whole life of the garrison. When Second Lieutenant H. B. Leonard misinterpreted his orders about slaughtering animals for meat, he was placed under arrest, and, instead of sorting the matter out verbally with his commanding officer, wrote an elaborate letter of apology:

Sir, In explanation of my involuntary disobedience of your orders. I beg leave most respectfully to state that I was not aware that the order issued by you extended to the Goats, and having understood from Sergeant Constant that the Bullock would not be sufficient and that two would be a great deal too much for one day's allowance, I thought it would be good for the Service if Goats were killed, and Sheep not.

To which the Commandant had the Adjutant reply:

Sir, I am desired by the Commandant to inform you that in consequence of the explanation contained in your letter of yesterday's date, and the regret you have expressed for an act of what he is glad to find you are able to assert was 'involuntary disobedience', you are relieved from that arrest in which you have been placed.

And the Commandant now desires that you will distinctly understand that you are not, under any pretext, to interfere with the agricultural arrangements, or with the stock of the land – for which he will provide as he deems best for the interest of H.M. Service.

It was partly as a result of the row between Leonard and Dwyer that a new system of command was adopted from 1844 onwards. In that year H.M.S. *Tortoise*, a store ship, was commissioned at Chatham, and sailed to Ascension, where she remained for the rest of her life, anchored in the bay. Her captain became the Commander of the garrison, so that command of the island passed from the Marines to the Navy; in the official records, the island became the tender of the guardship, and the members of the garrison the tender's crew, all borne on the guardship's books. In 1859 the *Tortoise* was replaced by the *Meander*, and the *Meander* in 1865 by the *Flora*, so that there was always some hulk rolling off the pierhead – until 1872, when the *Flora* was removed to Simonstown.

Even this new system of command did not entirely solve the problems of discipline on Ascension, and the Admiralty occasionally had to consult legal experts about what was and what was not admissible. In 1851 Sergeant J. Perkins of the Marines was murdered by an engine fitter called Peel, and both the murderer and witnesses were sent to England for trial. After this incident the Board of Trade in London agreed that the Captain-in-charge should be invested with the powers of a civil magistrate; yet in 1857 the Admiralty was still unhappy, and directed that

> seamen and marines borne on the books of H.M. ships are not amenable to Naval Court Martial for offences committed in Ascension other than those classed under the head of mutiny, desertion and disobedience of lawful command; it appears doubtful whether marines so borne are not liable to be tried under the Marine Mutiny Act, so the case was to be reconsidered with the law officers of the Crown.

On the island the advent of the guardship made little difference, as the great majority of the garrison continued to be Marines. The Captain-in-charge lived in Bate's cottage, on the side of Cross Hill, and the entire establishment was run 'for the good of the Service', to which everything else (including, often, reason) had to be sacrificed. When Dwyer wanted to put down some worn-out draught animals he could not do so without first taking a formal survey.

'The undermentioned Board of Officers,' said the daily order of 13 March 1844,

> will assemble at the Mountain on Friday morning next at 12 o'clock for the purpose of holding a strict and careful Survey on all the worn-out Horses and Donkeys, preparatory to their being destroyed:
> 1st Lieut. Moore: President
> 1st Lieut. and Acting Adjutant Fraser
> Dr A. Elliot: Assist. Surgeon.

The board duly reported on 'all the unserviceable Horses and Donkeys, which we find', as follows:

Description	Number	Remarks
Mares	1	Old and unfit for work and past breeding. Age upwards of 15 years.

| Poneys | 1 | Worn out by age and disease. |
| Mules | 1 | So vicious that she is unavailable for draught or saddle, has already kicked and bitten in a dangerous manner several Men and Animals. (Is nearly blind.) |

The report was approved by the Commandant, and in due course some twenty-five animals were put down.

Humans died without permission from anyone. Although the anti-slave-trade operations on the coast of Africa were less intensive than they had been a decade before, fever-stricken ships still repaired intermittently to Ascension to let their invalids recuperate. Even though one of Georgetown's two hospitals was reserved exclusively for fever cases, sickly ships were still sent into quarantine in Comfortless Cove, and, as in earlier years, far more people probably died there than the tiny graveyards suggest. In the so-called Trident Cemetry, for instance, there are only three graves marked, but written records show that at least twenty-five of the ship's officers and crew died during 1839.

In the garrison Africans were buried without ceremony. ('At 3.15 departed this life Embouroco African belonging to this Establishment,' said the island journal for 4 March 1844. 'At 5.15 interred the remains of the late Embouroco African.') But soldiers of all ranks were buried with military honours. 'A Funeral Guard,' said a typical daily order,

consisting of one Lieutenant, one Serjt. and 30 Rank and File will parade this morning at 10 o'clock to fire over the remains of the late Mr Henry W. Pope.

Fear of fever was ever-present, and even more so on ships than on the island. The following letter, sent home to his sweetheart, Mary Smith, by a private in the Marines, tells more than a hundred pages of official records about the terrors engendered by the slave trade. I give it all, and have retained the original spelling and punctuation, because the document says so much about the good-natured simplicity of its author.

I' LAND OF ASSENSON,

December 1, 1845.

ionce more take the opertunity of righting these few Lines to you hopeing to find you in good health as this leaves mee at Preasant thank God for it witch wee hout to Bee verry thankful for and verry much so, in this Part of the world for ican ashure you that health is a verry sCarce thing for any long time tothether DM ibelieve that itould you in my last that you might expect mee in England the latter part of this heare But our ship is going under a great repaires so that icannot tell you when you may expect to see mee But ican allmost make shure that it will not Bee for more than 6 or 7 months MD

ishall Bee verry happy when ifind my self in ould England once more and then inever intend to go from it any More MD i am quite ready to goin our ands and harts together when ever wee meet if it should Bee.to morrow

And you need not think any thing About the expence for iam doing verry well at preasant But theire is allways adreat on amind continialy for you see aman well and haty getting is dinner and in about one houre after you might see im in is Cot or dead and MD when we take any of these slave vessels theire is asmall party of oure Crue and then when the come back th in genrally that the have sickness at the time and then it gets amongst the rest of the Crue so that wee are never cleare But icannot grumble for ihave had verry good health in genreally But ihave seen 73 buried in in less than 4 hours there is but 3 officers in the ship that left England and wee have buried twice the compliment and whee have but 6 marines that left woolwich with us But thank God iam foolish to beelieve that ishall not die in the service MD iam verry sorry to inform you that ihave had but 2 letters from you since ileft England and one of them igot in march 44 and one in April 45 wichit makes mee have manny unhappy hours you tould mee you send one in April 44 but ihave not got it yet MDM imust conclud for the preasent by wishing you all the Comforts this world can afford Pleas to except of kind love yourself so iremain your true and sinseare Lover till Death doth us seperat

JOHN EDMONSON

give my love to your mother and to all enquiring friends

> In this vain world how happy should ibee
> to spend my life my love with thee
> A cottage would to mee apalace prove
> could injoy it with the Lass ilove
> faire the gay and the darling of my hart
> Long is the time since you and idid part
> Parting with you hooe iloved so well
> the sorrow of my hart no tounge can tell
> May garden angels ever on you atend
> may you never want but allway find a frend
> in everry stage of life how happy should ibee
> wheni are far distant gone to heare you think on mee
> the rosses are read and the leaves are green
> those days are past that wee have seen
> Lets hope the days are yet to come
> that you and imay bee as one
> Join 'and join hart join love for ever
> Your mind might change but mine cant never
> if you doee these lines refuse
> Pray burn the paper and mee excuse
> Once to have a song all round
> sweet Valentine would sooner drouned.

The 'comforts this world can afford' were few indeed on Ascension, but one of the main pleasures was to escape to the cool heights of the Mountain, which, then as now, offered a delicious contrast to the heat of the plains. Simon Fraser recalled his stay on the heights with enthusiasm:

We were allowed during our stay on the Island to spend a month on the Green Mountain, during which time we occupied the Mountain House, taking our whole establishment with us. The Island gig, a small carriage without springs (the only approach to a carriage at Ascension) was sent for the ladies. It was drawn by three mules. A small cart, also drawn by a mule, carried our baggage; and horses were sent for the rest of the party. . . .

The base of the Green Mountain is four miles from the garrison, it rises almost perpendicularly, the summit being reached by a rugged road along its side, very zig-zag and about three miles long, it is named 'the ramps'. It is a dangerous road in some parts, and one morning the mountain cart fell over the edge, and the two poor mules were killed.

The gate at the top is always guarded by a Marine sentry; and we – poor dwellers in the perpetual heat, dust and desolation below – were rejoiced at the sight of what seemed to us like a paradise; the sweet cool air was so refreshing, and round the mountain cottage were clustered the only trees to be found on the whole island.

The flower garden was a special delight to us, it seemed so long since we had seen roses fuchsias and other flowers...

The pleasures in which the Fraser family took such delight – of walking in the wind, of exploring the mountain paths, of breathing the air – are exactly the same as those which refresh Ascension's plain-dwellers today. Even with the heat mitigated by air-conditioning and refrigerators, the cool green mountain still offers a miraculous change from the aridity of Georgetown.

In the 1840s the mountain settlement was manned by a detachment of about thirty men. Altogether. the island's garrison was about 330 strong, and in 1844 it included forty-three European women and forty-nine children. Evidently the school started by Bate in the 1830s had been allowed to lapse, for a testy order of 1840 laid down that a new one should be opened immediately:

The Commandant forbids the children being allowed any longer to run riot in the Garrison, and expects that they will be made to attend school. As superior instruction will be given, a charge of sixpence a week is to be made.

The 'superior instruction' seems to have been given by a sergeant. But the curriculum cannot have been very arduous, and its is a safe bet that the children were the happiest, least bored members of the community, as they grew up on an island permanently bathed in sun.

THE CAPTAIN'S VIEW

1858–61

A vivid picture of life on the island emerges from the letters of
Captain William Burnett, a Scot from Aberdeenshire who was
posted to Ascension as Commandant in 1858, at the age of forty-
three. 'This is one of the strangest places on the face of the earth,'
he wrote to his mother on 22 March, a week after he had arrived.

On this cinder we have at present about 250 or 300 souls, the
bodies of which are some white and some black, and consist of
men, women and children, all under the charge of the Captain
of the *Tortoise*, who is styled by the Lords of the Admiralty
'Captain of H.M. *Tortoise* in charge of Ascension'.

There are four or five of my officers married who have their
wives and some children, these, with officers of men-of-war and
occasional ships calling, form the society of the island. We all
have good houses and separate, mine stands about 400 feet above
the sea overlooking the little bay and the so-called 'Georgetown'.
. . . I have a dining and drawing room, two bed rooms, a good
cellar, a large verandah, a constant fresh breeze day and night,
and a few yards below my house a stable where at present stand
the Captain's cow and the Captain's mule.

My household consists of a good little German who has charge
of everything, a cook (a white man), a jack of all trades (a black
man), and a Marine groom (a good Scotchman) who looks after
the mule and the cow and some pigeons, fowls, pigs etc. . . .

I get about £600 a year, and I suppose you will say what more
do you want. As far as I can see I would willingly take a good
steam frigate with £450 a year in exchange, but I am not going
to tell their Lordships that, so I shall try and make the best of

what they have given me. The good points about Ascension as far as I yet see are, a fair, healthy though hot climate, as much fish of fair quality as you like to pull out of the sea, and plenty occupation. The bad points are scarcity of water and of a green blade of any kind, flies which are a great nuisance and some other things besides.

Describing the turtles and their great size, he went on:

I saw one on the sand this morning and pointed it out to my Scotchman, and it was so large that although he is a powerful young man he had hard work for 2 or 3 minutes to get it on its back. I observed just as it was on its side that it reached as high as his chest, he then quietly seated himself on his fat friend.

In July he wrote again, saying that he was short of music, and that he was expecting his harmonium to arrive soon.

We have little here except some very good voices, principally nigger voices, most of the niggers like to sing. I had six nigger boys and girls in my verandah today, who just came in to show some nice clothes they had on and to say *Good Marnin*, Sir. And as I gave them some dried fruit, I dare say they will soon be back to say *Good Marnin* again.

My greatest want here is water – and what greater want can we have in this world? ... I live on a hill as dry as a chip the greater part of the year round, and although I am in mid ocean, horses and carts must toil up to me with the water of the sea even.

By August Burnett was still not used to the novelty of his surroundings:

You will hardly know what to think of such a place by my accounts, I dare say, and to tell you the truth, it is about as strange a place as there is on the face of the earth. It is of course part of H.M. Dominions, but we have no lawyers or such folks, and the only man in the shape of a magistrate is the Captain of the *Tortoise*, and we look to the Lords of the Admiralty and the Commander-in-Chief of the Station as our immediate masters, and live principally under the Acts which govern Her Majesty's Fleets. And if a man brings his wife and as many children as he may be blessed with and his maid and servants, etc., they are always rationed by the Government unless they behave themselves very badly, when I might ship them off at very short notice if I am sure I am right.

We have marriages and christenings, and when an addition in the shape of a baby appears, it is rationed from the day of its birth. We have two schools, one in the *Tortoise*, and one on shore, with not less than fifty old and young attending them and with a school mistress for the girls.

In fact, a man may bring here his wife or his near female relations by simply asking permission and paying their passage, and then they will be fed by the Government, and if I had Dick here, for example, she would be allowed so much beef, pork, biscuits, tea and sugar per day and be given so much turtle and vegetables per week besides, so I leave you to make out what kind of a place it is to live in.

Some ladies seem to like it, some don't know whether they do or not, some make themselves very happy and comfortable and others the contrary. They have a good deal of time on their hands generally, I should think, and must depend a good deal on the little changes and amusements that the place will afford, and the Captain may make himself very disagreeable if he is so inclined and does not take great care and perhaps humour people a little now and then, more than would probably be done in any other place, we are so strangely circumstanced.

I am now sitting at 9 p.m. in a deliciously cool evening, with the thermometer at 72, the trade wind is blowing briskly, and I wear a comfortable flannel jacket and trowsers and live principally in the verandah.

My books all reached me in good condition and are my

principal friends just now, thanks to Newell for having them so
well packed and sent. . . . Tell him Hogarth's preserved meats
are capital, but that the wine cooling stuff got a little damp
somehow and thereby I lost a small portion of it. . . .

God bless you my dear Mother,
Your ever affectionate son,
W. F. Burnett.

In a letter to his sister Helen, written in September 1858,
Burnett described his efforts to have the island's children vaccinated against small-pox:

When I came here I found scarcely one of my white or black
children (in all about forty) vaccinated, and was told that the
oldest inhabitant had always declared that it never would take on
Ascension. Whereupon I sent to the vaccine Institute in London
and the Cape and Sierra Leone and got vaccine matter, and some
of the black children took it first, and white mothers declared
they would not have their darlings vaccinated from a nasty
black thing, and so we went on for a while and I was obliged to
'vow vengeance', but now they are all done. . . and this Ascension
idea about vaccination has gone, and the small pox if it
should come will not probably make such a sweep amongst my
children.

By the spring of 1860 Burnett was evidently feeling the isolation
and lack of female company. 'You ask what the period of service
here is,' he wrote to his mother on April Fool's Day. 'My predecessors have stopped here from 3 to 5 years. I begin to think
three will be enough for me. . . . A man in my position ought to be
married and have his wife with him. There is but little society, as
you may suppose, and were it not for the abundance of occupation
for mind and body it would be dismal.'

In July he wrote to Helen suggesting with great enthusiasm that
she and her husband Thomas should come out and stay with him
during the English winter:

Your direct passage here would be, strange to say, by the Cape of Good Hope, for such is the present admirable arrangement that the outward packet frequently passes within signal distance of the island carrying mails and passengers for Ascension to the Cape, to be landed here a month later. . . .

If you do come, bring with you the finest and lightest flannel belts to wear next your skin, good thick ankle boots, as many books as you like, a basket of good potatoes, a light tartan riding skirt of the Ballater pattern for donkey purposes, one or two nice caps (not mutches) to wear in-doors where there is always a fine current of trade wind, a light colored bonnet of the 'soeur de charité' pattern . . . and trust to me for the rest. The caps, I beg leave to say, are an idea of my own for this place. I am certain they will be approved of and will be found comfortable. The flannel belts, neither man, woman or child should be without in these climates if they are of European blood.

As for Thomas, if he brings music and light flannel jackets and trowsers, 4 scarfs of light muslin each about 3 yards long and a pith hat, which he can easily get in London, he will do well. If he wishes to stalk wild goats ask him to bring his rifle or to trust to me for an Enfield of the latest pattern. Finally, sturdy independence of maid servants and washerwomen – the former in Ascension are nil, the latter few and proportionately saucy and always glad to avoid the getting up of fine linen if they can obtain large washing bills of male attire. The very lightest texture woollen is best for Ascension.

I expect my term of servitude here will expire about March 1861, but I don't know for certain and am trying to find out.

For reasons that cannot now be determined, Helen never managed to make the projected trip. But on 5 October 1860 Burnett reported a most distinguished visitor:

Yesterday we had a visit of twelve hours' duration from H.R.H. Prince Alfred, now a young midshipman on board the *Euryalus* frigate. He landed here much like any other midshipman and took a ride as far as time would allow.

As he is only a midshipman and the Cinder and folks on it are all part of the *Meander*, and commanded by a post captain, we had no salutes beyond loyal bows to a boy in a midshipman's jacket who is very respectful to the Captain of his ship, never addresses him but as Sir, and who on a few words' conversation with and not knowing anything of his high birth, one would say, in common conversation, is 'a well brought up boy'.

He did me the honour to bring a basket of fir cones for planting on the Cinder and to give me his likeness.

In April and May 1861 Burnett played host to the Bishop of St Helena, who came to Ascension to consecrate the church and burial grounds, and whom he described as 'a quite agreeable man'. Fortunately the esteem was mutual, and in an account of his visit written for *The Mission Field* the Bishop paid tribute to Burnett 'for his kind readiness in carrying out all my wishes, and for his own excellent arrangements'.

The ceremonies were spread over a number of days; the first, on 30 April, consecrated the graveyard on Monkey Rock, beside the Mountain Hospital. Having been called at 5 a.m. and dressed by candle-light, the Bishop ascended the Mountain in a cart drawn by two mules. After breakfast at the Garden Cottage he inspected the farm, and then proceeded to the ceremony:

We all assembled at this point [the Mountain Hospital], and when I had robed formed a procession to the little spot. . . . The consecration was a striking scene. On this wild hill we stood, a sheer precipice on one side, and high rocks rising above us on the other, and as I concluded the service, the Africans sang one of their quaint hymn tunes, whilst the sound was almost lost in the wind; and this, with the wide Atlantic far below us, was something that I shall not forget.

Next day, together with Burnett, the Bishop made a reconnaissance of Comfortless Cove and was much struck by the strangeness of the little graveyards. But for the main event – the consecration of the church – he waited for the arrival of Ascension Day, 9 May.

I was anxious that the day from which the island took its name (probably not observed from that time to this) should be marked by this local celebration if possible.

At ten o'clock Captain Burnett came and reported to me that everything was ready. Accordingly we moved in procession from the house to the Church under a salute from the guns of the fort. It was a lovely morning; and looking on the bright sea and the dark rocks on the other side of the bay, the scene was one that none could easily forget.

All the officers, and marines, and sailors attended, and with the few ladies and children, and the Africans, formed a very goodly assemblage. The Church was very neatly decked with branches and flowers; and though it is not a very ecclesiastical edifice, it shows very creditably among the white houses of the garrison. . . .

Between services the Bishop spent his time energetically confirming and converting whites and blacks alike, and after one punishing session with the Africans found himself trapped:

After I had done talking, they began, at a signal from one of their number, to sing a hymn. The day was very hot and the room not very large, and as their voices were loud and I was rather weary with long talking, I began to hope it might not last long. The wish was vain! The leader of my little choir after each cadence repeated his signal, and I saw no prospect of recovering my liberty. At last, in despair, I got up, and, a moment of silence obtained, I succeeded in dismissing them (I hope) without offence.

On 14 May the Bishop consecrated the main cemetery below Georgetown, and the small ones at Comfortless Cove. Soon afterwards he returned to St Helena, well pleased with his visit.

Burnett did not stay long on Ascension either. A note on the island records that he was invalided home in July. Whatever the illness he had, he soon recovered, for a year later he was in Australia. But in 1863 his ship the *Orpheus* hit an uncharted reef off Auckland, and together with many of his crew he was drowned – a sad waste of a good man and one of the best-natured commandants that Ascension can ever have had.

NEW FLORA AND FAUNA

1815-40

So far I have described the Marines' efforts to establish a permanent township, to service visiting men-of-war, and to secure the island against possible attacks. All this activity could reasonably be said to have had a military purpose. Yet at the same time the Marines were engaged in the totally un-military task of grappling with Ascension's hostile terrain and trying to make it productive. As the years went by, the attempt to establish an ecological balance where none had existed before became more important than any other ploy on the island, and in the official records far more space is occupied by the exploits of Royal Marine shepherds, gardeners and gamekeepers than by news of gunners, signallers or storemen.

Before the occupation, Ascension was extraordinarily barren, preserved almost empty of plants by its tremendous isolation. James Cunninghame, who carried out the first botanical survey in the 1690s, found only four kinds of plant – a spurge, a creeper, a hibiscus, and a grass of the genus Aristida which he named 'Adscensionis'. Other lowly mosses and ferns must have escaped his attention, for more than thirty species are now known to be peculiar to the island; even so, the original flora were extremely simple.

Apart from the sea birds, which roosted and nested in thousands all over the western half of the island, and the green turtles which arrived between December and May every year to lay their eggs in the hot sand of the beaches, the 'ruinous heap of rocks', as one visitor called it, was originally inhabited only by land crabs. What these sidling, bug-eyed little creatures lived on, it is hard to say;

but presumably the detritus from the sea-bird colonies formed the basis of their diet.

Then humans upset this simple pattern. The Portuguese explorers of the sixteenth century put goats ashore with a double purpose: first, to see whether the place had water and would support life, and second, to provide a supply of meat on the hoof for anyone stranded there – a function which the goats performed admirably for William Dampier and his crew after they had been wrecked in 1701.

By 1725, when the Dutch sailor was abandoned on the island, the herds were several hundred strong. In 1775 members of Captain Cook's crew observed them grazing on 'a prodigious quantity of purslane' round the base of Green Mountain; and in 1798 William Davies, surgeon of the American brig *Atlantic*, recorded in his diary how surprised he was to find them right down by the sea, 'upon the extreme point of the land'.

'There are a good number of wild goats on the island,' he wrote

... but they seem in very poor condition. Indeed, I cannot fully satisfy myself how they exist at all: as I observed but two species of vegetable and those perfectly dried up and but very few plants of them.

The low state of the animals is hardly surprising: they must by then have been hideously interbred, no new blood having been introduced (as far as I can trace) since the first flock was landed.

As soon as the British sailors arrived in 1815 they began to shoot and eat them, and goat was a regular item in their menu. James Holman, the blind traveller who was entertained by Colonel Nicolls during his visit in 1828, dined on 'a large loin of wether goat, which, in my opinion, was equal to the finest mutton: indeed, had it been called mutton, I should not have known the difference, it was so fat and highly flavoured'. Holman must have been exceptionally fortunate, for the records show that most of the goats killed were little more than gristly skeletons, whole carcases often weighing no more than eleven or twelve pounds. Fined down by inbreeding, by the constant heat and by endless scrambling over the lava and cinders, they must have tasted more like old boots than mutton.

Poor though they were, the goats at least were put to good use, which is more than can be said of the rats. These came ashore at some early date, either from wrecks or from the ships of visitors; and, finding in the sea birds thousands of sitting targets, increased at a horrible rate.

The stranded Dutch sailor found them in such quantities that he was afraid they would eat him – and this they almost certainly did, for all that was discovered of him was a sun-bleached skeleton. William Davies, too, remarked on their 'amazing numbers', and recorded that they were 'so daring as to come round us and feed upon our possessions at the distance of a yard or two'.

The Navy's answer to the rats was cats, which they deliberately brought in for pest-control; but the solution was not so easy as it seemed, for the cats found the birds more palatable than the rodents, lived on them, and almost at once went wild, establishing themselves in the lava, which their grey, long-legged descendants still haunt today.

The answer to cats was dogs: in the 1820s Nicolls imported a pack of bull-terriers, and set about cat-hunting with the enthusiasm that characterised his whole life. Writing to the Admiralty on 8 November 1824, he protested:

We should have thousands of guinea fowl and wild cocks and hens instead of hundreds, were it not that we are overrun by wild cats as bad if not worse than the island formerly was by rats (a rat is rarely to be seen now) and I hope soon to put down the cats by the assistance of my dogs. The cats have killed the geese and their goslings on their nests. Turkeys in the same way. So numerous are they that I have killed sixteen in a day and should have killed more but that the dogs were knocked up for intense heat and want of water.

Cat-hunting, it is clear from a visitor's report, was one of the soldiers' principal recreations. The cats (recorded James Holman) 'afford no little amusement to the officers of the establishment . . . the gentlemen sportsmen of the island declare that a battle between these belligerent powers (the dogs) and natural enemies, presents a scene of unusual excitement and interest to the lovers of animal gladiatorship'. Fifty years later the sport was still flourishing, for the commandant of the day had a large pile of earthenware drain pipes rearranged so that dogs could work right through and flush the cats into the open.

Crab hunting, too, was a fancied pastime, as Brandreth reported. The dogs, he wrote, were specially trained to hunt the land crabs

which are similar to those in the West Indies, and burrow high up in the mountain district. They are found crossing the tracks from hole to hole, with their claws bristling with defiance: the dog, when set on them, makes a spring, gives one cranch, and then tosses the mangled carcass away; but an occasional sharp howl indicates an unsuccessful attack, and that the crab has pinned his opponent by the nose. The land crab in the West Indies, after being penned up physicked, fattened and dressed with divers condiments, is considered a delicacy. I endeavoured to persuade my friends at Ascension to introduce it among the island delicacies, but in vain.

In thinking he had almost exterminated the rats, Nicolls was optimistic, for they continued to be a menace throughout the occupation. In the 1830s his successor, Bate, ended most of his weekly reports home with the bag of vermin killed:

Destroyed this week: 12 cats
                         35 rats.

Incentives were offered in the form of money or spirits:

3 May 1841. The Commandant is pleased to increase the quantity of spirits for killing a cat, to one gill instead of half a gill, as heretofore.

and the pack of 'Vermin Dogs' was maintained well into the 1840s, although it was not always used for the purpose intended:

27 May 1841. The Commandant cannot help expressing his surprise at the scarcity of Guinea Fowl compared with the numbers seen by him in former years. .... It is to be distinctly understood for the future that no party for the Mountain be permitted to take out the Vermin Dogs under the pretence of killing cats and rats unless accompanied by a non-commissioned officer, who will be held responsible.

In spite of new regulations, depredations on the guinea-fowl continued:

24 August 1842. Henceforth all shooting or killing of the wild-fowl around the Mountain district is strictly forbidden without a special order or permission from the Commandant. And were it not that the extreme fag to be incurred in guinea-fowl shooting is in itself a tolerably good barrier against abuse in that sport, the Commandant would feel it right to establish certain regulations. But even as it thus is, he will so far order that the space within a mile and a half around the Mountain quarters be respected as a preserve, in no pretence whatever to be violated without permission in writing from the Commandant.

Poaching or not, the cats had to be kept down: 'The Commandant has no objection to the men having Saturday to themselves as heretofore for the purpose of cat-hunting.'

2 August 1841. It is the Commandant's direction that Sergeant Constant will from this date forward to Headquarters every Monday morning the tails of all the cats and rats for which he may have to issue spirits.

Meanwhile a great variety of other plants and animals had been introduced. The Commandant of the first garrison party, Lt.

William Roberts, brought plants and seeds with him when he arrived from St Helena in 1816, and at once set about executing his orders to establish a garden.

The physical labour which this entailed is not easily imagined. The only cultivable soil which the Marines could find was six miles from the settlement and more than 2000 feet up Green Mountain; even to reach the place meant a walk of several hours, first through the gently-rising, rock-strewn clinker desert, and then up the precipitous shoulder of the Mountain. Even when the Marines had cut the chain of short, sharp straights, linked by hairpin bends, which they christened 'the Ramps', the climb remained a formidable one, in many places with a gradient of one in three. Nowhere along the route was there a single patch of shade: it is not surprising that a water-tank at about the half-way mark was christened 'God-be-Thanked', or that the two halves of a naval cutter were stood on end as shelters either side of the road at the foot of the really steep climb, giving the place the un-likely name of Two Boats.

The ascent, however, was well worth making, for at about 2200 feet, on a tiny plateau sheltered from the hustling trade winds, the pioneers found a good depth of fertile soil, and in it they soon had vegetables growing. The fact that this patch, of just over one acre, now known as the Home Garden, is the only piece of ground on the entire mountain that could reasonably be called level gives a good idea of how difficult cultivation was – and is. On it the Marines built two wooden houses – one for an officer and one for other ranks – for the garden was valuable also as a look-out post, and its distance from the garrison made it essential that the place was manned by a separate detachment.

Behind the Home Garden the land rises steeply again to a ridge at 2400 feet, and this in turn leads to the peak of Green Mountain. Today many of the steep upper slopes are cloaked with scrub and trees, and the peak itself is crowned with a dense grove of bamboos, so that it takes some effort of imagination to see the place as it was in 1815, entirely naked except for grass and a few other ground plants, grazed close by the wandering goats. (Darwin, visiting in

1836, described it as being like the worse parts of the Welsh mountains.)

Besides the Home Garden, the Marines managed to open up one or two other small patches, and soon they had more than two acres under cultivation. But they were severely hampered by lack of water and labour, and a report of 1821 described the gardens as 'much overrun with weeds and shrubs'. The houses, too, had fallen into bad repair, and the place had been generally let go. The live-stock were similarly out of control: two 'unserviceable' mules had been turned loose, and there were eight or nine oxen wild on the Mountain. The number of goats was unknown, but certainly over 150, and guinea-fowl, introduced by Sir George Collier, were thriving in considerable flocks. A few goats and pigs were being kept in captivity, and some members of the garrison had their own chickens, geese and turkeys.

Enthusiasm for horticulture revived with the arrival of Colonel Nicolls as Commandant in 1823. He himself owned a farm in England, and knew what he was about. He quickly sent in a demand for seeds of turnips, radishes, carrots, lettuces, leeks, parsley, cabbages, mustard and cress, cucumbers and broccoli, and so well did the garden flourish under his direction that in 1825 it produced 5708 pounds of vegetables and fruit, including french beans, sweet potatoes, turnips, leeks, spinach, pumpkins, water-melons and bananas. Heavy root-vegetables like potatoes and turnips clearly made up the great bulk of the produce, while more delicate things were comparatively rare. All the same, a considerable transforma-tion had been wrought: instead of being a sterile heap of rocks, Ascension had become able to furnish passing ships with water, turtle meat and vegetables.

By no means all the importations were deliberate, for many weeds came in, either mixed with seeds or in the roots of growing plants. By 1828, when W. H. B. Webster, surgeon of the *Chanticleer*, compiled a report on the island's botany, the wild species were so numerous that he found it impossible to say which were indigen-ous and which brought in. On the plains the most common plants were purslane (*Portulaca oleracea*) and spurge (the original

Euphorbia origanoides); on the Mountain, Cape gooseberries (*Physalis edulis*) and castor oil plants (*Ricinus communis*) flourished in abundance, besides at least three kinds of grass, thistles and some exotic weeds. The gooseberries, Webster records, were much fancied as a filling for tarts, and the Mountain garden produced 'cabbages, lettuces, potatoes (indifferent ones), calaloo, an excellent substitute for spinach, tomatoes and capsicums'. Another reference for the same year shows that pineapples and water-melons were grown 'with tolerable success'.

Apart from the turtles and goats, the island's only fresh meat came up from St Helena in the form of live cattle and sheep. Unscrupulous merchants clearly took advantage of the bad communications, knowing that recrimination would not reach them for months, if at all, and sent old and unsound animals, about which the Marines made continuous complaints. Some of the cattle were slaughtered in the garrison, but some were driven up to the Mountain and turned loose on the open pastures. Even there they were far from safe, for they were not accustomed to the hazards of living on the peak of a volcano, and many fell to their deaths. In 1827 Nicolls wrote to the Admiralty mourning the loss of a 'very fine buffalo cow' which had been sent from India, only to topple over a precipice. In the same letter he stressed the need for home-bred cattle, able to negotiate the violent slopes, and it was not long before some breeding stock was established.

Nicolls was a keen shooting man – his war on the wild cats was clearly inspired by a desire to preserve the guinea-fowl for sport – and one sad little note of 1827 shows that he was busy trying to import and establish other forms of game:

I am sorry to inform you that only one Hare (a male) has reached us alive, four of the Partridges died, and one of the Pheasants ... a great mortality has occurred among the bees.

Two years later, almost exactly the same thing happened again: after a slow passage of eighty days from England, the transport *Henry Porcher* arrived with most of its consignment of partridges, hares and rabbits dead, 'and not one of the Bees alive'. The red-legged partridges fared better, and a few of their descendants still inhabit the island. It was almost certainly Nicolls who introduced rabbits; from the 1830s onwards they crop up now and then in the records, although they never became numerous enough to be a nuisance until the end of the century.

The attempt to import bees (for pollination) was repeated again and again over the years, but every effort failed, and today there is not a single bee on the island. Those that survived the voyage were blown away by the ceaseless trade winds.

Many much tougher creatures succumbed to the rigours of travel under sail: sheep, cattle and several horses died *en route*, including two stallions sent out to breed animals for transport. Enough survived, however, to provide the garrison with food and transport, and by 1831 the island's quadruped population included

> 1 Bull, 16 Oxen, 15 Cows, 14 Calves, 2 Rams, 80 ewes, 20 wethers, 14 lambs, 25 billys, 303 nannys, 144 barrows, 85 kids, 6 horses, 6 mares, 6 geldings, 4 foals, 13 asses, 3 foals and 2 mules.

The great difficulty was to confine the animals and keep them under control. Materials for fencing were extremely scarce, and even when stakes were available, it was usually impossible to drive them in, the ground in most places being solid rock. The result was that one species after another escaped. Cows, or 'oxen', ran wild for several years, and the capture of a wild pig in 1826 was enough of an event to be recorded in the island journal; but this was evidently by no means the only one at large, for its offspring continued to be a nuisance for years:

> *16 July 1841*. It having been reported that several pigs belonging to the Garrison mess are still running wild, the Commanding Officer directs whenever they may be fallen in with every possible means to be taken to secure them, and the parties will receive a gratuity of 5s for the mess for everyone captured.

11 August 1841. In consequence of the mischievous nature of the Wild Pigs and their consumption of Government Pasture, together with the danger of young persons going to Wideawake Fair for eggs falling in with them, the Commandant grants permission for such men as may wish to go out on Saturdays for the purpose of ridding the island of the nuisance, and for their encouragement, the Pigs that may be caught or destroyed will become the property of the captors. The Goating dogs may be used for the purpose.

The distinction between Government and Mess property was all-important. The island belonged to the Government, and so did everything on it, except for a few private possessions which were officially sanctioned. (In theory each officer was allowed one cow and three goats, but in practice a number of animals were kept under the general title of 'Mess Stock'.) Such was the monotony of the rations, however, that most of the men tried to supplement them in some way or other, usually at the Government's expense. Hence frequent orders calling for an end to various abuses:

It having been reported to the Commanding Officer that the Africans are in the habit of feeding their fowls with oats and bran, which must be obtained clandestinely, for the future he strictly forbids poultry being kept by any of the garrison save the officers.

The wild cows and pigs were exterminated without too much difficulty, but donkeys, which first escaped in the 1830s, proved altogether too elusive. Once they had run wild into the rocky fastnesses of the Mountain, they proved impossible to recapture and some two hundred of their descendants still roam the island today – big, sway-backed, smooth-coated animals which, besides braying in the usual way, use a loud, menacing hiss as a means of warning off intruders.

In 1839, under the direction of an exceptionally energetic young officer, Lieutenant Wade, a horizontal path was cut encircling the upper slopes of the Mountain at a height of 2400 feet. In 1840 it was formally opened by Admiral Elliott, Commander-in-Chief of the West Coast of Africa Squadron, and it has been known ever since as Elliott's Path, or Elliott's Pass. Its original purpose was defensive – to enable the Marines to keep an all-round look-out; now its main use is recreational, since it makes a lovely walk. On a narrow ledge carved from the flank of the Mountain, the path skirts some tremendous drops; and in many places the inner wall is a sheer, porous face of black volcanic rock, as bare as on the day the Marines cut through it. Tunnels carry the path through the shoulders of the Mountain, and always, in whatever direction one faces, the views are immense.

ROOKS FOR ASCENSION

1840-95

While the animal population was increasing, the farm itself also expanded modestly. By the beginning of the 1830s some thirty acres were under cultivation, and small fields had been opened up at 'the Weather Garden', round the shoulder of the Mountain from the original Home Gardens, facing south into the teeth of the perpetual wind. Some time in the next few years a satellite farmstead called Palmer's was established in a south-facing ravine at about 1200 feet above sea level.

In the early days the object of importing plants and seeds was simply to produce fresh food; but later commandants were inspired by an altogether higher ecological aim – that of increasing the island's rainfall. This, it was thought could be achieved by mantling the summit and slopes of Green Mountain with trees and shrubs, and thus 'reversing the direction of the electricity'.

A Commodore visiting the island in 1844 wrote:

It is imagined by the officers resident on the island that if a plantation were formed on the summit of Green Mountain, where the soil is tolerably good and sufficiently deep, the vapour by which it is so frequently enveloped might by thus changing the direction of the electricity be induced to descend, and with a succession of plantations, the vegetation gradually extended over the island.

Whether or not the presence of trees increases precipitation is a matter of argument to this day: but on Ascension the electricity remained intractable and the rainfall continued extremely scant and irregular. Even so, the covering of trees and shrubs did creep slowly down the flanks of the Mountain from the top, and people returning to the island after an interval noticed considerable improvements. 'Decomposition has been going on regularly though slowly,' reported Captain Henry Bennett, R.M., when, fifteen years after his first visit, he returned to Ascension to take command of the garrison in 1841. 'Vegetation has extended over a much larger space than I had at all calculated upon.'

Repeated importations from every point of the compass – from India, Mauritius, South Africa, St Helena, Brazil, the West Indies and England – gradually produced an extraordinary mixture of trees, shrubs, flowers, fruit, and vegetables. At first the selection of species was completely amateur, and depended on the whims of the commandant or his senior officer, the Commodore of the West Coast of Africa Squadron. But, as a result of a visit in May 1843 by Dr Joseph Hooker, an altogether more professional approach was adopted.

Hooker, at the time, was Assistant Surgeon on board the *Erebus*, and botanist of the *Erebus* and *Terror* expedition, which was on its way home from the exploration of Antarctica. More important for Ascension, however, was his connection with the Royal Botanic Gardens at Kew, of which his father, Sir William, was the Director. Joseph's brief sight of Ascension clearly fired him with enthusiasm, and thereafter Kew took a close interest in the attempts to find plants which would thrive in that peculiar environment.

In a report dated 1 October 1847 Dr Hooker recommended the appointment of a skilled gardener, and outlined a programme of work for him. The planting of large trees high up the mountain, he said, would directly increase the rainfall. The steep sides of the ravines should be clothed with brushwood, to achieve decomposition of the soil, to prevent evaporation and to increase the amount of organic matter. (For this, he suggested bramble, briar rose, prickly pear and aloes.) Promising spots in the lower dry valleys should be planted with eucalyptus, casuarina and acacia.

The first professional gardener, William Wren, got his orders in November 1847. Not only was he to increase the productivity of the farm and to plant large numbers of trees: he was charged also with 'the gradual recovery of the coast district of volcanic cinders, which is now wholly unproductive'. This, his instructions conceded, was a task outside most ordinary gardeners' scope. 'No cultivation, properly so called, is at present feasible,' the orders admitted. 'The immediate object is to render the district gradually susceptible of cultivation. To effect this, the cinders must be pulverised and vegetable soil must be introduced among the fragments.'

Poor Wren! No one who has seen Ascension could imagine a more daunting task. Still, apparently undeterred, he signed for twelve 'books of practical use' (including *Brewster's Treatise on Optics*), a portable barometer, six thermometers of various descriptions, and one large copper rain-gauge, and set to work at a salary of £100 a year.

He stuck it for five years, but after that he had obviously had enough. In September 1852 he asked to be relieved, using a petty quarrel as a pretext for getting home. 'A clever horticulturalist and flower gardener,' reported the Commandant, 'but a very litigous troublesome person. . . . I have been continuously pestered with frivolous vexatious complaints couched in the most disrespectful terms.'

Wren's successor, Wallace, seems to have been little better. The Commandant described him as 'a very irritable man', and by 1855 he was threatening to shoot both himself and the gamekeeper. His wife was a menace in her own right, deliberately fomenting trouble in order to get him repatriated. Mrs Wallace, the Commandant wrote to the Admiralty, had asked an officer's wife where her 'fancy man' was, meaning Lieutenant David, 'it being generally understood that an unfortunate intreague had been carried on for some time between Lt David and the lady named'. The Commandant described the row at some length 'so that their Lordships may conceive of the egregious nonsense I have to contend with'.

Wren and his successors seem to have followed Hooker's instructions faithfully; and if they could not tame the arid low-ground, the results of their labours are still clearly visible in many parts of the island: the ravines are satisfactorily choked with brush-wood; brambles, wild raspberries, ginger and aloes grow freely high on the Mountain. Eucalyptus, casuarina and acacia flourish on the lower slopes, and prickly pears are scattered widely through the island.

During the fifteen years after Wren's arrival, a large programme of planting was maintained, and Kew initiated numerous botanical experiments, sending out bougainvillaea, bamboo seedlings and sisal hemp plants in 1847, and a case of para grass in 1849, besides immense numbers of seeds. Tropical plants and trees were pro-cured from thousands of miles afield: one hundred orange trees were brought from Rio de Janeiro and 'fresh-gathered cones of pitch pine' were shipped from the Bahamas.

In sending plants from England, the Royal Gardens were dependent on Naval transports, and the Admiralty would inform Hooker whenever a ship was available:

I am commanded by my Lords Commissioners of the Admiralty to acquaint you that H.M. Sloop *Flying Fish* will leave Devon-port on the 4th of September for Ascension, and that any case addressed to the Commanding Officer at that island and marked 'by *Flying Fish*' and sent down to the Admiral's office, Devon-port, shall go by that vessel.

In spite of repeated instructions about how the plants and seeds should be packed and handled, a great many perished during the voyage; and on the island progress was scarcely helped by the fact that gardeners came and went, often with considerable periods between them. The records themselves are intermittent, so that it is hard to see exactly how long each man lasted; but Wren and Wallace were succeeded in 1857 by John Bell, whose name survives on the island in Bell's Cottage, in the Mountain settlement.

'He is young, healthy and unmarried, and undoubtedly quite sober,' reported Dr John Lindley, a horticultural expert who had advertised the post on behalf of the Admiralty in the *Gardener's Chronicle*. Even more to the point, Bell obviously had green fingers, for under his direction the produce of Green Mountain rose from 59,000 lbs in 1858 to 90,000 lbs in 1860. In the last four months of 1860 alone he planted out 27,000 trees and shrubs. After numerous good reports from the commandant, the Admiralty raised his salary to £150 a year but added with characteristic meanness that any successor could not expect more than £100.

Bell's main work force was a gang of forty Africans, although he also had help from the Mountain detachment of Marines, which consisted of some thirty men and a sergeant. Being a civilian, he could not order soldiers about, and his post must have required considerable tact. In his reports to the commandant he maintained a precise formality, no matter what he was discussing: 'I now beg to draw your serious consideration to the subject of Manure.'

In October 1859, when he had been on Ascension for nearly two years, he described in a detailed report to the commandant the whole state of the farming and silvicultural enterprise. 'I do not consider myself a writing gardener,' he began modestly. 'I am more conversant with spade and hoe than with the pen.'

'The greatest feature of the establishment' was the Home Garden, of one acre twelve poles, the only patch that could be called anything like level. There, in a border, he was growing seedling palms. Should they succeed, 'the aspect of the Mountain would be materially changed, as at present those magnificent vegetable productions the Palm tribes are not cultivated here to any great extent'. He described many individual shrubs and trees in loving detail, proudly giving the dimensions of trunks and roots. Among his vegetables were carrots, lettuce, endive, cucumbers and radishes, and he had borders full of herbs, for which there was a great demand from the hospital.

The path to the peak of the mountain he described as passing through an enclosed piece of ground four acres in extent. Some 1600 shrubs and plants had been put in round the peak itself, and a belt of shrubs and trees had been planted round Elliott's Pass. The Weather Gardens consisted of seven acres bounded by a single fence, growing mainly sweet potatoes. Palmer's had 'a very convenient cottage surrounded by shrubbery but ... struggling against the wind. Twenty *Ficus elastica* [rubber trees] planted recently, small gardens of sugar cane, banana. Castor oil plant thrives, prickly pear in great numbers.'

Palmer's is now a ruin, overrun by a jungle of prickly pear and acacia; but a few of Bell's rubber trees remain, and elsewhere on the island there are many monuments to his industry. A number of the palm trees must be his (there are about fifty altogether), but it is impossible to be certain which he planted and which were the work of his predecessors. All the cultivation, he added, was done with the spade; not a single agricultural instrument was in use because of the steepness of the ground.

Another report, compiled by the Commandant, Captain F. L. Barnard, in 1862, throws light on some of the Marines' horticultural methods:

There is no limit to the broken ground available for the planting of shrubs, and during the dry season a party is constantly employed digging holes four feet wide three deep; there are upwards of 1,000 now open for the reception of the Australian wattle, to be planted between Michaelmas and Lady Day. This shrub has been most successful at Ascension, and in a few years will change the aspect, and probably the climate, of the island, from its rapid growth and facility of propagation. I lately measured one that was planted last November twelve months, in the shape of a small layer, and it is now from six to seven feet high, covering a circle with a circumference of thirty-six feet; about 1,000 of these have been planted within the last three years.

Mr Bell fortunately hit upon the simple plan of laying the small branches into preserved meat tins, butter firkins and boxes, in which they can be carried to any distance. . . . Mr Bell having represented to me that numbers of young shrubs and trees required protection when first planted out, I have caused a large number of guards to be constructed from firewood and the hoops that come off the trusses of hay; they answer most admirably.

Having described how he had brought guano from Boatswain Bird Island as fertiliser for the farm, Barnard went on to sing the praises of Para grass, which was 'doing wonders, increasing in the most astonishing manner' on the North East plains, 'growing down all weeds and inferior grasses wherever it is once established'.

The method Mr Bell is adopting for planting the grass is by cutting turf into junks, which are carried to the spot in bread bags, on the heads of Africans, and trod in at equal distances; the runners grow by inches in one week after rain, and form a perfect mat which no animal can root up.

Barnard's report was addressed to Kew, where Sir William Hooker became so interested by it that he persuaded the Admiralty to print some copies. Altogether, Barnard was regarded as something of an expert on Ascension, and a more detailed account which he compiled in 1864 was also printed by the Admiralty.

No doubt much of the success which he and Bell achieved was due to the exceptionally heavy rains. In the single month of June 1857, 20½ inches were recorded at the Mountain settlement, nine of them in one day; and the total for 1859 was 108 inches – four times the annual average. Admirals and commodores congratulated each other on having finally out-witted the recalcitrant electricity, not realising that they had simply been fortunate enough to get some of the freak downpours to which Ascension is periodically subject. Only two years later, in 1861, such a severe drought set in that the garrison had to resort to its 40,000 rations of compressed vegetables.

It may well have been this drought that caused a visitor in 1861 to take such a dim view of the whole farming enterprise. 'I found the garden and grounds in a very bad state of cultivation, the gardener employing his time shooting instead of at his work,' wrote Thomas Saumarez, a naval officer, in his diary for May that year:

I regret to state that never have I seen a place gone so much back as this Mountain, and the employing of Africans in the room of Marines a great mistake. Everything connected with the Mountain is faulty in the extreme, and it is not to be wondered at considering there is no officer to overlook the work done, and the Captain Superintendent never having slept a night up there since he has had command. It always takes two hours to ride up, and as much to descend, and considéring the fatigue of the journey, how can the only officer who can interfere walk or ride in one day round the various fields in cultivation?

We found all the families complaining, and though all the work below as regards stores is faultless, yet anything could be done with half the trouble. Red tape prevails here beyond anything, and with it, of course, discontent.

Such strictures are hard to equate with all the other generally good reports of Bell; nor do they fit the excellent impression given elsewhere by the commandant, Burnett. But other pages of Saumarez's journal show that his attitude was often critical, and it may well be that he exaggerated Ascension's deficiencies.

However much time he spent shooting, Bell must have worked like a Trojan. After rain-making, his next most difficult task was to establish a balance of nature. The attempts at this were unending and never entirely successful, for, just as rats, cats and donkeys had all run amok in the absence of natural restraints, so insects and plants bred out of control whenever they found the peculiar conditions congenial.

As early as the 1830s the whole north-east side of the Mountain was reported overrun by what the harassed commandant called 'wild balm' – probably greasy grass, which is long, rank and useless, and has a strong sweet smell like molasses. The commandant's remedy was to fire it – a risky process if any animals were about, because of the brisk trade winds – but he failed to get rid of it, and it remains a nuisance to this day, for nothing will eat it. Another troublemaker was buddleia, a purple-flowered shrub which was introduced from Cape Town in 1858 and did so well on the Mountain that it choked large areas.

By far the greatest menace, however, were the insects, generally known for want of any more exact description as 'the grub'. From the 1830s onwards crop after crop succumbed to them, particularly in dry weather, and one farm superintendent resorted to the desperate measure of spreading a large amount of dried grass over his fields and setting fire to it in an attempt to roast the vermin in the ground. 'The principal enemy,' said one report, 'is the black grub, which passes over the land like a devouring army, leaving nothing behind it.'

At an early stage it was realised that the only long-term answer to insects was birds which would eat them, and many attempts were made to establish suitable species. The guinea-fowl, partridges and pheasants brought in for sporting purposes ate their fill of grubs, and a flock of Muscovy ducks gorged themselves daily, but they needed far better reinforcements than they ever got. Most imported birds either failed to survive the voyage from England or found the heat, drought, wind and lack of cover on Ascension too much for them.

A dozen starlings, for instance, were released on the Mountain in 1852, and by 1861 they had multiplied to about 200; but twenty years later they were all dead, and further importations had also failed. Amadavats (or advadavats) – small Indian birds like weavers – were introduced during the 1850s, but although they survived for a number of years, they were too small to do much good. A better alternative was proposed – with the caution due from a member of an organisation as bureaucratic as the Navy – by Captain Burnett, the commandant in 1861:

Although their Lordships are not pleased to direct me to offer any suggestions, I venture to state that the bird called Minor, and said to have been so destructive to insects at Mauritius and St Helena . . . would be of great service at Ascension, and would live well about the Mountain.

From then on the idea of mynahs (or 'minors' or 'myners') was mooted intermittently for years, but no one roused himself sufficiently to obtain a supply until the late 1870s, when repeated *cris de coeur* from the farm superintendent, Joseph Spearing, finally brought action.

'The caterpillar and black grub are now so numerous that it is useless to put in any crop in the outlying gardens,' he wrote in 1878. 'The pastures are alive with them.' His report was passed to Kew, where Sir Joseph Hooker had succeeded his father as Director. Hooker asked for specimens to be sent to England, and in reply Spearing forwarded an assortment ('I beg to hand you a collection of the different grubs and caterpillars of this island.') labelling them A to E. A was the notorious black grub, whose habit was to nip off young plants just before ground level. With the specimens Spearing enclosed a list of the island's land birds, which included 25 pheasants, 400 partridges, 100 guinea-fowl, 50 canaries, ten cardinals and 1500 waxbills.

Exhibit A, diagnosed Robert McLachlan, F.R.S., of Kew, was *Agrotis segetum*, the larva of a moth, and the 'most to be dreaded on account of its abundance and concealed mode of life' – it was nocturnal, withdrawing underground during the day. The best answer to it would be rooks, and the next best starlings or ducks. Sparrows, said McLachlan, were quite useless:

> It appears to me that the best thing that can be done is to increase the number of ducks to an enormous extent and turn them out into the fields.

Hooker himself recommended birds from Africa or Mauritius, pointing out that the English species (thrushes, sparrows and so on) introduced to St Helena in 1869 to deal with the white ants had all proved disappointing.

So a mynah hunt was set up in Mauritius, and at the same time a search was begun in England for rooks, jackdaws, starlings and owls, which Spearing wanted to tackle the rats and mice. Since Ascension was a naval station, all its requests naturally passed through naval channels. The demand for vermin-eaters went first to the Director of Victualling, and he in turn passed it to the Royal

Victoria Yard, whose Superintending Storekeeper had to venture out into the by-ways of Dickensian London in search of his quarry. The first man he tried was Mr Charles Jamrach, described as a 'naturalist', who declared himself unable to obtain any barn owls at that season of the year 'owing to the prohibition of the Privy Council'. The Wild Birds Protection Act of 1872 was something for which their Lordships had not bargained. 'Owing to the strictness with which the Bird Act is carried out, the Bird Catchers do not care to go out catching birds any more, hence the scarcity of owls and rooks,' wrote Jamrach, adding slyly: 'I have some foreign owls, Great Eagle Owls, which I sell at £4 each.'

His offer was ignored, and other bird-copers were approached. One, Mr Thomas Irons of Kennington, did not answer, but then Mr W. T. Ims of Bloomsbury confidently announced that he could get the birds required.

He seems to have had some difficulty, for the matter dragged on for months, with the navy putting increasing pressure on him to deliver. On 26 April 1880 he wrote to say that in a week he would have three pairs of barn owls (for £3 15s.), six pairs of rooks (£3. 0. 0.) and nine cages costing £3 10s. But when an official from the Royal Victoria Yard visited him on 22 June, he had only three pairs of rooks, one pair of barn owls and one singleton, and one pair of brown owls. Eventually, in July, two pairs of barn owls and one of brown, together with five rooks, were put aboard H.M.S. *Tyne*. During the next ten days Ims was harried mercilessly for the outstanding seven rooks, and cables headed 'Rooks for Ascension' flashed back and forth across London between the Royal Victoria Yard and the Director of Victualling. Ims eventually found the birds, but too late to catch the *Tyne*, and they had to be put on the August packet.

Meanwhile an even higher-powered operation had set twenty-four mynahs in motion on their way to Ascension from the opposite direction. On 22 May 1879 Robert Hall, Secretary of the Admiralty, had written to Commodore Sir Frederick Richards, Commander of the West Coast of Africa and Cape of Good Hope Squadron:

Sir – I am commanded by my Lords Commissioners of the Admiralty to acquaint you that the Commander-in-Chief, East Indies, reports that twelve pairs of these birds have at his request been procured by the Governor of Mauritius, and that they will be forwarded by the first opportunity to the Senior Officer at the Cape of Good Hope for shipment to Ascension.

A second shipment of twenty-five and a half pairs followed a year later, and by 1881 the mynahs were already breeding well. So securely did they become established that large flocks frequent the island today. Not so the wretched rooks, which never bred at all. 'There are eleven on the Peak, which are to be seen daily,' said a report of June 1881; but none of them nested – either through the lack of tall trees, or because of the climate. By 1883 there was only one left. 'As no remains have been found,' reported Spearing sadly, 'I fear they must have taken too long a flight and failed to again make the land.' More rooks, together with some jackdaws, were received the next year, but they too disappeared. The owls, procured with such difficulty and at such expense, did little better, soon dying out in spite of the abundance of prey.

The whole programme of introducing birds to deal with vermin was thus a failure, and Spearing was left to struggle on as best he could. He was clearly a man of ideas and energy: because the Mountain climate was too cold for the Kroomen from the West coast of Africa, he suggested the importation of twenty families of Chinese labourers. 'I would recommend the Chinese,' he wrote, 'because they are excellent gardeners and easy to feed.' Another of his plans was that the wild donkeys would be rounded up and put to work, 'as horses cannot be induced to go up the Ramps more than once a day, and next to vermin and caterpillars the greatest difficulty in cultivating the farm is spreading manure over the fields, which is now done by men with hand barrows.' Neither idea was adopted, but Spearing tackled the various problems with such vigour that in 1880 the farm produced 137,000 lbs of vegetables – 62,000 for the crews of visiting ships and for the garrison, and 75,000 for the animals.

The husbandry of livestock was, if anything, even more amateur than the horticulture. To provide fresh meat, cattle and sheep were imported regularly, and repeated but on the whole unsuccessful attempts were made to breed hardy island races: the main difficulty was always to introduce good new blood, and the island strains kept degenerating through in-breeding. Nor were the successive farmers helped by the whims of admirals who, from a safe distance, were apt to make remarks like: 'I have always been of the opinion that more Mutton should be consumed on the Island of Ascension than Beef.'

Beef cattle, shipped from St Helena or the Cape, almost always arrived in a shocking state. 'The weight of the Oxen is made up in immense bones, and will not exceed an average of 370 lbs for the present year,' said a report to the Admiralty in 1865. 'This is so remarkable that their Lordships will, I am quite certain, hardly believe it.'

Animals that arrived on steam-ships were much more expensive than those that came by sail, for the recipient was allowed to inspect the cargo of a steamer and approve or reject, whereas every creature that reached Ascension alive under sail had to be accepted.

Once arrived, these bags of bones had to be fed up enough to make them edible. Controversy raged ceaselessly about whether it was better to stable them in the garrison and fatten them there, or drive them up to the farm. Each scheme had severe disadvantages. If the beasts were below, fodder from the Mountain had to be carted down to them, and their manure hauled up: if they were aloft, imported food such as corn and hay had to be lifted 2000 feet above sea level.

In 1877 an attempt was made to settle the argument once and for all by holding a comparative test: six beasts were kept under observation in the garrison and six up the Mountain. The result, as usual, was inconclusive: the garrison-reared beef came out considerably the cheaper at 1s 7½d a pound, and was ready to hand when needed; but the mountain-reared beef, though a good deal more expensive at 2s 3¾d a pound, was of far better quality.

In all these considerations, manure carried substantial weight. Its presence in the relentless heat of the garrison was intolerable ('several thousand loads of manure . . .' wrote one commandant, 'the non-removal of which excites the attention of strangers') yet hauling it up the Mountain was an Augean task. 'Each load so carted up,' reported a farm superintendent, 'brings with it a swarm of flies from off the clinker, making the Mountain almost uninhabitable for man and beast.'

A further disadvantage of the large Cape oxen was that each one of them yielded too much beef at a time: fresh meat would not keep for more than a couple of days, and whenever the number of men in the garrison was low, a good deal must have been wasted. 'There are now on the island,' wrote Spearing, the farm superintendent, 'fourteen of the last shipment . . . eating their heads off for want of sufficient mouths to eat them.'

The answer to this problem lay in finding smaller animals, and in the 1880s the Admiralty arranged a supply of 'Mossamedes cattle', which were shipped from Portuguese West Africa (Angola). Besides being a more useful size, these were nimbler and better able to negotiate the mountain pastures; a gratified commandant reported that their arrival had reduced the price of beef by no less than a farthing – from 1s 1¾d to 1s 1½d a pound.

Sheep were on the whole a better proposition than bullocks; those that came up from the Cape were often toothless and decrepit, but the ones bred on the island did better than the homegrown cattle – so much so that senior naval officers frequently ordered the commandant to increase stocks enough to make Ascension self-supporting in meat.

Systematic breeding was begun by Spearing in the late 1870s; the flock was built up by keeping the ewes which were occasionally sent in mistake for wethers, and by June 1882 it consisted of 215 wethers and 130 ewes. Pure-bred Merino ewes and rams were imported from the Cape, and under the care of a professional shepherd the flock flourished. 'A most excellent shepherd,' said a report of 1878. 'The work done by this man is prodigious. He never knows, when he rises in the morning, on what part of the island he will meet his flock, and yet he unfailingly does find them and examines them for the fly.'

Unfortunately, like everything else on the island, the sheep were subject to changes of policy and personnel. The good shepherd left and was replaced by Private Clifford of the Royal Marines – a man 'entirely ignorant' of sheep and their habits. Through his negligence a large part of the flock was lost. The half-yearly survey taken in July 1885 showed that 135 ewes and lambs were missing; the entire island was searched, but the absentees were never found. 'Over eighty of these sheep went away in a flock and I fear have followed one another into some hole or over the cliff and have not been able to get back,' reported Spearing. He placed the blame squarely on Clifford and went on: 'The duty of shepherd on this island is no sinecure; he has daily to travel over many miles of rough ground, and must therefore be strong and active.'

By Spearing's day the farm superintendent had become the island's gamekeeper as well. In the 1850s a full-time gamekeeper had been appointed, with fourpence a day extra pay, eight shillings a month shoe money, two African assistants, a fowling piece with powder and No. 4 or 6 shot, and twenty-four spring traps. But the post had disappeared in one of the reductions of strength, and by the 1880s agriculture and vermin control had become inextricably combined. This was logical enough, for the principal enemies were as much of a menace to farming as they were to game; the cats killed pheasants, which otherwise usefully ate insects; the rats ate root vegetables as well as eggs, and land crabs honey-combed the surface of the fields with their burrows.

A memorandum from the Commandant, Captain A. G. Roe, dated 8 April 1879, appointed two men as vermin-killers and laid down:

The tails, heads and claws of the vermin killed are to be sent to Garrison every Saturday morning for the Sergeant Major to count, and report the number to the Marine Office. He is then to cause them to be thrown into the sea.

The bounty paid – originally rum – became 1s 6d a head for wild cats, a halfpenny a head for rats, and 1s 6d a hundred for mouse-tails and pairs of land crab claws. These incentives produced a prodigious bag, which for 1879 included 66 cats, 7683 rats, 4013 mice and 80,414 land crabs. With the place still overrun by rats and mice, Spearing began to wonder whether he should continue to destroy the cats, but he soon decided that the answer was 'yes'; for one thing, as a result of the cat-purge there had been a sharp increase in the number of pheasants and partridges round the cultivated land, and they ate a useful number of insects; and for another, he pointed out that the Ascension cats' favourite food was *not* rats and mice, 'as on the arrival of the wideawakes they leave all other parts of the island and draw in towards the fairs'.

So the all-out war continued. In January 1887 the Commandant gave the grand total of vermin killed in the past eight years: 580 cats, 70,148 rats, and the phenomenal number of 335,535 land crabs. 'But for this destruction,' he wrote,

I believe not a bird would be left on the Island. Rats would have devoured all crops and landcrabs would have honeycombed the ground to such an extent that much vegetation would have been destroyed and the pasturage rendered unfit for sheep. Vermin have been much got under. Land crabs are still a large item, but the men have to go very far afield to get many.

Even if the larger species had been decimated, the insects were still a menace, and a call went out for bats, frogs and hedgehogs. No one could procure any bats – 'It will be very difficult, I think, to meet the wishes of the naval authorities in respect to the supply of live bats for Ascension,' wrote the Curator of the South African Museum in Cape Town – but some frogs were sent up from the Cape on board H.M.S. *Orontes* and soon produced a mass of spawn and tadpoles. In the same year – 1887 – two dozen hedgehogs were sent out from England via St Helena on the mail steamer *Warwick Castle*, but only three reached Ascension. One expired soon after landing; the others were put in a greenhouse 'to get strength', and then loosed into the Mountain garden, but both were struck by blow-fly and died.

Thus, by fits and starts, Ascension gradually acquired its unique collection of flora and fauna. Some time in the second half of the century a circular dew-pond was excavated near the peak of the Mountain, its original purpose having been (presumably) to act as a last-ditch water supply. When it was first made, the pond was in the open; but today it is surrounded by the dense grove of bamboos that cloaks the entire peak, and their waving stems are pleasantly reflected in the patches of clear water between the lilies. Near the pond, at the very summit, lies a rusty anchor·chain. Naval miscreants are said to have been ordered aloft to put in an hour or two of chain-whirling – an activity thought likely to produce rain.

In the end, the effort of trying to balance nature proved too much even for the energetic Joseph Spearing, who clearly became devoted to the island in spite of the harsh blows it dealt him. At the beginning of the 1890s he was invalided home with, among other ailments, paralysis of the right side. But in 1892 he wrote to the Admiralty begging to be allowed to return:

I have held my present appointment for over 16 years and, as I was 26 years old when I entered on the same, it has absorbed the best years of my life.

The Admiralty let him go, on condition that he would pay his own passage home should he be invalided again within two years. Out he went, only to crack up completely: his collapse is vividly recorded in the log of the Garrison hospital, filled in by the surgeon:

A signal was received from the Mountain settlement at 3 p.m. on Saturday 17 August [1895] to the effect that Mr Spearing was 'in a fit'. I immediately rode up, taking with me a bleeding lancet and a few grains of calomel. . . .

He was in a condition of quiet dementia . . . at 3 a.m. the symptom of Formication came on, this led him to believe that not only his bed but his whole house was swarming with ants, every familiar object, such as a dark painted stripe above the dado on the wall, was to his disordered imagination an 'ant run' . . . he became very violent, but then calmer.

Thereafter Spearing disappears from the archives. What, if anything, the galloping surgeon managed to do for him is not recorded; but to have succumbed to formication seems a poor reward for all the long years of hard labour that he had put in on the island.

WHITE ELEPHANT?

1860–1901

One of the most absurd facts about Ascension during the occupation was that the island was never remotely defensible. Although a British naval station, its armament was inadequate from first to last, and it could have been captured with ease by anybody who wanted it.

The eastern and southern coasts were – and are – defended naturally, by lava cliffs and pounding waves. Had any attack come, it would have fallen on the beaches along the sheltered west coast, and in particular on the main anchorage beside the settlement. From 1815 this one beach was covered by guns of a kind, but the batteries were never sufficiently powerful or well enough protected to have repelled a determined assault.

The first emplacement, begun as soon as the British landed, was on the small hill at the southern end of Long Beach and was called Fort Cockburn (its name was later changed to Fort Thornton). During the 1830s another small battery was set up on the side of Cross Hill, near Bate's Cottage, commanding the beach from a greater height and distance: two bulbous muzzle loaders which still stand there are dated 1839. In the garrison itself a high-walled Naval Yard was constructed, measuring 188 feet by 50 feet. It was during the completion of this yard, in 1839, that one of the few notes of urgency crept into the Commandant's reports home: he had heard rumours of wars between England and America, so he was using every available man to finish the yard as soon as possible.

In 1860 a visiting commodore reported that Captain Burnett had 'greatly improved the arrangements for defending the island, should it ever become necessary'. Fort Thornton had by then been reinforced by a second emplacement, Fort Hayes, a couple of hundred yards to the south. The garrison's main armament consisted of two guns 'furnished with appliances for throwing Hot Shot'. There were also two 'pivot guns' placed to good advantage not far from Bate's Cottage; the road to the Mountain had been covered by nine guns 'placed in the most advantageous positions and well protected with sandbags', and spots had been chosen for riflemen, in the event of their having to retire from Georgetown.

Evidently Burnett did his best in the circumstances, but his efforts did not impress Commodore G. Phipps Hornby, who visited Ascension six years later and scathingly remarked:

> Ascension is at present open to destruction by a couple of gunboats. Everything is so dry that the place would be on fire in a couple of minutes. . . . The island would need vast expenses on the defences to make it secure. . . . In fact, one frigate or more must, if Ascension be held as a depot in war time, be always kept there for its protection.

The Admiralty seem to have paid scant heed to his advice, and ten years later the new Commandant, Captain East, gave a highly critical account of the defences he had inherited. Fort Thornton he described as a horse-shoe fort, eighty feet above the sea, equipped with old 24-pounders. The guns were almost unprotected and open at the rear; the small service magazine was partially protected, but the large blockhouse full of ammunition and stores was fully exposed to view and 'would be blown up by the first shell fired'.

A small richochet battery 100 yards away to the north-east was in bad order, with no guns. On the side of Cross Hill, 1400 yards from the anchorage and 220 feet above sea level, were two 24 pounders; some forty feet above and behind these were two much larger weapons – an 84 cwt ten-inch gun and a 95 cwt 68-pounder, but the carriages and platforms had been neglected for years. 'I believe,' wrote East, 'the former would go to pieces on the first shot being fired.' Finally, on top of Cross Hill stood another 68-

pounder, rendered useless by the fact that it had no magazine nearby.

'Since the reduction of this establishment,' East concluded,

... all the defences have been totally neglected, but this is of little consequence as they would be utterly useless against a ship armed with moderate artillery ... which could destroy the place and stores from a distance without landing.

If a couple of heavy guns, say 12 or 18 ton guns, were mounted on Fort Thornton, either in a turret or on the Moncrieff principle, a good account could be made of any hostile cruiser.

Some of East's advice was taken, and new guns were eventually mounted in Fort Thornton; but in 1879 there were still 60,000 lbs of green powder lying in the open, and the island remained a sitting target for anyone who cared to take it.

The fact that nobody ever did can only mean one thing: that nobody thought Ascension worth having. Indeed, as the nineteenth century wore on, the reasons for England maintaining an expensive base there became increasingly tenuous. Originally there had been reasonably solid strategic grounds for occupying the island: first the British had to deny the place to any possible rescuers of Napoleon, and then they needed a base and sanatorium to support the blockade against the slavers. Furthermore, in the days of sail there were certain commercial advantages in holding Ascension. Ships returning from the Cape of Good Hope – many of them British – frequently arrived in distress, having missed St Helena, and Ascension could furnish them with essential supplies. Also, the island was potentially a good base for whalers. 'I understand the Americans would give anything for possession of this island as a rendezvous for their ships engaged in the South Sea fishery,' wrote the Commandant, Captain Roger Tinklar, in 1839. 'They also know it is a great route to Europe for commerce.'

By the 1860s, however, with Napoleon long dead, the slave trade dwindling and steam rapidly taking over from sail, the full-scale occupation of Ascension became harder and harder to justify.

For years, whenever the cost rose too high, successive commandants had been ordered to reduce the size of the establishment, but it was not until 1866 that any serious attempt was made to abandon the place altogether.

In that year Commodore Hornby, commander of the West Coast of Africa Squadron, sent the Admiralty a detailed report, fifteen pages long, listing the 'many grave inconveniences' of Ascension and contrasting them strongly with the amenities of St Helena. Hornby was clearly a committed St Helena man, and he made the most of his evidence; even so, many of his points could not be refuted.

The burden of his analysis was that St Helena would make a far better base for the Navy in its operations off the African coast. Not only did it have far more water, a better harbour and incomparably superior defences; it was also better placed for ships wanting to reach the Congo or Loanda quickly – because of the south-east trade winds, a sailing vessel could cover the greater distance from St Helena more quickly than it could beat across from Ascension.

As his trump card Hornby played the state of Ascension's hospitals. 'I was painfully struck,' he wrote,

> ... with the suffering the men undergo in the lower hospitals from causes beyond our control. The plague of flies is like that in Egypt. Attempts are made to protect the men by throwing light mosquito nets over their faces, or by tying up their faces or hands in net or curtaining. I need not say what annoyance and irritation this causes. ...
>
> Again, the buildings are infested with Bugs or Clinker Lice to an extent that must be seen to be believed.

Although everything was kept scrupulously clean, he went on, and the general cleanliness of the hospital could not be surpassed, the beds 'literally swarmed with vermin'.

The Mountain hospital was little better. The timber-framed building was on the point of collapse, and

... the medical men complain of its damp situation (it is generally in the clouds), it is cheerless and depressing in itself, and in common with the rest of the island, is very scantily supplied with hospital necessaries such as vegetables, milk, eggs, poultry, good meat, etc.

As a result of Hornby's remarks, a committee of four senior officers was set up in the Admiralty to report on the expediency of reducing or abandoning Ascension as headquarters and depot of the West African Squadron. Unanimously they decided that abandonment was impossible as long as the squadron was kept at its present strength. Among their arguments for retention was the fact that men with fever would not be allowed to land on St Helena in any case, for fear of spreading disease to the much larger population, so that it was essential to maintain hospitals on Ascension, no matter how bad they might be.

And so, instead of disbanding the garrison, the Ascension Committee set about reducing it from its total of 442 men, women and children to a total of about 360. They decided to dismiss the gardener and the liberated Africans, and to reduce the number of wives and dependants as much as possible.

From then on, the records are full of reductions and attempts at economy, all bedevilled by the contradictory ideas of different senior officers. All wives and children should be got rid of, wrote one; or, if they were allowed to stay, they should be made to pay for the privilege:

Such people are quite useless, and frequently mischievous as they foment the slightest rub upon duty between husbands, as would be obliterated at the first mess meal, into a bitter family quarrel, greatly to the obstruction of duty.

Three years later another commanding officer reported that Ascension was feeling the lack of women and urged that more married Marines be sent out: 'I am sure they (the wives) exercise a beneficial effect in keeping the men steady.'

Persistent efforts were made to discourage merchant ships from calling to collect water, since the island did not have enough for its own needs, let alone those of strangers; and in order to reduce traffic, high dues were charged – 1s for every cask, case or package shipped from the island; 5s per ton raised by the steam hoist; 7s 6d for the Health Officer's fee, and 2s 6d for a certificate of clearance. In spite of the high prices, some 500 ships were calling every year in the early 1860s, and as a further measure, all the rates were suddenly doubled in 1868. Inevitably the move brought complaints, and to counter them the Admiralty produced a printed notice which was sent to ship-owners, pointing out that it had become common practice for homeward-bound vessels to run past St Helena deliberately, in order to escape paying the port dues there, and to call at Ascension 'on the plea of being in distress'.

'Ascension is not a place suited for private trade, being only a rock on which sufficient stores are kept with reference to the requirement of Her Majesty's ships,' said the form. Private vessels were therefore required to keep off except in real emergencies.

It is hard to escape the conclusion that, from about 1860, Ascension must have been an exceedingly dreary place in which to serve. Labour and materials were permanently short; the food was notoriously bad, the water often rationed; the station had less and less of a *raison d'être*, and almost never did any excitement break the monotony of the day-to-day routine.

After 1860 very few new buildings were constructed, with the important exceptions of the Mountain Hospital (see page 140) and the Mountain Barracks. This handsome two-storey stone structure with a small clock-tower at one end, was beautifully sited on the same level as Home Garden, and replaced the earlier, higher barracks which had been completed by Bate in 1832 but had never been a success because it was so often enveloped in cloud. Today the lower barracks is known as the Red Lion, and houses the St Helenians who work on the farm; its pleasing shape and magnificent position – the clock-tower outlined against the background of volcanic craters 1000 feet below – have made it the most popular photographic subject on the Mountain.

A smaller but equally essential innovation was a gaol. Until the 1860s no purpose-built prison existed on the island. In 1839 the Commandant reported the completion of a 'dead house', or mortuary, 'which will, if necessary, be adapted for the reception of lunatics or prisoners', and a year later there are references to the building of a new guardroom 'with a black hole on either side of it'. But several commandants felt the need for a proper gaol – 'The want of a jail for the confinement of refractory characters is much felt on this Coast,' said a report of 1863; and eventually, after the Admiralty had repeatedly refused to sanction the cost of building a prison, in 1864 the Commandant, Captain William Dowell, took the law into his own hands and put one up. A year later it was first used and officially recognised, and Dowell made out a set of rules, including the times at which prisoners were to exercise.

Far from wanting to sanction new buildings, the Admiralty became ever keener to flatten as many as possible, thereby saving the cost of maintenance; and their Lordships evidently acquired a taste for long-range demolition. 'My Lords approve of the immediate razing of the Carpenter's Shop, Farrier's Shop, Plumber's Shop, . . . Married Quarters, Seamen's Quarters, the Greater Part of Vindictive Row,' said a letter from the Secretary of the Admiralty in 1881.

To order buildings razed from a distance of 4000 miles was one thing, but to see that they actually came down was another, and the commandants managed to defy the orders more or less successfully, not only preserving most of the buildings but also clinging to their personnel. In spite of repeated instructions to reduce numbers, they pleaded the necessity of having an extra cook here, an extra storeman there – and after every purge the strength crept up again.

Although chronically short of materials and labour, the garrison made the best of things in a thoroughly British manner. 'A rigid economy is observable by the ingenuity with which old materials such as broken iron, staves and packing cases are worked up to make tramways, ovens, storehouses, etc,' said a report of 1863.

The ships of the West Africa squadron were refuelled from a

huge heap of coal (some 4000 tons), and repairs were carried out in the factory, which, by the 1860s, contained a 'moulding room, modelling house, tinsmith's and plumber's shops, painter's room, smelting furnaces, one for brass and the other for iron, and a capacious machinery room'. Like everything else, however, the factory was frequently crippled by lack of some vital part, and for years the machinery was powered by Africans, 'with the help of large flywheels', because the steam engine had broken down.

A further modest service was provided by the fly-ridden lower hospitals. Yet such was the fear of infectious diseases that sufferers were landed on the open beach at Comfortless Cove right into the 1890s. Although senior officers regularly recommended that some buildings should be put up there, nothing more substantial than a tent was ever established to shelter the sick.

Not that patients were necessarily better off if they *were* taken into hospital. In 1865 Mr Henry Francis, the Dispenser (who was in charge of the issue of drugs), was suspended from duty 'upon the representation of the Surgeon that he is on the sick list suffering from "Delirium Tremens"'. Asking for a more sober replacement, the Commandant observed that 'so young a man as Mr Francis is not well suited to the peculiarities of service at Ascension'.

Most of the nursing must have been rough, to say the least, for the hospital orderlies were ordinary Marines, struck off other duties for three months at a time. When, in 1864, after one of them had been dismissed for drunkenness, the Surgeon, Dr Cronin, wrote to the Admiralty for regular blue-jacket nurses, all he got was an Olympian rebuff:

> The Lords direct that Dr Cronin shall be informed that he takes a very erroneous view of the position. It is no part of his duty to select the Marines for nurses.

One surviving volume of the hospital register gives some hair-raising insights into what it was like to be ill during the 1880s and 1890s. Apart from the fact that Chlorodyne was used to treat dysentery, not much of the medical practice strikes a familiar note.

Fever was the most common complaint, but 'rheumatism-gonnorheal', 'rheumatism-syphilitic', 'gout (suppressed)' and 'insanity (temporary)' all struck frequently.

Accidents were common, particularly during blasting operations, and anybody injured was given a 'hurt certificate' which listed the details of his injuries and included the phrase 'the man was sober at the time'. Often the mules were as dangerous as the dynamite. In August 1895 Sergeant G. Moran came into hospital with 'broken rib, large flap of scalp detached, ear almost severed' after his team had bolted while he was unloading cement from a cart on Cross Hill; and in August 1908 Private Thomas Jenner was killed when his mules bolted near God-be-Thanked tank, on the road to the Mountain.

Violence in the hospital was by no means rare. William Dawson, coxswain of the island steamboat *Trinculo*, had an epileptic fit at the wheel, and was brought into the ward, whereupon he went berserk and rushed out on to the clinker barefoot. Eventually he was coaxed back, reported the surgeon,

> ... but not before his legs – and feet – were covered with small wounds ... at 2 a.m. I found him in a state of acute mania, and with his lower extremities covered with blood. I at once got a strong escort from the barracks and had him conveyed to a cell in the police station.

Some of the cases had a happier ending – for instance, that of Tom Peter, a Krooman who was brought into hospital by his messmate at 7.30 one evening in a coma and giving off a strong smell of peppermint. His pupils were contracted and fixed, and his appearance one of 'deep repose'. The surgeon's hour-by-hour reports give the scene a nightmarish clarity:

> *7.40 p.m.* A strong infusion of coffee, containing eight grains of Bicarbonate of Ammonia, was introduced by means of the stomach pump, and was followed in about ten minutes by another basin. Ammonia was applied to the nostrils and general shaking

persevered in. . . . He was also douched with cold water. The symptoms remained unchanged, however.

8 p.m. Smell of peppermint still strong.

9 p.m. A strong smell of peppermint fills the whole ward.

2 a.m. Since the last report he has been steadily roused by relays of assistants; by pinching and pricking of the skin, and from time to time walking him up and down the verandah.

Gradually poor Tom Peter came to his senses, and

. . . on enquiry it was found that the Krooman employed in the Stables gave him about midday a large quantity (about half a tea-cup full) of oil of peppermint to relieve griping pains in the bowels. The oil is kept for the use of the horses.

The Mountain Hospital, built in a magnificent position on a spur 2000 feet up, where the air was much cooler, was never regularly used. The first structure was of wood, and seems never to have been finished. A report of 1864 shows that the main ward had no roof, and that the lavatories were badly sited, immediately up wind. In 1867 the ramshackle hut was replaced by a pleasant stone building which stands to this day and is still known as 'San'. Yet almost from the beginning shortage of funds and manpower meant that the mountain hospital could not be properly staffed, and in 1873 there came an order to close it immediately. Thereafter it was kept shut until a ship came in with fever on board, whereupon the crew were sent aloft to recuperate.

One such vessel was the *Flirt*, which arrived in February 1883, with fever caught on the Niger. The Mountain Hospital was specially opened, and members of the crew spent ten days up there in relays. The scheme was a great success, as the men benefited visibly in health and physique, and simultaneously did a good deal of useful work for which the garrison had no time. Later the same year another crew cleared Elliott's Path, weeded the roads and paths, yellow-washed the barracks and other buildings, and repaired all the lavatories and palings. The Commandant of the island was delighted, and so was the ship's captain, who wrote:

> There can be no doubt that the change of air, healthy exercise – and the fact of having one bottle of beer a day each and the perfect regime of working hours etc. – has not only renewed their health but has turned them out even stronger than when they left England.

Hygiene at the Mountain Hospital was scarcely improved by the fact that all rubbish was tipped into a steep ravine nearby. Almost always the steady trade winds carried the stench safely off, but in 1884 a rare variation of the breeze rendered the whole place uninhabitable. Fifty-eight officers and men of the *Opal* were there at the time, convalescing from yellow fever; but after ten days an exceptional east wind set in, and the sanatorium had to be closed 'in consequence of the unpleasant odours emanating from the place appropriated for the deposit of refuse matter'.

From many such hints in the official records, it is obvious that life on Ascension was odd, to say the least; yet the island's eccentricities, and its reputation for them, emerge far more clearly from the reports of visiting outsiders. The fullest picture comes from the redoubtable Isabel Gill, who in her book *Six Months in Ascension* describes how in 1877 she accompanied her astronomer husband David to observe the opposition of Mars, and so to try and establish the exact distance between the earth and the sun.

Her subtitle – 'An Unscientific Account of a Scientific Expedition' – just about sums the book up. She was a curious mixture – naïve yet sometimes humorous, prudish and prejudiced yet occasionally also humble; maddeningly feeble for most of the time, yet now and then showing considerable resource.

Her first sight of the island reduced her to palpitations of horror: sighing for the mists and rain of her native Scotland, she called Ascension 'the Abomination of Desolation' and took off into flights of purple prose:

Doubtless there were stirring times here once on a day when Vulcan's forge was alight, but that was before we short-sighted mortals dared to peep into this now deserted workshop of the grimy god.

She was appalled by the absence of gardens or greenery, by the lack of shops and food, particularly milk. Milk, she reported, came down from Green Mountain in the mornings, when there was any: 'A bell rings at seven o'clock and everybody runs for a gill, except when there are many sick in hospital, when they get it all.'

Meat, too, was scarce, 'for the sheep and bullocks are starving for food and water. Hardly any are killed that have not fainted first'.

Not even a Rothschild could buy a juicy leg of mutton here, nor enjoy the luxury of a fresh salad with his cheese. That mutton! Shall I ever forget it? Our first 'gigot', of hock-bottle shape, would have made an English butcher faint, and ought to have been sent to the British Museum, there to consort with time-toughened mummies, and testify to the high state of training achieved by Ascension sheep in 1877.

Arriving with twenty tons of baggage, the Gills established their first base in Georgetown. The heliometer – according to Gill, 'the most exquisite of all angle-measuring instruments' – was set up in its own little house, with a canvas dome: the smaller transit telescope was in a wooden 'transit hut' and the professor and his wife lived in Bungalow No. 6.

Soon, however, it became clear that the site was badly chosen, for every night, when Gill tried to take his vital measurements of Mars, clouds trailing downwind from the summit of Green Mountain obscured the view of the heavens. After several frustrating and sleepless night Mrs Gill struck off southwards over the moonlit clinker to see if the clouds covered the whole island.

For someone who was plunged into despair by running out of tea, and who was horrified at having to take over the cooking when her African boy was crippled by rheumatism, these nocturnal explorations across the roadless lava desert must have been considerable feats of intrepidity and endurance. Hitching up her skirts, she stumbled about for several miles until rewarded by the discovery that over the southern half of the island the sky was completely clear.

At once the Gills moved camp. The stores went round by sea in the turtle boat, but the delicate heliometer tube was lashed to a spar and carried overland by the Kroomen, to a site in what the Commandant of the time called Mars Bay. There, in a setting of real desolation, among loose cinders and jagged lumps of black basalt, a new observatory was built and another camp laid out. The brick pillar of the telescope mount, the sandy paths that connected the tents, and the pile of white shells that Mrs Gill collected, are all visible to this day.

For five months she stuck out the considerable discomfort, harassed by mosquitoes, prowling cats and the weakness of their Marine servant for rum:

He is a thirsty animal, the British tar . . . it was only when this evil came under our immediate notice that we fully realised the necessity of strictness in this matter of rum-giving.

Another problem was their tame Krooman, Sam. At first Mrs Gill treated him as a nice, amusing animal, but one day she was astonished and humbled to find him trying to improve his English with a book. Thereafter he was more on her conscience, until he had a fight with the Marine servant and had to be sent back to hard labour on the pierhead.

Preoccupied though she was with her own problems, Mrs Gill had time to make several tours of the island and to describe its main curiosities. One of the graveyards at Comfortless Cove moved her to transports of emotion, which she recorded thus:

Here a waking dream stole over me, born of the sad scene and of the words of our guide – 'A ship in quarantine for yellow fever landed her sick here, and many of them died.'

Strong men are busy pitching tents in nervous haste, for wives and comrades are sickening in the sun, and there is none to help – no friendly neighbour to offer a cup of cold water to parched lips, no kindly hand to smooth a fever-tossed pillow. They are alone with God and with their sorrow, and some of them are sick unto death.

Now I can see a sad company of men, bearing living, dying burdens up the steep shores from where the plague-stricken ship lies anchored; but not a sound breaks the stillness, save an occasional moan which the toilers are too sad to answer, for they are bearing the future – the heaviest burden of the human soul. . . .

Again and again I see sad, silent processions wending their way down into this sheltered nook, growing smaller, more sad and more silent each time that another and another member of the doomed company is borne to his last resting-place, until at last my eyes grow so dim with tears, that past and present are blotted from my sight.

History and topography apart, Mrs Gill recorded several of the garrison's idiosyncrasies, among them the fact that, during a prolonged drought, the chaplain refused to pray for rain until the Admiralty sent out some more efficient condensers for distilling salt water. She also told the story (often repeated afterwards) of how the five white women on the island squabbled for precedence in church, and of how the chaplain settled the arguments once and for all, by pronouncing that the front pew should be occupied by the *oldest* lady, whereupon a determined rush set in for the back.

Although often irritating and not a little absurd, Mrs Gill leaves the impression of having been thoroughly good at heart, and it is pleasant to know that her husband's expedition was a scientific success, the observations taken from Mars Bay helping to establish the distance between earth and sun with far greater precision than before.

'Stay-at-home travellers who pass an agreeable evening over Mrs

Gill's narrative,' wrote William Wickham, reviewing the book in *The Academy* of 19 April 1879, 'will have the satisfaction of feeling that they have learned all that there is to be learned about Ascension from her, and that they rather gain than lose by not having visited so repulsive a place.'

A far more cynical visitor than Mrs Gill was Major A. B. Ellis of the First West India Regiment, who stopped at the island twice between 1871 and 1882, and described it in a chapter of his book *West African Islands*, published in 1885. He practised a sharp line in sarcastic exaggeration, and (one suspects) lifted a good many of his facts from Mrs Gill's narrative. Having briefly described Ascension's discovery in 1501, he went on:

> From that day to the present we have retained possession of Ascension, at the trifling cost, to the British taxpayer, of some forty thousand pounds a year. . . .
>
> The hospital, by polite fiction, is considered a kind of sanatorium for the seamen of vessels employed on the Coast of Africa. To an ordinary mind, a locality in which nothing to eat can be obtained, and to which rations have to be regularly supplied, would appear a curious one in which to establish a sanatorium . . . but it seems to satisfy the Admiralty.
>
> Ascension produces nothing but turtles, rats and wideawakes. The latter are not very tempting, even when disguised by the most skilful *chef*. Europeans seem to be generally prejudiced against eating rats; while turtle, though a very excellent thing for invalids, aldermen and other persons who require fattening, is apt to become wearisome when served up thrice daily. . . . Consequently, cattle, sheep and vegetables have to be imported from St Helena; two of the sheep are killed weekly, usually just in time to save their lives.

One of Ellis's anecdotes (though almost certainly exaggerated) is worth quoting in full, for it illustrates the level of fatuity to which some members of the garrison had sunk. Civilians were not normally allowed to land on the island, and when one did – an

American acquaintance of the author's – he met with a curious reception:

He had gone on board the island, and was walking past the barracks in Georgetown when he nearly stumbled against a fair young naval officer of forty, with flaxen whiskers, who came suddenly out of a building.

The officer raised his eye-glass, looked at the American with astonishment, and, before the latter had time to commence an apology, called out: 'Simmons.'

A voice replied 'Ay, ay, sir!' from the interior of the building and a bearded seaman appeared on the scene. The officer continued: 'Simmons, do you know what this person wants, or who he is?'

'No, sir; I can't say, I'm sure, sir.'

This absence of ceremoniousness aroused the latent spread-eaglism of my friend, and he began: 'Sir, I am a citizen of the United –' when the naval man, who appeared to be unaware that he was speaking, interrupted him, and asked: 'Simmons, do you think he is a stowaway?'

'Can't say, sir, I'm sure, sir,' replied the imperturbable Simmons.

'Is there a merchant seaman at anchor there?'

'Yes, sir. Cape mail, sir.'

'Well, Simmons, just go to the officer of the watch and ask if he has given permission to any person to board us. And – er – see what this person wants.'

The American, now very angry, again began: 'Sir, I am –' when he was again interrupted by the officer, who said: 'Simmons, I am engaged now. I cannot see this person. Perhaps you had better take him to the officer of the watch,' and he went off before my friend could launch all the terrors of the United States at his head.

And so the occupation dragged pointlessly on. Small wonder that the clock on the Marine barracks in Georgetown was said to chime 'Oh Gawd!' four times before it struck each hour, in sympathy with the members of the garrison, or that in 1890 the Admiralty considered swapping the whole island for German South-West Africa. By 1895, according to the Royal Marines' journal, *The Globe and Laurel*, the ladies in Georgetown corresponded with each other only in writing, not deigning to speak for months on end. None of them can have had any inkling that Ascension was about to enter a new and far more useful phase of its history – that of communications.

The lethargy prevailing on shore was fully apparent to Captain Joshua Slocum, the first of the many single-handed circumnavigators who have called at Ascension on their way home. In his celebrated book *Sailing Alone around the World* the Canadian mariner described how he arrived on board the *Spray* in April 1898, and how, when he expressed a desire to ascend the Mountain, he was immediately given a horse to ride and a sailor to lead it:

> There was not a man on the island at that moment better able to walk than I. The sailor knew that. 'Let me take the bridle,' I said, 'and keep the horse from bolting.' 'Great Stone Frigate!' he exclaimed, as he burst into a laugh, 'this 'ere 'oss wouldn't bolt no faster nor a turtle. If I didn't tow 'im 'ard, we'd never get into port.'

Slocum soon made friends with the officers of the garrison, and spent hours swapping yarns. Before he left he increased the island's strength slightly by marooning (as he put it) a goat that had been misguidedly given him as a ship's pet in St Helena. From the moment it came aboard it had proved a menace, since it ate everything within its reach: Slocum's Panama hat and his indispensable chart of the West Indies merely whetted its appetite for the rigging. 'Alas,' he wrote, 'there was not a rope in the sloop proof against that goat's awful teeth.'

His visit, brief as it was, must have provided the islanders with a welcome distraction. But just after the turn of the century the monotony was at last broken by an incident of drama. On the morning of 29 August 1900 a small boat was spotted drifting out to sea. The island launch put out, and found that the vessel contained survivors, far gone with thirst and exhaustion, from the wreck of the *Primera*, a ship of 600 tons which had left London on 31 May, bound for the Cape with a cargo of coal, forage and general stores.

Safe in Georgetown's hospital, the castaways soon recovered, and they left a charmingly-written account of the disaster. Their troubles had begun on July 7, when the Captain died after a short illness, and the Mate had to take command. Then on August 3 smoke had started billowing out of the fore hatch. Thinking their hay was on fire, they brought several hundred bales up on deck before realising it was the coal which had begun to smoulder:

> At 1.10 a.m. everyone was brought to a lively sense of their position by the fore and main hatches blowing up, the report, which shook the unfortunate vessel from end to end, being followed by a hissing noise and clouds of smoke, with hundreds of sparks.

The boats were lowered with all speed, ten men taking to the lifeboat and four to the dinghy. The crew hoped, by careful rationing of their water and ship's biscuits, to drift to St Helena; but the wind was persistently unfavourable, blowing all the time from the east. For ten days they drifted in sight of their burning barque; but then on August 13 the two little craft parted company to give each a better chance of being picked up by a passing vessel. Five men chose to go in the dinghy, and to aim for St Helena; the rest, in the lifeboat, set out for Ascension. 'So, with three good cheers on either side, the two boats parted company.'

The men in the dinghy were eventually rescued by a foreign sailing vessel and landed on an island in the West Indies. But the lifeboat at last got good winds, and, though much troubled by the attentions of whales, sighted Ascension on the evening of August 28. Having spent the night at anchor, the boat was towed in the following morning.

'Small as the island of Ascension is,' the survivors' account

Lionel Bartlett riding on a turtle, about 1934

Fairy tern

White booby feeding chick

View down from farm settlement, over the Red Lion. The Sisters' range is to the left, with the village of Two Boats in the col below it

Dorothy Morgan, daughter of the commandant, Capt. R. H. Morgan, with her Krooman nurse in 1905

continued, 'its inhabitants have the soul of a continent, and our own flesh and blood could not have treated us more kindly than they did.'

The fact that the crew reached the island at all was clearly due to the skill and courage of the Mate, Evan Harvard, an old sea salt of sixty-six, who forced his companions to obey his code of discipline, particularly his orders for rationing. Their gratitude shines out in the splendid tribute they wrote:

The more one thinks of how he brought us through that wearisome time, the more one realises what a lion-hearted old man he was, his chronometer was his watch and his charts his memory.

At the turn of the century it became fashionable in England to display on one's sitting-room table albums filled with picture-postcards from far-flung places; and in 1901 Ascension entered the stakes with one of a series of cards printed to commemorate the royal tour of the Empire by the Duke and Duchess of Cornwall and York. Unfortunately on the proposed day of the visit – 30 August 1901 – the rollers were up, and the royal party was unable to come ashore; all the same, many of the cards were cancelled in the island's post office on that day, and the intention, if not the actual landing, was suitably immortalised.

COMMUNICATIONS CENTRE

1860–1922

From the time of the earliest commercial voyages Ascension's position made it a natural centre for communications. I have already described how, in the seventeenth and eighteenth centuries, the bottle post was used by ships' captains to exchange information about recent visitors to the island; and throughout the naval occupation the commandants took advantage of any homeward-bound vessel that called to send news of themselves back to England. 'The *Cassiopeia* Brig from Singapore to London has just entered the bay and waits an hour for letters,' said a typical note from Bate in November 1830.

For many years the posts were maddeningly irregular. Packets for England generally reached their destination fairly soon, as the carrier vessels were already on their way home. John Edmonson's letter of 1845, for instance, took only six weeks to reach his sweetheart in Lancashire. Yet outward mail took far longer because it almost always went straight past Ascension to St Helena, where, depending on the inertia or energy of the postmaster, it might hang about for several weeks or even months before coming north again. In February 1829 Bate complained to the Admiralty of the 'very great negligence' of the postmaster, who had missed at least five opportunities of forwarding a letter which had reached St Helena on 6 November the previous year; and complaints of this nature occur frequently throughout the records. Even when steam began to take over from sail in the 1850s and 1860s, southbound ships still went straight to St Helena first.

The development of Ascension's post is a subject of burning interest to philatelists, and to Major E. H. Ford, whose little book on the subject was published privately in 1933, it was outrageous that formal arrangements were not made far earlier. 'No post office establishment in 1860!' he trumpeted. 'And yet Ascension was known among most of the mariners of the world as "The Sailors' Post Office" even in the seventeenth century!' Ordinary British stamps were being used unofficially on the island as early as 1845, and Penny Reds combined with Ascension postmarks are now philatelic jewels of the first water. But Major Ford records how in 1860 the Rev. A. G. Berry, chaplain of Ascension, wrote to the Postmaster General in London complaining that there were still no stamps to be bought on the island. The answer came back that there was no need for letters to be stamped at that end – whatever was due could be levied at the destination.

Later the same year the Commandant tried again, pointing out that:

> Foreigners of all nations wish to post letters for Europe, but there is no post office establishment and no stamps, and I request that instructions may be sent.

He too was brushed aside, and a further attempt to obtain stamps in 1863 was similarly dismissed. Not until October 1866 was the breakthrough made. By then Ascension had a postmaster of its own – one Hugh A. Haswell, who wrote to London saying:

> I . . . have the honor to request that, as continual application is being made to me (not only by the Residents on this Island but also by people on board merchant ships as well as men of war calling here) for stamps, I may be supplied with a portion of shilling, sixpenny and penny stamps for the convenience of the public.

At last, on 9 January 1867, the Postmaster General granted the request, and sent out £20 worth of ordinary English stamps – £5 worth of 1d, £8 of 6d, and £7 of 1s – which reached the island on 3 March. 'Philatelically, then,' Major Ford remarked, '3 March

1867, was the most important day in the history of this "ship that never sailed the seas".'

Not even the existence of stamps and a postmaster, however, could speed the passage of the mail. In 1863 a contract had been made between the Postmaster General in London and the Union Steamship Company, whereby, on their return voyages from Cape Town to England, the Company's packet boats would call at St Helena and Ascension once a month. The entire voyage was to take not more than thirty-eight days, including twelve-hour stays at each island.

The contract also provided for stops on the outward voyages, should the Postmaster General specifically order them. But until 1903, when arrangements were made for the steamers to call regularly from both directions, Ascension never benefited by this optional clause, no doubt because the price was so steep: the extra service would have cost £8000 a year if the ships had called at both islands, £5000 if they had stopped at St Helena only, and £2000 if they had visited Ascension. As a result, letters from England took three times as long to reach Ascension as others took to get home, and the arrival of a mail boat became such an event in the lives of the garrison that whenever one was expected a lookout was posted to signal its approach. Often, when one did come in, all work stopped so that the islanders could get their letters at the first possible instant. Once, in 1874, the steamer was sighted during divine service, whereupon the Chaplain immediately closed the church and the entire congregation adjourned to the pierhead.

The introduction of regular homeward steamers enabled Ascension to furnish another modest service: from the 1860s Lloyd's in London paid £6 a year for a lookout to be stationed permanently on Cross Hill in order to report shipping movements. The intelligence, reaching them at least a month after the events recorded, can have been of limited value, especially as the Marines chosen for look-out duty were by no means infallible: in 1885 the Commandant wrote acknowledging the receipt of one year's wage, but added:

As the proper signalman has been imprisoned for three months óf the year for misconduct, I have awarded $\frac{1}{3}$ of the payment to X.

Not until 1899 did Ascension acquire the speed of communication likely to be of real interest to Lloyd's. Then, with the arrival of the first submarine cable, from the Cape and St Helena, the island suddenly ceased to be merely an out-of-the-way naval station and became instead the crossroads of an international cable network.

The need for swift communication with distant parts of the Empire had first been demonstrated by the Indian Mutiny in 1857; and the Boer war, starting in 1899, once again showed the paramount advantages of speed and reliability. Until a direct line was laid, messages from South Africa had to be transmitted either through the maze of West African cables, or through the East Coast cables to Aden and thence via Suez, Alexandria, Malta and Gibraltar to England. In the words of *A Century of Service*, K. C. Baglehole's brief history of Cable and Wireless, the Eastern Telegraph Company therefore

... decided to lay a cable from Capetown, touching only at St Helena and Ascension Islands, to St Vincent (CVI) where it would join the main lines to Porthcurno.* The Telegraph, Construction and Maintenance Company sent the cableship *Anglia* to Capetown loaded with over 2000 nauts of cable, and a second ship, the *Seine*, with 800 nauts to St Helena. The *Anglia* completed the St Helena section on 26 November 1899, and returned to England for further cable while the *Seine* laid the St Helena-Ascension section which she completed on 15 December. That date marked the opening of a new station at Ascension which has ever since been manned by company personnel.

The *Anglia* returned with a further 2000 nauts and laid the final section Ascension-St Vincent between February 10th and

*The Company's training college in Cornwall.

21st 1900. In the following year the speed of transmission over this cable was further increased by a new section laid from Porthcurno to St Vincent via Madeira, and Ascension Island was, for strategic purposes, connected direct to West Africa by a cable laid to Sierra Leone.

Disappointingly few details survive about how the cables were brought ashore – quite an operation, on that coast and with that sea – or how the staff of the Eastern Telegraph Company established themselves and their equipment on the island; but it is clear from the scanty records that the old hands of the Marine garrison did not exactly put themselves out to make the civilian interlopers feel at home.

The cables came ashore in Comfortless Cove, some one and half miles from Georgetown, and landlines had to be laid between the cove and the E.T.C. office in the settlement. The Marines were supposed to help with the daunting task of burying the lines by providing and directing their Kroo labourers – and indeed they did, though not without mischievously creating a number of difficulties.

By 1904 the job was still not finished, and the E.T.C. superintendent, C. A. Paine, was evidently having trouble on various fronts. The ground near Comfortless was chaotically difficult, and in order to avoid as much blasting as possible, the line of the landcable twisted about, following the ash-beds between the piles of black basalt slabs. But it was easier to outflank the terrain than to outmanoeuvre the senior officer of Marines, Captain R. H. Morgan, a plump, moustachioed and monocled officer who seems to have pulled his considerable weight whenever possible.

In order to get labour for the trench-digging, the wretched Paine went to formal interviews with him, the results of which he reported to the E.T.C. in London. In August 1904 he wrote:

On the morning of the 11th the Captain informed us he could not spare labour without referring the matter to Admiralty, which he did on 12th inst., consequently work was not commenced . . .

19th. Captain came over and informed us that we could have the men on Monday 22nd and remarked that he could easily have spared the men in January last.

Even when the labour became available, the E.T.C. experienced great difficulties. The Kroomen were extremely careless: the heat and dust wore out all the Europeans, and loose ash was continually sliding into the newly-opened trench. At the end of September work could be carried on in the mornings only, for in the afternoons the garrison carried out its annual firing on the Long Beach ranges, and the area through which the trench was being cut lay directly behind the targets. Faults kept developing in the land-lines, either as the result of rock-slips or because of the heat, and a further hold-up occurred when the storeship *Wye* arrived with small-pox on board and had to be put into quarantine in Comfortless Cove.

The next year, 1905, work on the E.T.C.'s buildings was further retarded by a reduction in the strength of the Marine garrison, and Paine was forced to recruit volunteer labour out of working hours. 'Volunteer labour is precarious,' he reported to his office in London, 'but may be facilitated by liberal liquid refreshment in part payment.' The cement tunnel protecting the cables where they entered the sea in Comfortless Cove was largely the product of generous issues of rum.

Luckily for the E.T.C., Paine was a man of considerable patience. When he wrote home to the Managing Director, his letters carried strong echoes of the official naval dispatches: 'Dear Sir, I have the honour to report that all the electrical apparatus received here per S.S. *Westminster Bridge* has been unpacked.' And when he dealt with Captain Morgan he was the very essence of tact.

In spite of all the difficulties, traffic built up quickly after the first cable, from Cape Town, had been extended to the United Kingdom via the Cape Verde islands. From the Marines' point of view, the electricians, with their new-fangled equipment and endless requests for help, were obviously a nuisance; but it was in no way the fault of the E.T.C. that morale among members of the garrison was far from good. In a memoir written later in life for his family General Morgan (as he became) recalled his arrival on Ascension in 1904:

> We landed at the Pier and walked up to our bungalow. . . . We saw not a soul on the way up and not one of the officers' wives was there to greet us, but we felt that we were being surveyed from behind the jalousies of the various bungalows. . . . We found that there was a lot of friction in the island between the naval Captain-in-Charge (McAlpine) and his officers, and he made it so unpleasant for anyone he disagreed with that all the wives were afraid to take any step before Mrs McAlpine showed the way.
>
> The next morning I reported to McAlpine, who immediately asked me to explain why I had brought my wife and child with me, as it was entirely contrary to his orders! I pointed out that I did what the Admiralty ordered and had no knowledge of *his* orders.
>
> This was not a good start, and we soon found that both he and his wife were impossible. She called herself the Queen of Ascension and was a marvellous production. . . . We found the island a strange place, with everyone at sixes and sevens.

Early in 1905 Morgan received an official letter asking if he would take charge of the garrison, as the Admiralty had decided that the command of the island should once more be taken over by a major of Marines. Although only a captain, Morgan was given the job, and his journal continues:

> Soon after, I heard unofficially that I was going to be appointed, and some time later I was sent for by McAlpine and informed that for some unknown reason the Admiralty had very foolishly decided to put a Royal Marine officer in charge of the island, and I was to be the one. He was furiously angry and said the most outrageous and insulting things to me, but luckily I kept my

temper and said nothing. In fact I was so pleased with my good fortune that nothing would have bothered me.

In April McAlpine left, only handing over the keys and charge of the island to me as he left the Pier. He had behaved like a disgruntled child ever since he had heard that I was to relieve him and had never given me any help or shown me a single official paper. What was much worse was that after he left I found a telegram from the Admiralty instructing him to hand over to me in the middle of March. He had not even shown me the telegram, and so had done me out of a month's command pay.

And so, for the first time since 1844, Ascension was once again under the command of a Royal Marine officer, with the whole island now – bizarrely enough – borne on the books of H.M.S. *Cormorant*, which was stationed at Gibraltar. Gradually the garrison settled down into a much happier state, and Morgan made such a good job of running the place that in 1907 his tour of duty was extended for a further year. To judge from his own records and photograph album, he was not exactly overworked: he seems to have devoted much of his time to goat-shooting, his passion for which took him repeatedly over the roughest ground in the island. His photographs combine with an account printed in the E.T.C.'s house magazine *Zodiac* to give a vivid impression of this exacting sport.

The party would leave Georgetown at 6.30 in the morning and walk up to the Mountain settlement, which they reached at about 8.30, their baggage having been taken up in advance by an African with a donkey or mule. Then the real action began – a day of violent climbing, scrambling, slithering and creeping through the cinders and lumps of lava. Only shot-guns were allowed (the dangers of ricochets being too great from rifles), so that the hunters had to get within fifty yards or less of their quarry before it was worth taking a shot. Hours of patient approach work would either be wasted by a last-minute mistake or rewarded by a few seconds of lightning action – perhaps a right-and-left at an old billy and a kid. The bodies were liable to tumble over cliffs and smash themselves to pulp, and often they could not be retrieved at all; even so, a bag of six in a weekend was not uncommon.

Another energetic task on which Morgan had to spend a considerable amount of time was prospecting for phosphates. Ever since 1851 intermittent attempts had been made to harvest the rich deposits of phosphates and guano (both the product of sea-birds' droppings), particularly on Boatswain Bird Island; but the expense and physical difficulty of extraction had brought several contractors to grief. One was William Thorpe, a merchant in St Helena, who claimed to have lost nearly £2000 as a result of the fiasco in which his operation ended, and during the early 1900s he tried unsuccessfully to sue the Admiralty for some redress.

Their Lordships, ever anxious to defray the cost of running Ascension, were keen to encourage a new venture; but at the same time they were nervous about allowing any commercial organisation free rein on an island that was run by and for the Navy. An Admiralty minute of 1906 raised the question of whether the Board should allow commerce on an island ruled by naval discipline, and pointed out:

> There are at present employees of the Telegraph Company there, but an importation of labourers would be a different matter.

In spite of its doubts, in 1907 the Board allowed companies to put in new tenders. Among them was James Morrison and Co. of St Helena, and the Admiralty was no doubt influenced by the fact that the economy of St Helena was then in an extremely bad way. That same year the Governor wrote to the Secretary of State for the Colonies pleading the 'acute distress' and 'semi-starvation' of many families. A few St Helenians were already working for the E.T.C. But to send large gangs of labourers up to Ascension was an attractive idea, for it would provide the southern island with much-needed relief.

For several months the Admiralty prevaricated in a typically maddening way, never managing to commit itself. Mr G. O. Cannon, a representative of the St Helena firm, was allowed to prospect on Ascension, and together with Captain Morgan he scrambled about measuring the phosphate deposits. Morgan's photographs show the pair of them perspiring heavily among the villainous lava on the north-west corner of the island, particularly round English Bay. Morgan himself was asked by the Admiralty to prepare a report on the feasibility of the whole project, and he wrote back to say that he thought a commercial venture perfectly possible, provided that certain conditions were observed: first, all work would have to be done without the help of the naval establishment; second, all men on the main island would have to be under the control of the Marine Commandant: third, no 'spirituous liquor whatever' was to be brought ashore by the company.

Rather than make a decision, the Admiralty took refuge in detailed objections. Since only about forty St Helenians would benefit from the scheme, was the whole thing worth it? Who would lock them up if they caused trouble? Where would they live? Presumably in some old hulk – but if so, where would it be moored? How many natives could safely be taken from St Helena? How far would the influx of 'a number of (probably coloured) labourers affect the administration and discipline of the island'?

Some research was put in hand to establish the position of civil law on Ascension. The answer was that there had never been any: everyone had always come under naval discipline. Whereas the civilian gardener was on the books of the guard-ship for both victuals and pay, the employees of the E.T.C. were on its books for victuals only. 'They therefore appear to be on the Island in the capacity of private individuals,' said an Admiralty minute, 'and occupy a somewhat similar position to that of the wives and children of the garrison, who are not "officially recognised".'

If the staff of the E.T.C. – already present – were not officially recognised, what hope was there for some bare-facedly commercial firm? The answer was none. After months of masterly stalling, the Admiralty at last, in December 1908, sent out a letter regretting that the difficulties of the whole operation were too great, and that no concession would be granted.

By then the cable station was well established. In January 1908 the Ascension relays passed on over 27,000 messages, and on 28 January, when the Suez landlines were interrupted, they handled 1716 messages – a record to that date.

In May 1908 Morgan left for home, taking with him his three baby daughters, the youngest of whom had been born and christened on the island, and all of whom had run happily barefoot about the clinker, being made much of by their Krooman-nurse, Tom Cole, and the rest of the garrison. Muriel, the middle girl, had her name given to Muriel Avenue, a double line of palm trees at Two Boats. It is pleasant to find Morgan, in his family memoir, paying tribute to the men of the cable company: even if he had teased them at first, he had later come to appreciate their worth. 'I was most loyally backed up by everyone in the island,' he wrote, 'including the Superintendent and staff (forty including servants) of the Eastern Telegraph Company.'

During his spare time Morgan had shown a lively interest in Ascension's history and made extracts from old records, some of which have since disappeared. Also he wrote treatises on the behaviour of the island's two oddest species – the turtles and the wideawakes.

By 1909 the original cable hut in Comfortless Cove was evidently obsolete, for a search was made of the island's beaches for a better site. The electricians inspected English Bay, South West Bay and the beaches round Georgetown, but concluded after all that Comfortless Cove was much the best place. The route for a new landline was accordingly surveyed and pegged at twenty-yard intervals, and excavations began in November. 'Blasters Moyce and George arrive from St Helena with explosives and miners' tools,' said the E.T.C. diary for 10 November. 'Nov. 11th. Commence opening trench close to Office. Unable to proceed past Long Beach owing to musketry course being carried on at Rifle Range by H.M.S. *Dwarf*.'

In 1910 a further important link was added to the telegraph network when the cable was laid from Buenos Aires to Ascension, and in October that year the island's scientific equipment was reinforced by the arrival of a seismograph. Quite possibly the instrument would have given some warning of a brewing eruption, but for several months its operator was much harassed by its instability. 'On the 9th inst,' he wrote, in a letter typical of many, 'I noticed a very marked disturbance, which at present I am quite unable to account for, but I think very probably that it is due to the very strong prevailing winds.'

With the arrival of the cables, Lloyd's strengthened the signal station on Cross Hill with the addition of a second observer. The job could hardly be described as 'action-packed', and for day after day the entries in the log are almost identical:

6.10 Nothing in sight.
6.45 Milk cart from Mountain.
2.00 Daily cart to Mountain.
6.00 Nothing in sight.

While the signalmen on Cross Hill slumbered, up on the farm immense progress was being made by the man who, perhaps more than any other, left his mark on Green Mountain. Few details survive about the reign of Hedley Cronk, who came to Ascension in 1896 and remained head gardener until 1922. To the junior members of the garrison he was a king-like figure, reigning supreme in his lofty domain. His name survives in Cronk's Path, which he cut in 1921 from the Home Garden round to North East cottage, and along which (tradition has it) he liked to stroll in the evenings, contemplating all his works. But the day-to-day journal which he kept of his twenty-six years on the island has alas disappeared, and little remains except some notes which he compiled after he had left.

Even so, it is clear that he brought to the cultivation of Green Mountain more skill and perseverance than any of his predecessors. At the time of his arrival, he recalled, there were no more than fifty full-sized trees, and he himself imported and established Norfolk Island pines, eucalyptus, casuarina, cypress, limes, oranges, bananas, coconuts and others. The Norfolk Island pines came from Buenos Aires, to which he made two visits in the old storeship *Wye* about 1900, and today a fine stand of them still graces Breakneck Valley. The oranges did well at Palmer's and below the San, and although most of the citrus trees have now died out, bananas still flourish in many of the ravines.

Cronk also greatly extended the area of grazing by bringing in various new grasses – *Paspalum dilatatum* from Australia, Rutherford Grass from South Africa and Guinea Grass from South America. Each extension represented a major effort, for every new patch had to be fenced against the rabbits, and this, with the ground composed mainly of rock and loose cinders, was in itself a formidable task. Cronk's battle against the rabbits was unending, but in the end successful: continuous shooting and ferreting eventually wore them down to a tolerable level.

Other pests abounded, many of them vegetable: wild guava, buddleia, periwinkle and prickly pear all had to be kept under control, the last by the highly poisonous and sinister-sounding '"Jansen Process", which was purchased by the Government from a German Professor and used in South Africa.

Oddly enough – on an island chronically short of women – Ascension acted as a kind of marriage market for the Cronk family. Hedley's sister went out to keep house for him and married one of the officers, Lt. Eagles; and when the sister of the Commandant's wife, Mrs Blaxland, went out to stay, she married Hedley.

The outbreak of war in 1914 did not at first affect the island greatly. The only difference from peacetime was that the forts were manned day and night, and guard-posts were set up on Long Beach, at the Needles (the site of one of the main water tanks, above and behind Georgetown), and at Gallows Hill, a short distance south of the township. Apart from keeping a look-out there were few precautions that the islanders could take, although the Admiralty, believing that some German warship might attack the cable station any minute, insisted on a telegram being sent home every day to report that the garrison was still alive and well.

It is worth recalling at this point that although Ascension had become a vital link in a cable network which spanned the world, its own internal communications were still extremely poor. After almost exactly a century of occupation, there was still only one road – a rough track – from Georgetown to the Mountain settlement. Apart from this, only footpaths wound through the clinker to Comfortless Cove and South-West Bay. There was no mechanical transport of any kind, and not even any wheeled vehicles apart from a few mule carts. A primitive telephone kept Georgetown, Cross Hill and the Mountain Settlement in touch with each other, but anyone on duty in other parts of the island had to rely for instructions on flags hoisted on top of Cross Hill. Except in the E.T.C.'s offices and quarters, there was no electricity: all lamps were oil, and all cooking was done on coal.

To the thirty young men of the first Royal Marine Mobile Force who reached Ascension in January 1915 the place seemed exceedingly strange. And from the moment they swung ashore by rope on to the pierhead they were put hard to work. With the arrival of reinforcements, guards were set every night in the outlying bays – English, North East and South West – and this meant a strenuous schedule for the men on duty. The North East Bay party, for instance, was stationed at San, the Mountain Hospital. First they had to walk up to it from the garrison: four miles and a 2000 foot climb, carrying their rifles, equipment and food. Then detachments of two men at a time made the long trek down to North East Bay, using, for part of the way, the original track said to have been cleared by the early Portuguese explorers.

In the bay there was nothing to do but keep a watch and fish. 'There were plenty of good-sized cod,' remembers Ernest Smith, one of the Marine infantrymen.

We'd fillet enough to make a nice parcel to take back to the camp at San, feeding the carcases to the monstrous sharks, which abounded. When our time was up we'd set off for home, passing our relief on the track on their way down, and so the routine of bringing fish back each day was established.

One could imagine that our life was very strenuous, and yet we revelled in the exercise, and at no time were we ever distressed. On our day off we were usually invited down to Garrison to play in a football match, starting the game at four o'clock in the afternoon. Then our mates would have the necessary reception ready – perhaps a pigeon pie and drinks to follow well into the night – and the next morning back up the long trail to San ready for the North East Bay trip again in the afternoon.

Meanwhile, as the old-fashioned (and, one suspects, largely futile) guard-routines were faithfully carried out, an important technical innovation was taking place on Ash Plain, a mile inland from Georgetown; the construction of the first wireless station.

Radio communication was then in its infancy, and in order to keep in contact with its ships in distant waters, the Admiralty in London needed a chain of relay stations. Ascension was ideally sited for passing messages to and from the fleet in the South Atlantic which was protecting the South African and South American shipping lanes, and the island was one of the first places to be chosen for a relay.

William J. Howlett, who was serving in the Royal Navy as a Warrant Telegraphist at the time, recalls the clandestine origins of the project:

The strictest secrecy was observed before we left England [in 1915]. We were told that the mission was secret, and given the option of refusing or volunteering. Even when we had joined the ship no one knew our destination. It was not until we were several days out from Liverpool, when the captain opened his sealed orders, that we knew where we were bound. And even when we heard the name 'Ascension', most of us still had no idea where we were heading.

Because of the total lack of facilities on the island, the project had been planned with immense care. There was absolutely nothing that Ascension could offer to help in the building of a wireless station – there were no power supplies, labour, transport: nothing but the site.

So the operation had been planned literally down to the last nut and bolt. We had on board the complete project, including the wireless equipment, six 300–foot tubular steel masts, generating plant and all the necessary building materials for housing the station and its staff, together with the contractors to build the station and the staff to operate it.

Ample spare parts had been included, as any replacements would have taken weeks to come out from England, and it was obviously no use building a wireless station to keep contact with the fleet in wartime if it was going to be out of action waiting for a spare part.

After calling at Sierra Leone to pick up a hundred Kroo labourers, the ship reached Ascension safely and anchored in Clarence Bay. The crew soon discovered that one of the most formidable problems awaiting them was to get all the heavy equipment ashore: the pier had only one antiquated ten-ton crane, fitted with a hand winch, and the incoming rollers made the transfer of big loads from lighter to land extremely hazardous. The landing was accomplished without any serious accident, but it took a month to unload the 3000 tons of stores. First to come ashore were three five-ton coal-fired Foden steam lorries, which did almost all the hauling to the site. The station quickly went up on Ash Plain, beside the road to the Mountain, and in three months it was finished. The fifty white contractors' men fitted in admirably with the garrison, but the hundred Kroomen – 'the sweepings of the Sierra Leone gaol', according to one of the officers present – were an entirely different proposition, and a continuous source of trouble. When they struck for more pay, their manner was so threatening that the British had an armed party standing by while negotiations were in progress.

The huge aerial masts were set up in pairs, with cross wires slung between them, and these brought down many wideawakes on their way to and from the fairs in the southern corner of the island. The station's equipment, though primitive, seems to have functioned remarkably well. Valves, recalls Howlett, were used only for receiving:

> They were designed with a pip on the top which had to be heated before they would function, and we applied the heat with lighted matches. Transmission was carried out by passing a high voltage across a small gap – a system known as spark transmission.

Shaky though the performance sounds, the station operated continuously, twenty-four hours a day, with only minor break-downs. Thus armed with both cable and radio links (and also with new internal telephone lines to English and South West Bays), Ascension settled down to a war of watching and waiting which soon became dreadfully boring. The garrison's armament was obsolete, and any German cruiser or battleship could have blown the defenders off the face of the clinker in a few minutes, or driven them to seek sanctuary up the mountain; but no attack ever came, and most of the men found their existence one of stupefying tedium. 'The strain of the isolation and privations,' remarked one person who was there, 'eventually led to a state of utter despair.'

For those with energy to spare, the main recreation was clinker-crawling – walking or climbing over the island's rugged terrain. The clinker-crawl *par excellence* was to the traditional site of Letter Box, on South East Head, where there was indeed a wooden letter box, in which the walkers left notes, much as the bottles had been used in the past.

Walking apart, there was football, cricket, tennis and hockey, and, from 1915, golf. The nine-hole course, with its fairways of lava and greens of sand bound with oil, was disfigured by no blade of grass, and it was soon known with some reason as the worst in the world. A well-struck shot which happened to hit a rock was liable to come back past the striker as fast as it had left him, or to ricochet wildly off into the lava. Balls were cut to pieces by the rocks and sometimes barely survived a single round. Even so, people played with enthusiasm, and when they grew bored with the course itself, challenged each other to golfing steeplechases, one popular contest being a race from the settlement to the top of Cross Hill – 868 feet up extremely steep slopes of loose, sliding red ash.

Another of the principal recreations was fishing. The sea round Ascension teems with life, and fishing had been the most profitable local sport ever since the beginning of the occupation. Rock cod and cavally were (and still are) the kinds most easily taken from the rocks, but bonito, yellowtail, albacore and wahoo all abounded, to say nothing of the sharks. Almost all Ascension's fish are edible, with the notable exception of the ubiquitous blackfish, which swarm in thousands round the coast. So voracious are they that they clean the bottom of any ship that stays at anchor for two or three days, and so rough is their skin that, once dried, it makes serviceable sandpaper. But even the excellent fishing palled during the war years, and the monotony of diet was exactly the same as had jaundiced the garrison for the past hundred years. On several occasions supply voyages were interrupted, and once, when the mail steamer *Alnwick Castle* was torpedoed in the Bay of Biscay in 1917, the E.T.C. were reduced for three months to a diet of corned beef and biscuits, supplemented only by turtle meat, wideawakes' eggs, occasional goat mutton, and such fresh fish as they could catch.

In the middle of so much restriction, rum was at a premium. The E.T.C. staff received a good allowance as part of their rations, and its usefulness not merely as a spirit-raiser but as hard currency is recalled by a former Eastern man, Mr H. K. Jolley:

If we needed a haircut or our boots repaired or any other service, the Marine would never accept money in payment. So a bottle of rum would disappear up his jumper, to be kept for the Saturday singsong. It was strictly against regulations, but authority turned Nelson's blind eye on Nelson's blood, and no harm ever came of it.

Social life – never particularly varied – was further restricted by the fact that all the women left on the island had been evacuated to the Mountain settlement, where they hovered out of immediate harm's way, telephoning their shopping orders down to George-town. Undeterred, some of the brighter sparks of the Navy and the E.T.C. began to specialise in female impersonation for the fancy-dress balls, soap operas and pantomimes. The *Aladdin* of 1918 was a memorable event: prepared by Mr A. E. Burnham of the E.T.C., with paint and canvas for the scenery provided by Colour Sergeant Doree and the Royal Marines' armourer's shop, and 'modernised by a wealth of topical allusion', the production raised £53 on Ascension and £50 on St Helena, being hailed as a winner on both islands.

Oddly enough, the one violent event that did occur on Ascension took place when the war was over. The trouble came from the Kroomen, whose predecessors had been brought from the West Coast of Africa to work on the island ever since the 1830s. Although the men temporarily imported in 1915 to build the wireless station had proved unsatisfactory, the regulars had almost without exception given loyal and trustworthy service, particularly as domestic staff; many of them took on English names, adopting whatever patronymic they fancied: John Long, John Hard, Tom Cole, Tom Peter were typical, and one man styled himself Lord Jellicoe. A nice story survives of a man presenting himself for the first time to his new English mistress and, on being asked his name, answering: 'Tom.'

'Tom what?'

'Jus' Tom.'

This was not enough for the lady, who, glancing at the clock and noticing that it stood at four o'clock, said: 'I know – we'll call you Tom Four o'clock'; and so the man was known thereafter.

In April 1920 the easy relationship was seriously undermined when most of the Kroomen on the island went on strike, claiming that their contracts had expired. The men were arrested and imprisoned in the fort, and in due course the trouble blew over. In 1921, however, three separate attempts were made to assault white women, and tension slowly mounted until the climax burst in September, when, between ten and eleven one night, a riot broke out in the Kroo cantonment below Fort Hayes.

The shouting and banging roused the garrison, and the troops were called out. As the noise increased, the Commandant and officers were sent for. The Commandant ordered the rioters to be given up, but the only answer he got was that if he wanted the offenders he could come and get them. The Kroomen then barricaded themselves into their quarters and defied anyone to enter.

Ordered to clear the Kroomen out, the Marines fired a volley over the building. Since this produced only yells of defiance, a second volley was fired, through the windows. The result was the same, so the troops closed up and tried to force their way in. Suddenly the door was thrown open, and a sergeant-major who had his weight against it was hurled into the building. Immediately he was thrown out again senseless, having been hit so hard on the head that he remained unconscious for more than an hour.

But the door was open, and the Marines rushed inside. Even then, the Kroomen fought so fiercely that the struggle lasted nearly an hour before the last of them was overpowered and marched off under escort to Fort Hayes, where they were kept behind wire and watched over by armed guards.

The incident finally convinced the Admiralty that Kroo labour was undesirable on Ascension. On 6 October 1921 H.M.S. *Dublin* arrived with a force of St Helenians, and in their place took on board the Kroomen, who were repatriated to Sierra Leone. Since then the Saints, as they were soon christened, have been Ascension's only permanent work-force.

When the war was over, the naval occupation of the island became a mere formality. Its high military seriousness is well indicated by the log of the *Dublin's* ship-to-shore radio messages on the day when she called to pick up the Kroomen:

I should like to call on Mr Cronk at Green Mountain in the afternoon. Could you please provide a horse for me to ride? Possible number of officers attending picnic about 6 or 7. . . . What time does cricket match start tomorrow? Can you lend us six hockey sticks for this afternoon as we can muster only five all told?

As the last dregs of its naval value ebbed away, Ascension's commercial importance was further increased (in 1919) by the laying of another cable, this time from Rio de Janeiro. Sitting at the cross-roads of a network that now spanned the Atlantic not only from north to south but also from east to west, the cable men had a real job to do. Clearly, it was time for the Navy to depart.

On 30 September 1922 the signal station on Cross Hill closed with the characteristic final entry: '4.45 p.m. Nothing in sight'; and at last, on 20 October, the Marine garrison withdrew, leaving the E.T.C. in sole possession of the island. Several of the sailors transferred their allegiance to the cable company and stayed on to work as civilians. Naval stores were auctioned off, and the withdrawal was celebrated by an immense firework display which consisted of the detonation of all surplus flares, rockets and shells, and the firing of an immense heap of cordite.

No doubt the Marines were delighted to be off. But one man was heartbroken by the abrupt departure. For reasons that are not now clear, the Admiralty dismissed Hedley Cronk almost a year sooner than he had been anticipating. 'I rather expected to be retained till next August, when I originally was to retire,' he wrote in a letter to the Governor of St Helena dated October 1922, 'but there appears to be nothing doing.'

The restrained tone of the letter does not conceal Cronk's bitter disappointment:

There is a great deal to do still to keep the Island progressing towards more vegetation and water. I have seen it through its worst period and have spent a big slice of my life trying to bring it to more usefulness – it has been difficult, hard work, and now to end it this way is most disheartening.

The pension I now look forward to appears to have been worked out on the same scale as applied to Civil Servants in home offices and only amounts to a little over £100 a year. I was hoping my particular appointment here (which is the only one of its sort) might have been worked out a little more generously on a better scale, more by results.

At least Cronk had the satisfaction of knowing that he had left an indelible mark on Ascension: his twenty-six years of hard labour changed the aspect of Green Mountain for ever, and the mantle of lush growth which it wears today is his living memorial.

The Marines, too, are remembered in a hundred different places. In 1937 a stone commemorating the occupation was brought to Ascension by H.M.S. *Penzance* and erected beside the entrance to the church; but all over the island there are far more eloquent tributes to the skill, endurance and sheer sturdy worth of the men who for a hundred years manned the one ship of the Royal Navy made entirely of volcanic rock.

In the solid yet gracious buildings, in the heavy brass taps of the sheep troughs which still turn at a touch, in the fine masonry of the water-tanks and the magnificent siting of the Mountain settlement – in all this one can see and feel an uniquely British quality.

THE CABLE MEN'S HEYDAY

1922–39

With the departure of the Navy, Ascension ceased officially to be a ship, becoming instead a dependency of its southern neighbour, St Helena. To mark the occasion sets of St Helena stamps, overprinted with the word 'Ascension', were placed on sale in the island's post office on 2 November 1922. At once the postmaster was inundated with requests from all over the world for sets of the stamps, many of the letters containing money orders. But as there was no bank on the island, and money was not normally used, most of the applications had to be returned, thereby causing an immense amount of work. Two years later – on 20 August 1924 – Ascension got the first definitive issue of stamps of its own, and ever since then its eagerly-sought and collected issues have been a considerable source of income.

And yet, in 1922, although the island had become a colonial dependency, in every practical detail it belonged to, and was run by, the E.T.C. The company's Manager became the resident magistrate, the harbourmaster and the lay preacher rolled into one. The company took over Green Mountain Farm and the garrison hospital, and organised their own school.

To celebrate the new acquisition, in December 1923 the company's house magazine *Zodiac* published an 'Ascension Number' which contained twenty-six pages of excellent photographs, a little history, and a considerable amount of advice for any of the staff who might have to serve on the island. 'Fever and colds are unknown, and children flourish,' said an article entitled 'Domesticities':

There is no school. Servants come from St Helena, and married folk, on appointment, should write out for two to be engaged. A three or four-burner 'Perfection' oil stove should be brought out, the use of oil being cheaper than coal. . . . Living is expensive. For a family of five, 45 pounds a month is a moderate estimate, and this sum does not include clothing etc. Tussore, zephyrs and casement cloth are the best wearing apparel for ladies' dresses. The laundry is bad and soon ruins anything dainty. There is no resident dentist, and teeth are apt to go bad quickly.

In the years that followed Ascension became very closely identified with the E.T.C. (later Cable and Wireless) since it was, to all intents and purposes, *their* island. The essence of these years is admirably caught in *Bartlett's Book*, a portrait of Ascension compiled by Lionel Bartlett, Cable and Wireless's Manager there from 1934 to 1936. The book has never been published, and probably never will be, for the author had – as he himself was the first to admit – no great talent for literary organisation. But it remains a marvellous labour of love; lavishly illustrated with sketches and photographs, its text is typed with meticulous accuracy, individual words having been cut from other sheets of paper and stuck over the top of the original whenever the author wanted to make a correction.

From this unique volume there emerges a vivid picture of the peace and happiness which Bartlett and his fellow-exiles found on their volcanic cinder, with its relics of naval history scattered all round them.

'The line of married bungalows on the right is known as "Scandal Terrace", and that to the left as "Teapot Alley",' he wrote, describing Georgetown.

The bungalows themselves are most picturesque, with red or grey-tiled roofs, ample verandahs and patches of garden. Hanging maiden-hair ferns, banks of palladium and other tropical growths impart an atmosphere of coolness and restfulness as one steps inside from the outer sunshine. An idyllic peace reigns. . . .

The broad verandah is invariably the reception room, with lounge chairs of cane and wicker and small tables bearing vases of fresh flowers. The bright sunshine filtering through the green rush blinds gives just the right contrast and atmosphere of coolness.

The verandah is the rendezvous of the morning tea-party, when the ladies gather together armed with sewing and knitting to discuss modes and means. Here, too, in the evening is held the 'Bitters Party', a form of entertaining, consisting of the dispensation of appetisers and 'small chop', peculiar to the tropics. . . .

Life flows along easily, notwithstanding a certain amount of monotony and constriction. Everyone is ready to make the best of everything, and there is little discontent. It is not unlike being in a large ship, for the roll of the sea is never far distant, and the same individuals meet every day.

Like many Ascensionites before and after him, Bartlett was much stirred by the island's physical strangeness – by the extra-ordinary colours and textures of the shattered volcanoes, by their desolation, and by the brilliance of the southern sky at night. Often he would sit out on the verandah of Governor's Lodge (formerly Captain's or Bate's Cottage) up on the side of Cross Hill, looking down over Long Beach and watching the sun plunge into the Atlantic, loath, as he said, to leave such a splendid scene.

Nightfall viewed from the Mountain settlement was still more magnificent:

The hour before sunset is woven with mystic changes as one watches from the heights, the horizon barely distinguishable from the skyline. . . . Faintly at first, and then more strongly, the evening mists rise from the heated plains. The hard outlines of the craters and hills become softened until they resemble a crumpled velvet blanket.

The sun, creating marvellous transformation scenes, changing from gold flame to blood red, sinks lower, and, dipping into the sea, leaves the world to a sudden peacefulness. . . .

One may stand on the heights in England, or any other country, watching the same moon and the same stars, but in Ascension there is that extra thrill of the realisation that one is on a tiny island in the middle of a vast, floodlighted ocean, a mere spot of land, almost insignificant, lapped by waves a thousand miles from anywhere.

Bartlett's affection was shared by many of the cable company's staff, and his rosy account of morale on the island is strikingly confirmed by a little book written in 1934 by the Rev. C. C. Watts, Bishop of St Helena. In *In Mid-Atlantic* he drew a painful contrast between the misery and squalor of St Helena and the relaxed prosperity of its northern dependency: 'Ascension today,' he wrote,

> . . . is inhabited entirely by servants of the Cable Company, with about 100 people from St Helena. About forty cable employees form the island community, and I should say they are one of the happiest groups in the world. There is no unemployment, the houses are good, and there is plenty of food to be had.

By the time of Bishop Watts's visit in 1934, the cable men were thoroughly settled in. But an early E.T.C. log-book reveals that when they first took over from the Navy they were not entirely at ease in their new possession. In 1925, on their own initiative, two members of the staff set up a small radio receiver and transmitter in Fort Thornton in order to be able to contact passing ships; but when they wanted to move the apparatus to Fort Hayes, their superintendent first wrote home to head office:

> We presume there will be no objection to our using Fort Hayes, but would suggest that it would be advisable to obtain permission from the proper authorities, in view of there being other interests on the island. . . . The installation could be entirely dismantled and removed in an hour or so if required. . . . We do not know

whether any licence or permit is required to operate a private station here.

The 'other interests' were a new generation of guano-hunters in the form of the English Bay Company, set up in 1923, with a concession for removing guano and phosphates from anywhere on Ascension and Boatswain Bird Island. Ill-fortune dogged the venture almost from the start. Labourers from St Helena arrived in October 1923, and a year later the first shipment went out – 1000 tons of phosphates, 300 tons of guano and 15 tons of pumice. But the phosphates had been drenched by a freak storm in 1924, which washed out most of the essential minerals, and when the cargo arrived in England it proved almost unmarketable.

In 1926 the Union Castle liner *Garth Castle*, coming in with the mail, mistook the lights of the company's colony in English Bay for those of Georgetown and ran aground. The passengers were not allowed ashore, but had to stay on board, rolling in the swell, until a relief steamer took them off about a week later. The *Garth Castle* itself was eventually refloated after pumps and divers had been brought up from the Cape.

In 1929 another storm sank the *Derby*, the phosphate company's trawler which had been plying to and fro between English Bay and Boatswain Bird Island, and three smaller vessels.

In spite of these disasters, occasional shipments of guano and phosphates were made; but as the easily accessible stocks ran out the company began to float far-fetched ideas – among them that synthetic vanilla could be made from the uric acid in the guano, and that commercial quantities of platinum and gold could be extracted from ore mined on the island. By 1932, however, all but the wildest hopes had faded, and all the staff except a caretaker were withdrawn.

Today the evidence of their precipitate departure is still un-cannily fresh. Part of their light railway line still winds through the tumbled lava, but it is the little dumps of excavated phosphates that make one stop and wonder: the cast-down baskets and shovels lie where they fell forty years ago, and hessian sacks, filled to the brim with greyish-white powder, stand neatly stacked together, ready to be collected, preserved in astonishingly good condition by the hot, dry climate. Why, one longs to know, did the English Bay Company abandon ship in such a rush?

Whatever the reason, a still more bizarre episode followed. A year later, in 1932, the German chemist who had been the prime mover of the whole enterprise startled the public by announcing that from the volcanic deposits of Ascension he could produce enough gold to pay off the entire national debt in one instalment. Estimates of his process, he said, showed that it would produce £25 million a year from only £1 million capital.

Challenged by almost every metallurgist in Europe, he stuck to his claims with such conviction that he raised £100,000 of support, only to see the new company go bankrupt soon afterwards. Undismayed, he put out feelers for yet another firm, this time with capital of £1 million. But at last fate intervened to save the investors from further punishment, and the chemist was killed in an accident in March 1935. On Ascension, English Bay stood abandoned, and on Boatswain Bird Island the sea birds once more were left without competitors.

In Georgetown the E.T.C. had been beset by many of the difficulties that had troubled their naval predecessors. In 1924, for example, there had been freak rains, which produced waist-high grass all over the low ground. This in turn brought a plague of insects, as the company's superintendent reported on August 2:

> The whole island has recently been overrun by innumerable crickets. All other insect life on the island has also multiplied enormously owing to the abnormally heavy rains in the early part of the year causing rapid growth of vegetation.
>
> More recently the number of mice has very noticeably increased. On the 29th ult. a stoppage on HL-AO-SVI occurred owing to the insulation of leads to the main Gulstad windings having been eaten through, the conductor being exposed and a short circuit resulting.

In spite of their difficulties, the staff of the E.T.C. were always ready to respond to the challenge of a major sporting event. On 3 June 1926 special arrangements were made for flashing the result of the Derby to Cape Town in record time: by 'joining up a translator which was switched in as soon as the line was cleared', the delay on the London-Cape circuit was reduced from thirty seconds to fifteen.

Meanwhile, 4000 miles away in Whitehall, the Board of the Admiralty had been fighting a dogged action to retain a privilege which its members had enjoyed intermittently for the past hundred years. Ever since the early days of Ascension's occupation, turtles had been shipped back to London for the delectation of their lordships and others, and even though a sailing ship might take two months or more over the voyage, many of them reached their destination safely.

When the mail steamers began to ply regularly from Ascension, the practice became established of sending back consignments especially for the Lords of the Admiralty. The custom was that the captain of the ship got one turtle for himself, and the rest were delivered on arrival in England to Messrs Ring & Brymer, the celebrated soup-makers of Cornhill, who brewed them up into clear green *consommé* and wrote to the Secretary of the Admiralty informing him of the size of each allocation. (About eight quarts of soup were produced from each live turtle, but even a dead one usually yielded four.)

'We beg to inform you,' said a typical letter written on 6 August 1912, 'that we have received 6 (six) turtle ex R.M.S. *Braemar Castle*, for the Lords of the Admiralty, for which we propose to allocate 48 (forty-eight) quarts of soup.'

Their Lordships themselves kept keen eyes on the allocations, bickering and complaining whenever they thought they were being short-changed, borrowing and lending each other's rations when they wanted to give large parties. The First Lord of the Admiralty received most, and the others descending amounts related to their importance. Elaborate records were kept, with every sub-division being written out in full. The list for 10 June 1913 began:

Right Hon. Winston L. Spencer Churchill, M.P.	6 quarts
Admiral H.S.H. Prince Louis Athlone of Battenberg	$4\frac{1}{2}$
Vice-Admiral Sir John R. Jellicoe	$4\frac{1}{2}$
Sir W. Graham Greene, K.C.B.	$4\frac{1}{2}$

and so on, with lower members of the Board getting less.

The system continued whenever possible right through the First World War. Several consignments of turtles reached London in 1916, and at least two – five and six respectively – came in during 1917, although on both occasions, as a laconic note from Ring & Brymer reported, 'the fish all arrived dead'.

Occasional letters preserved from these years show how strong was their Lordships' attachment to their soup. Yet it was not until Sir Vincent Baddeley became First Principal Assistant Secretary of the Admiralty that the depths of their greed were finally exposed.

Whether driven by their insistence, or goaded by his own partiality, Baddeley emerges from the Admiralty archives as the most sedulous turtle-coper in history. Constantly haggling about prices and amounts, he pursued details with fanatical precision.

One of his first actions was to depose Ring & Brymer in favour of Mr John Lusty, also of the East End (telegraphic address: 'Turtling, London'), as the official soup-maker. The reason for the switch is not clear, but may not have been unconnected with the fact that Lusty said he could make fifteen quarts of soup from each live turtle, against Ring & Brymer's eight. In any case, from 1920 Lusty had the job.

Only an extended quotation can illustrate the kind of bureaucracy in which Baddeley specialised: 'I understand,' he wrote to Lusty on 6 August 1921, after one turtle had died in transit from Ascension,

> that of the ten turtles shipped, one was intended for the Captain of the ship, one for the Directors of the Company (the

Eastern Telegraph Company), one for the Commandant of the Island and one for another Marine Officer, to be sold for his benefit.

As it is impossible to say to whom the dead turtle belonged, I propose that the remaining nine turtles should be divided as follows:

The Captain of the Ship, the Directors of the Company and the Commandant of the Garrison to receive 9/10 of a turtle each; the Lords of the Admiralty to receive the remainder – 6 3/10 turtle. At 15 quarts of soup per turtle, the Admiralty allocation will be 94½ quarts.

He was at it again in July 1922, when a captain who had not previously brought turtles from Ascension landed six at Dover instead of bringing them round to London, and sent them on by rail. Immediately Baddeley wrote to every member of the Admiralty Board, informing them that the turtles had inadvertently been sent by passenger train, so that

a heavy freight charge was incurred which, divided proportionately, will amount to 1s 6 1/5d per quart. I am in communication with the South Eastern and Central Railway in the matter and hope to obtain some reduction in their charges, but in the meantime I should be glad to know whether you would be prepared to pay a proportionate amount.

By then, however, Baddeley had a far bigger problem on his hands, for the Navy had abandoned Ascension, and the supply line itself was threatened. At once he set about trying to maintain the flow with a series of letters whose combination of greed, unctuousness and pomposity must surely be unique.

On 2 June 1922, in a private note to Rear-Admiral H. W. Grant, Managing Director of the E.T.C., he wrote:

We have ourselves no official concern in the future arrangements for Ascension. There is one thing, however, which I find My

A turtle laying eggs

The Bonetta graveyard behind Comfortless Cove

Evidence of successive eruptions: layer of white trachyte between sand-
wich of basalt

Georgetown, with the colonnaded Marine Barracks in the centre and
Cross Hill behind

The Cable and Wireless earth station on Donkey Plain

Lords are keenly interested in: As you probably know, for nearly a hundred years past certain turtle that visit the bays in the island have been captured by members of the garrison or ship's company, and, after being kept in turtle ponds, some of them have been shipped home. . . .

On arrival in England they are delivered to the King's Turtle Soup Manufacturer, who allows my Lords a regular quantity of turtle soup. This is divided up among members of the Board and the secretaries, and is a small privilege which gives intense enjoyment to the recipients. . . .

The Admiralty Board would be extremely grateful if the Company could find it possible as a matter of courtesy in view of our friendly relations for many years past, to continue the practice. . . . The result would give pleasure out of all relation to the intrinsic merits of the business.

Unmoved by such ill-concealed craving, Grant replied courteously, pointing out that the E.T.C. staff on Ascension was very small, and that there were too few men to ensure any regular supply. In July he wrote saying that his Board *hoped* to be able to go on sending turtles, but that he could not 'enter into any definite obligation to do so'.

Thwarted for the time being in this direction, Baddeley began intriguing elsewhere. Major C. A. Tennyson, who had been the last Commandant of the Ascension garrison but by then was unemployed, was himself trying to secure a turtling concession on the island, and approached Baddeley with an oiliness almost worthy of the Secretary himself. If he obtained the concession, he wrote, he would 'show his gratitude' by supplying the Admiralty free. Lusty, too, was after the rights, and Baddeley held discussions with both of them to see if some private arrangement could be worked out.

The E.T.C., however, knowing full well how difficult it was to house and feed commercial outsiders on Ascension, preferred to keep the rights themselves, and made an arrangement with the Government of St Helena whereby they took over the exclusive concession for £100 a year and a royalty of ten shillings per turtle caught.

While this arrangement was being worked out, some surreptitious lobbying had evidently been done, for on 18 June 1923 a Conservative Member of Parliament asked in the House of Commons whether the annual tribute of turtles would in future be enjoyed by the Colonial Office or by the Admiralty. This provoked from the Financial Secretary to the Admiralty a horribly facetious reply: in the absence of anybody in the employment of the Crown to seize the visitors to the island, he said, the turtles were unmolested. The Admiralty had

> no means of securing the continuance of the practice by which some of the turtles found their visit extended from that island to this.

An even more facetious correspondence broke out in *The Times*. Rear-Admiral Hopwood recalled how his gunboat used to take turtles from Ascension to ships off the coast of West Africa:

> Our guests were accommodated just before the port sea gangway, in charge of their keeper, who was one of the fore-top men. Exactly how or when he became qualified, I cannot say, but as is the custom in H.M. ships, the need produced the man. . . . That the turtles generally ignored such dainties as he provided from his mess . . . was universally held to be due to a lack of education on their part rather than on his. . . .
>
> I can see today the groups of seamen, smoking gravely and silently as they contemplated, with certain approval, the Captain of the Turtles polishing the upper works of his charges. . . . Too bulky to carry, they were eventually encouraged, and in some cases urged, to march in solemn procession to a small derrick, where, to the accompaniment of a bosun's call, they were hoisted out and honourably sent to their several destinations.

Nostalgia did little to favour Baddeley's cause. Yet, in spite of the various difficulties, the E.T.C. was able to gratify their Lordships from time to time, and in April 1924, after fifty quarts of soup had been placed at the Admiralty's disposal, Baddeley wrote to Grant:

> I can assure you that the amount of pleasure given by the receipt of this present is out of all proportion to its intrinsic value.

But his thirst soon returned, and in February 1927 he reminded Grant that no allocation had been made since December 1925. 'As you know,' he wrote, 'on sentimental as well as on other grounds I have been most anxious that the custom which has lasted for over a century should not be entirely dropped.'

Again Grant replied that he would help if he could, and three months later had fifty quarts presented. For the next three years the same amount – fifty quarts – was handed over regularly every autumn, but in April 1929 the E.T.C., together with its associated companies, had become part of the much bigger Imperial and International Communications Ltd. and supplies ceased.

By 1933 Baddeley could not resist trying his luck again, and he asked whether the company could 'resume this pleasant practice, or whether some circumstances of which we are unaware have arisen at Ascension which have prevented you from doing so'. All he got was a polite note from Edward Wilshaw, Managing Director of I.I.C.L.: 'I am sorry to say that the adverse economic conditions from which the world in general is suffering have embraced this industry also.'

Even that did not stifle Baddeley's gastronomic ambition. The next year he heard that consignments of Ascension turtles had been reaching England, and tried yet again:

> It is now four years since your company was last good enough to follow this practice, and the present Board of the Admiralty, which has been in office since the autumn of 1931, has had no enjoyment of it.

But once again Wilshaw gently fobbed him off, and that was the end of him as far as turtling went.

It was almost the end of the turtles' persecution, too, for thereafter the staff of the cable company turned very few – enough only for their own modest needs.

Life on Ascension continued gently in what one might call the Bartlett manner. The amenities gradually improved, but not so drastically as to rob the community of its cherished sense of isolation. The first car – a solid-tyred Trojan belonging to the E.T.C.'s general manager – arrived in 1923, but since it was too short-winded to tackle the Mountain road, its scope was severely limited. In the same year one of the staff imported an Indian Chief motor-cycle and side-car from America, fitted with a special sprocket to enable it to ascend the Ramps. Other motor-cycles soon followed, and some energetic members of the E.T.C. cleared a rough road the whole way to Wideawake Plain in order to facilitate the motorised collection of eggs.

Social life was brisk and (by today's standards) ridiculously formal, with everyone changing into the proper dress every evening. Local leave was taken on Green Mountain, where several of the houses in the settlement were used as holiday cottages. As in naval days, the event anticipated most keenly was the monthly arrival of the mail boat. Not only would the exiles get their letters: even more important, the ladies could go on board and have their hair done in the ship's saloon. Their chagrin is easily imagined when – as happened from time to time – the steamer's arrival coincided with a bad bout of rollers, and the ship, having waited in vain for perhaps twelve hours, went on her way again with no contact made except by radio.

Often the ships' passengers were startled by the appearance of the deeply-tanned 'natives', and one woman was heard to remark: 'Why – they're almost white!' while another is alleged to have commented on how well they spoke English. Sometimes, recalled Bartlett, the islanders took advantage of such gullibility by relating hair-raising stories.

With serious faces they would tell of blue-maned lions lurking in the fastnesses behind the Sisters Mountain; of the savage tribes inhabiting Green Mountain, necessitating barbed-wire entanglements when hunger drove them down during the snow periods; of the turtle races on Long Beach every Thursday, when large sums of money changed hands, and so on.

During the 1930s the island's physical appearance scarcely changed, except for a short period after an astonishing cloudburst in 1934. As in the celebrated downpours of 1924 and 1896 (when the naval captain's Japanese steward was struck down to the floor of the verandah by lightning while talking on the telephone to the Mountain, but promptly revived by brandy), the storm came on suddenly, with little warning. Its violence was vividly recorded by Bartlett:

At 7.15 on 30 April the bottom dropped out of the heavens, and a deluge, such as is known only in the tropics, falling hard and straight, enveloped the island. In the dark, little could be seen, but to my anxious ears the drumming of the rain on the roofs and the rush of swirling waters sounded disastrous: no lightning, no thunder – just the relentless rain and the increasing roar of the waters pouring from the highlands into and through Garrison.

All hands had been called out, and under the direction of the I.M.O. [Island Maintenance Officer] were busy trenching and clearing the threatened areas. In spite of tremendous exertions, working by electric torch-light, stores and bungalows were flooded and much damage done. The cinema hall was flooded to a depth of eighteen inches. . . .

Early morn promised no cessation. Roads and paths were non-existent; their surfaces had been completely removed, leaving bare the rocky foundations scored with pits and gullies. . . . At eight in the morning there was a decided slackening in the downpour, and shortly afterwards it ceased. Ten and a half inches of rain had fallen in twelve hours.

Gangs of men were quickly out on the road to the Mountain,

of which the whole six miles had to be restored. . . . Roofs, walls and fencing all had to be repaired, and it was months before we ceased anathematising the flood. It was a consolation that two years' water supply had been collected in the tanks. . . .

The aftermath soon appeared; a green mantle began to cover the normally brown clinker. A species of desert grass, of which the seed had been lying dormant for years, increased in height and thickness and turned yellow, until it seemed as if the land were covered with waving corn.

Again as in 1924, the grass brought a hideous plague of insects – mosquitoes, cockroaches, locusts and crickets which invaded the houses of Georgetown in millions, driving the inhabitants nearly frantic with irritation and eating a great many of their belongings. As Barlett observed, since there had been no major flood since 1924, it seemed that the eggs of the insects, like the grass seed, must have been lying dormant in the clinker for a whole decade.

No other natural drama of this magnitude disturbed the even tenor of the cable men's existence. At one point in his manuscript Barlett presciently remarked that Ascension would make a good stepping stone for aircraft crossing the South Atlantic, and that if planes did come, the place for an airfield would be on Wideawake Plain. But it was the very absence of anything so urgent and modern as an airfield that gave Ascension its charm during the 1930s. Every day thousands of messages clicked and whirred through the cable office; but outside it, life was deliciously uncomplicated. In trying to sum up why he found the place so attractive, one man wrote:

List all the drawbacks and frustrations which are part of present-day existence – bureaucracy, income tax, customs duties, the weather, sickness, overcrowding, noise, class pretensions, money worries, crime, violence. . . . Abolish the lot, and you had Ascension.

AMERICAN INVASION

1939-47

In June 1939, with the outbreak of a Second World War looming, the Colonial Office in London approached Cable and Wireless and consulted them about possible arrangements for the defence of Ascension; but it was not until April 1940 that the necessary legislation was passed and the island's defence force came into being under command of the company's General Manager, S. Cardwell. Directed by an officer and several N.C.O.s sent up from St Helena, the force trained enthusiastically with its rifles. A hole was dug in which the company's safe could be buried at short notice, and spare telegraphic gear was secreted under the lava. Yet the islanders could not help being aware of the utter frailty of their armament, especially as several German raiders, including the pocket battleship *Graf Spee*, were known to be at large in the South Atlantic.

With an attack on the cable station expected at any time, nerves were constantly on edge. So when, on Christmas Eve 1939, a submarine was spotted approaching, the alarm signal was given, and not until the vessel was close enough inshore for her White Ensign to be clearly visible did Cardwell respond to her cryptic request to send a boat. Going out himself in the one and only launch, he discovered that the visitor was H.M.S. *Severn*, returning towards her base in Freetown after her fruitless hunt for the German *Altmark*. Members of the Submarine's crew remember to this day the Christmas puddings and fresh vegetables which the members of the garrison bestowed upon them.

In March 1941 Ascension's armament was strengthened by the arrival of a detachment of Royal Artillery, and by the installation of two six-inch guns which came from the battleship H.M.S. *Hood*.

Without tractors or proper hauling gear, the guns were hoisted 300 feet up the loose clinker slopes of Cross Hill. They stand there now, with their armour plates impressively riddled by bullets or shrapnel – scars which all but the most avidly partisan Ascensionites admit were acquired before the weapons came ashore.

Until November 1941 Ascension depended on this still tenuous protection. But then there arrived a message which precipitated the greatest invasion the island had ever known – a secret cable from the Governor of St Helena asking Cardwell to make a survey of two possible sites for an airfield that the American Government was planning to build.

One, on Ash Plain, inland behind Georgetown, was quickly eliminated as being entirely unsuitable; apart from the unevenness of the ground, there was a major impediment in the form of the British naval wireless station. But the other site, on South West Plain, seemed to have everything in its favour. Pacing out the level area, Cardwell found that it was at least 1000 yards long and nearly 700 yards wide, and that the surface was not 'dusty', as the *Africa Pilot* described it, so much as hard packed. A further advantage was the exceptional constancy of the wind: on almost every day of the year, there was a fresh, steady breeze from the south east, the very direction in which the strip of flat ground lay.

The greatest potential snag, of which the Americans were already aware, was the presence of several hundred thousand wideawake or sooty terns. Since time immemorial they had nested on the bare, stony ground in that corner of the island, and their dense flocks could, it seemed, prove a serious hazard to aircraft taking off and landing. Neither the feral cats nor the egg-hungry naval garrison had seriously depleted their numbers, and for several months of the year they were present in an immense, vociferous colony.

Cardwell, however, was able to report that the wideawakes' main fair, or nesting ground, was no longer in the place marked on the Admiralty chart, but further to the south. 'It is now the height of their season,' he wrote,

and the birds are as numerous as ever. As during previous seasons within my experience, the birds are laying their eggs only on the triangular area bounded by Mars Bay, Dark Slope Crater and Pillar Bay. Although countless eggs are being deposited in this area, not a single egg is laid on S.W. Plain itself. This does not mean to say that there are no birds flying in the air over the Plain. There were a few flying close over my head, and they seem a bit inquisitive.

Cardwell sent off his report, and in due course was told that he would get word when the American reconnaissance party was on its way to Ascension. No such word ever came, and early on Christmas morning 1941, when he was up the Mountain, warships were suddenly seen approaching from the west. So careful had he been not to mention the secret project to any of his colleagues that no one else knew anything about it, and the ships were almost fired on before their identity was established.

A party of five officers and five ratings came ashore to inspect the site proposed for the airfield, and an aircraft from U.S.S. *Omaha* made an aerial reconnaissance. The Americans soon departed, but not before they had drafted an effusive telegram, to be sent to the Governor of St Helena, thanking Cable and Wireless for their help, and not before they had treated all the children on Ascension to an ice-cream-and-cake Christmas party.

The main task force, escorted by warships, arrived on 30 March 1942. That same day the Stars and Stripes was carried ashore ceremonially and hoisted above the United States' temporary head-quarters in Georgetown.

The thirty-five men of the cable company, together with their hundred-odd St Helenian workmen, must have felt as though they had been hit by a tornado, for the normally prevailing calm was blown to shreds by a whirlwind of activity. The first and most for-midable task was to land 1500 men and 8000 tons of equipment, including seventy vehicles, some of them bulldozers. All Cable and Wireless had for the purpose was one fifteen-year-old launch, a number of leaky lighters purchased at a knock-down price from the Navy in 1922, and an obsolete steam crane on the pier. For the first few days the staff had also to help feed the newcomer, and the island's one bread-oven – ex H.M.S. *Nelson* and a good fifty years old – worked as never before to take fresh loaves for a total of 1700 people.

To begin with most of the task force camped out on Long Beach. As usual, the weather was mainly fine, with only a few light showers, but occasionally an onset of rollers caused a rush for higher ground. At reveille one morning a man found baby turtles erupting from the sand beneath his cot, and is alleged to have remarked: 'You sure have some bugs here!' A more serious bug was dysentery, which broke out through poor sanitation, and for a few days patients filled the old naval hospital in Georgetown and overflowed into tents all round it.

On 4 April, with unloading still in progress, the U.S. 38th Engineer Combat Regiment went into action on three separate fronts. One company was assigned the task of building a proper road to the airfield site, some three miles south of the settlement, and they began clearing the rock away with hand-tools – a tough assignment in the tropical heat, especially as the water-ration was only a quart per man per day. Simultaneously other parties began work on the permanent camp site, beside the airfield, and on the vital tank farm, some distance inland from Georgetown and behind Cross Hill, where the aviation fuel was to be stored.

On the airfield the engineers had little difficulty in choosing the line of the runway, for only one was possible – through the saddle between two hills, in a direction almost exactly parallel with that of the prevailing wind. By 13 April enough heavy equipment had been brought ashore for bulldozing to begin, and from then on alternating shifts worked twenty-four hours a day. The floodlights which blazed at night were carefully shielded so that they would not be visible to any enemy ship that might be passing out to sea.

By 20 April the machines had uncovered solid rock, and drilling and blasting began. The difficulties proved considerable: the volcanic rock was so riddled by cavities that dozens of holes had to be drilled before the charges could be laid satisfactorily, and drill-bits broke by the score. The rock itself was so sharp and heavy that the tractors, bulldozers and trucks suffered continuous damage: tracks broke and were mended so often that they looked as though they were made entirely out of welding rods. As usual, the Americans improvised brilliantly. 'Mechanics and drivers of the bulldozers literally lifted themselves by their bootstraps,' wrote Lt.-Col. Frederick J. Clarke, commanding officer of the Ist Battalion, 38th Engineer Combat Regiment, in a later report:

> The rock was so large and hard to handle that front springs broke like toothpicks; so cables were rigged over the top of each machine, attached to the rear end, and the front of the bulldozers would be suspended to cushion the constant and terrific shock.

All day the boom of blasting gelignite rumbled over South West Plain, and a huge pall of red-brown dust went streaming away down the wind. At night the clouds above Cross Hill were lit by the flickering flashes of the welders' torches as the engineers fitted together the prefabricated steel plates of the petrol containers on the tank farm.

There were eight huge tanks, each of 11,000-barrel capacity, and since each had six rings of plates, every ring was given a name for ease of reference. 'Having eight tanks and forty-eight rings, we named each of the rings after one of the forty-eight states,' explained the lieutenant in charge of construction.

> We put Alabama on the bottom of the first tank, went up with Arizona, Arkansas, California, Colorado, and topped it off with Connecticut. The second one started with Delaware, the third with Iowa, and so on until, when we got Wyoming in place and welded, the field was complete.

The runway itself was impossible to disguise – it struck arrow-straight like a great blue-black scar through the lava. But the engineers took immense trouble to camouflage everything else. On the airfield the bomb-storage building was made completely invisible from the air, and elaborate precautions were taken to hide the tank farm, each tank being surrounded by a rough 25-foot wall of local rock and cinders. As a more positive deception dummy tanks, partially camouflaged, were built in the empty area at the back of Long Beach, where no amount of shelling could do any harm. Even the main water-pipe coming down from Green Mountain was painted or buried along some of its length so that its tell-tale straight line would not be so apparent.

The Task Force's orders specified that the island must be ready to receive aircraft by the middle of July. Spurred on by the shortage of time, three hundred men worked on the airfield day and night, and the heavy equipment was in use for more than twenty-two hours out of every twenty-four, being serviced during mealtimes.

At the beginning of May a new system was tried for laying the explosives: instead of drilling, the men dug tunnels with picks and shovels, and a major explosion on May 15, when eight tons of gelignite were detonated in ten such tunnels, proved highly effective. The biggest bang, however, came on May 19, when fourteen tons were let off in seventeen tunnels. The blast broke up immense quantities of rock and flung 50-lb lumps more than a mile, doing considerable damage to the camp.

In all, some 380,000 cubic yards of rock were removed from the runway cut, and more than thirty-five tons of gelignite were used. The landing strip that emerged was 6000 feet long and 150 wide, with fifty feet of shoulder on either side; to this day it has a slight hump in the middle, the engineers having decided – quite rightly – that the advantages of making it completely level would not have repaid the immense extra labour involved.

The bare rock was covered with a foot-thick layer of cinders and grit, and finished with a coat of asphalt. The tarring began on 25 May, and took nearly six weeks to complete.

3 June 1942 brought a spectacle as bizarre as anything the island had seen in naval days: the laying of the sea-pipe which would bring aviation fuel ashore to the tank farm. All other projects were halted for twenty-four hours so that every man was available, and some 1200 men literally carried the pipe down to the sea.

The history of the 38th Engineers records the event precisely:

The personnel were divided as follows: 21 men (boat crews); 160 men (float-riders); 20 men (float fasteners); 13 men (joint makers); 900 to 1000 men (pipe carriers).

First the rubber sea-hose was towed out by a launch, kept afloat by empty oil drums attached to it every thirty feet. Then its inner end was fastened to the beginning of the main steel pipe. At a signal from the officer in charge, the 1000 men picked up an 1100-foot section of pipe, using slings and baulks of timber, and marched on either side of it down to the water. The Engineers' history goes on:

> The officer in charge of the launching was standing on a sand dune near the beach so that he could watch how the pipe was entering. When he wanted the pipe to move forward he would signal to the flag officer, who would raise his flag and bring it down sharply. At this signal each section officer would warn his men to lay hold. At the second signal they would raise the pipe. At the third signal the pipe and 1000 men would start forward. If the officer in charge wanted to halt the pipe, he would signal to the flag officer, who in turn would give two signals, which were 'Hold' and 'Lower'. This system worked out very well . . . It was quite a sight to see the men pick up the pipe, and then 1000 men and the pipe slowly move forward like a great earthworm.

While the pipe was being launched, it was buoyed up by drums tied to it with rope every fourteen feet. The job of the float-riders (all volunteers because of the sharks) was to sit on the drums and, at a given signal, release the hitch-knots, so that the pipe would sink to the bottom. In the event, it was found that the rope had swollen so much that the knots could not be released, and the floats had to be sunk by rifle shots from the armed anti-shark patrols who had been standing by throughout the operation.

A few days later the pipe was connected up to the tank farm, and the fuel system was ready to service aircraft. But the first plane that came in turned out not to be American at all.

Since it was totally unexpected, it got a hot reception. Approaching from the east at about 1.30 p.m. on 15 June, the single aircraft was engaged over Georgetown by the anti-aircraft emplacements of the U.S. 426th Coast Artillery Battalion; and when it tried to touch down on the new airfield, it found the runway blocked with vehicles. Then it was identified as a British Fairey Swordfish, and the runway was cleared for it to land. Three bullet-holes were found in its skin, and a .30 calibre projectile had lodged in the pilot's shoulder-harness. The plane had come from the carrier H.M.S. *Archer*; its mission was to drop a message for the authorities in Georgetown, and after two hours it took off again to return to its mother ship.

Three more weeks passed before the first American aircraft appeared – a C-87 of Air Transport Command which came in from Accra early in the morning of 10 July 1942 to inspect the new field. The runway, hardly finished, withstood the impact of its landing successfully, and the crew received a resounding welcome from the men who had tamed the lava. The 38th Engineers had triumphantly carried out the task that many people had said would prove impossible – they had built an airfield on top of a volcano.

Thereafter a huge migration of aircraft passed safely through the island. Before the airstrip was opened, two-engined aircraft could make the 1,800-mile flight from Natal, in Brazil, to West Africa only if they carried extra fuel tanks, but with the provision of 'this anchored airdrome of volcanic rock', as the United States official history of the war called it, the ocean crossing was divided into two fairly easy stages and ceased to be a serious operational problem.

'If we don't hit Ascension, our wives get a pension,' went the pilots' song; but in fact the island carried a radio beam, and navigators had no trouble finding it. Hundreds of crews found the little stepping-stone successfully, paused for the night to refuel, and went on in the morning towards Africa and the war. The first flight of A-29s and B-25s dropped in on 20 July, and the arrival of squadrons out of the sunset became a nightly occurrence. The success of the Allied campaign in North Africa during the autumn of 1942 was due in no small part to the steady flow of men and munitions through Ascension.

Before the Engineers left in August, they completed many other projects besides the airfield. One was the American hospital – a complex of seven wood-framed, tar-paper-covered buildings almost exactly in the middle of the island, at the base of Green Mountain. Another was the construction of two radar-stations, one beside the Ramps, on the way up to the farm, and the other 2400 foot up on the south-east nose of the Mountain. In order to reach the heights at all, the Engineers had to make drastic improvements to the Ramps: they enlarged eighteen of the bends, cutting out the insides and reinforcing the outsides with steel mats, until 1½-ton trucks could negotiate every corner. Then they were faced with the delicate task of widening Elliott's Path – the horizontal foot-track which circles the Mountain and had been cut by hand in 1839 and 1840 for keeping an all-round look-out.

The slope which the path traverses is terrific – often 75 degrees or more, and in some places vertical, with drops of 1000 feet on the outside. Most of the widening was done by a bulldozer driven by a man named Reecer, who rode standing up, so that he could jump at a second's notice, and had a colleague watching his outer track all the time so that he did not go too near the edge. He improved the path enough for a jeep and trailer to be driven all the way out to the radar station on the south-east point, and the new highway was named Reecer's Road in his honour; but on some later occasion a bulldozer *did* go over the edge: starting a minor landslide, it slipped down a few feet and lodged again. Although still in view, it was unrecoverable and had to be abandoned – an episode not mentioned in 38th Engineers' official history of their exploits on Ascension! Today the machine is still there, rusting gently away under a waving blanket of ginger.

In August 1942 the engineers were relieved (in more senses than one) by the arrival of the permanent wartime garrison force, the third battalion of the U.S. 91st Infantry. As their ship, the *James Parker*, came in, the G.I.s 'were amazed at the grim, ragged look of the island,' their battalion history recalls. 'Most men had never dreamed a place could look so forbidding.'

Landing at dusk, they had to spend the first night in the open on the Parade Ground beside Lady Hill. 'Some time during the night,' the history goes on, 'some jackasses started to bray. There was great consternation among some of the men, because many of them had never heard such a noise before. It was a big joke next morning.'

The Infantry crackled into action, taking over and strengthening the 'meager defences' which were all the Engineers had been able to set up in the intervals of building airfield, roads and tank-farm. At English Bay the G.I.s found a 37-mm gun set up in such a way that

if the men had fired, they would have been killed. The trails of the gun were set up on piles of rocks. The first shot would have driven it back about twenty feet, right over the men manning it.

Echoes of naval days . . . but there was nothing old-fashioned about the way the G.I.s installed outposts at Pebbly Beach, North East Bay, English Bay, Comfortless Cove, South West Bay and Mars Bay. In most places they had to cut emplacements out of solid rock, and in order to save long overland treks, they put roads through to English Bay and North East. 'The Engineers said it would take at least six months to build a road to English Bay,' recalled a scornful note in the Infantry's history. 'It took K Company three weeks to put the English Bay road through.'

As K Company's outposts were six miles away from head-quarters, kitchens were set up at each one, some in tents, and some in proper mess halls, the one at English Bay being cannibalised from the remains of the buildings abandoned by the phosphate company in the 1930s.

Fresh water – supplied by distilling units – was extremely short, and since none was available for washing clothes, the men often took their laundry with them on outpost duty, flinging bundles into the sea tied to the ends of ropes. After twenty-four hours or so most of the dirt would have been beaten out by the waves pounding the garments against rocks or sand – if, that is, the rope had not come adrift and the whole consignment been lost.

For three months at the beginning of 1943 a listening post was established on South East Head – site of the present Letterbox and one of the island's remotest extremities. A telephone kept the men in touch with their company headquarters, but all provisions and reliefs had to be taken round by boat; and when it was decided to move the post back inland, the U.S. Navy picket boat went to collect the tents and other equipment left behind. As it was loading up, the official history records,

a tremendous and unexpected swell hit the boat, lifting it and crashing it against the rocks. The boat and most of the boat's equipment were lost, but the men got out all right, except one who had a bad head injury sustained while beaten against the rocks by the waves. The men had to carry him all the way in to the settlement on Green Mountain. He was carried on a stretcher made of pyramidal tent-pole sections, with field jackets slipped over them. Anyone who has ever been over the terrain can see what a backbreaking and dangerous job it was.

Apart from this, casualties seem to have been extraordinarily few, considering that by the middle of 1943 there might be, at any one time, nearly 4000 Americans on the island. The forces devised themselves such comforts and distractions as they could, continuously improving their camp, making baseball diamonds, a new golf course, basket-ball and volley-ball courts and outdoor cinemas, and even establishing an extremely expensive hydroponics station, in which vegetables were grown on beds of cinders watered by solutions of nutrient salts. Yet, in spite of the ingeniously varied training programme, the most insidious enemy was boredom. No attack ever came to break the tedium; no combat situation – as the Americans put it – ever developed, and the men were worn down by inertia. The official history of the 175th Station Hospital, which was in charge of medical facilities, carried this revealing paragraph, describing the troops in 1944:

> To a casual observer, the morale of these men who have been stationed on this isolated island for two years is excellent, but after a more intimate glimpse into their lives it is apparent that they have been affected. Their habits are more indolent than the ordinary soldier, they lack ambition for any enterprise, and everything they do is done without enthusiasm. They do their work satisfactorily, but there is very little to do.

From the military point of view the American occupation was an unqualified success. Apart from fulfilling the original role projected for it – that of a refulling-point for aircraft crossing the Atlantic – Ascension also proved a useful base for anti-submarine warfare. Together with two similar stations in Freetown and St Helena, its own radio station formed a deadly triangle, which on several occasions led to the destruction of German U-boats.

As soon as one station intercepted an enemy radio signal, it would flash a cable message, giving the bearing, to the other two corners of the triangle. Experience showed that an absolutely reliable five-second service could be maintained, with the result that plots of the enemy's position could be produced almost instantaneously. The U.S. Navy bomber patrol pilots were quick to appreciate the speed and accuracy of these target reports, and the sight of their big white Liberators rising from Wideawake Field to head out into the wastes of the South Atlantic was one of the finest spectacles on Ascension. Although often they returned disappointed, or with nothing better than a 'possible' to report, there were several occasions on which they could claim a full-blooded kill. In November 1943, for instance, they sunk two of the big 1600-ton U-cruisers, the U-848 and U-849.

Apart from the stream of military personnel, there also passed through Ascension a considerable number of celebrities, including many politicians, actors and film stars. Madame Chiang Kai Chek, Litvinoff, Sir John Dill, Noel Coward, Paulette Goddard and Sir

John Reith were among those who took a jeep-ride up the mountain, and the journalist John Gunther dropped in for a few hours – long enough to enable him to write a breezy and rather inaccurate report for *Time* magazine. For a few hectic months the world came through Ascension.

For the staff of Cable and Wireless the American invasion meant a fundamental readjustment. No longer could they call the thirty-four square miles of clinker their own: indeed, to have tried to do so would have been ridiculous, as they were outnumbered by more than ten to one. Instead, the cable men went out of their way to help the newcomers, and relations between the two communities seem to have been exceptionally good – apart from the occasions when the Americans opened up with machine guns on the turtles cruising off Long Beach.

In May 1942 a representative of the St Helena Government was posted to Ascension, and from then on he maintained liaison between the two communities. In a contemporary report, written mainly for old-timers who had known Ascension in its virgin state, Eric Symes, one of the cable staff, described the scene in 1943:

Roads everywhere. Numbered highways marked by neat sign-boards. Of course, we drive on the right . . . There is even a bus service to parts of the island, with bus stop signs on the highways! One is able to thumb one's way almost anywhere, except maybe to Cricket Valley and Letter Box.

Telephone wires trail everywhere about the clinker, even over the golf course . . . and the telephone directory is quite an impressive volume. Each officer's tent has its phone laid on, as well as those to our offices and quarters. There are four telephone exchanges, and we no longer, when the operator cuts in to ask 'Are you through?', mistake his query for one asking if we have got through to our number. He means 'Have you finished speaking?'

We have speed limits, military police in white topees, road signs, ice cream, Coca Cola and sometimes popcorn. A daily news sheet and a Sunday six-page paper complete with illustrations.

Nostalgia for the peace of the old days was more than cancelled out by appreciation of the comforts which the Americans brought with them, and by the feeling that the co-operation of two nations on their volcanic outcrop was making a real contribution to the war effort. The Englishmen's satisfaction at the small but important part they had played was shown to be well justified by a letter to Cable and Wireless in 1944 from Col. J. C. Mullenix, who had been commander of the island garrison. Complimenting the company on Ascension's usefulness, he wrote:

> Ascension Island has played a unique and vital part in the war. . . . Without the existence of Ascension, without its active facilitation of the movement of our airplanes, the indispensable aviation support for our troops in North Africa could not have been accomplished at the critical period when Rommel and his Afrika Corps were literally assaulting the gates of Cairo. That aviation passed through Ascension safely and surely played its decisive part in driving the German and Italian forces from North Africa.

After the war had ended in 1945, the Americans began to withdraw. The main force left in October, but a base unit of the Air Transport Command stayed on, and for the next eighteen months or so a regular Carasol (Caribbean and South Atlantic) line service was flown through Ascension to Roberts Field, Monrovia, one plane coming through every week. When the last of the United States contingent departed in 1947, they left behind an immense amount of stores and equipment, some of it packed up on the airfield and (theoretically) ready to be taken away, but much of it simply dumped. So much petrol was abandoned that it kept all the cars on Ascension going for more than ten years (at three-pence a gallon), and the cable staff salvaged numerous lathes, drilling rigs, pumps and motors, to say nothing of several radio sets and jeeps, a mobile crane and a dentist's chair in full working order. During the 1950s it was a regular Saturday afternoon outing to go and dig for American treasure in the side of South West Bay

Red Hill, whence many odd items were recovered, including crates of pliers and specialised aircraft tools.

Some considerable dumps of ammunition also came to light. Nearly 1350 powder-charges for the British naval 5.5-inch guns, together with 1160 high explosive and armour-piercing rounds, were discovered in Fort Bedford, and 540 American six-inch high-explosive shells were found in a pit, covered only by a tarpaulin, near Georgetown. Later, 121 cases of 20-lb fragmentation bombs, packed six to a case, had to be blown up as they were too dangerous to move. Of greater practical use were the dumps of tinned meat and other food which had been buried at strategic points round the island as a last resort in case of invasion; these were soon dug out and fed to the chickens.

Ascension suffered only two real casualties as a result of the American occupation. One was Bate's, or Captain's, Cottage, on the side of Cross Hill – a pleasant bungalow that had been occupied by the artillery regiment, and was badly smashed up. It stood derelict until it was replaced by a new building in 1971. The other casualty was the last of the goats, which, having survived for four hundred years, were exterminated by trigger-happy G.I.s. Their disappearance, though sad in a way, was by no means a disaster, for their destructive browsing over the centuries had probably done as much as anything to retard the spread of vegetation which the British had worked so hard and so long to achieve.

Everything else survived. But no survival was so extraordinary as that of the wideawake terns. A few weeks after the airfield opened, the wideawakes began returning to their nesting grounds right beside the runway, where, as the official American history of the war made clear, they were a real menace:

Every time a plane started down the runway the roar of the motors brought a huge flock of birds into the air right in its path. Heavier planes, unable to climb quickly enough, were obliged to pass right through the mass of birds, running the risk of a broken windshield, a dented leading edge, or a bird wedged in engine or air scoop.

Smoke, dynamite and a plane-load of imported cats all failed to shift the sqatters, and in desperation Army Air Force headquarters sent down a well-known ornithologist, Dr James P. Chapin of the American Museum of Natural History. He believed that the birds would leave the area if their eggs were broken – so some 40,000 were smashed, and the wideawakes did indeed shift their ground a little to the south. Yet the population as a whole remained unmoved, amazing ornithologists by its perseverance. Maybe Colonel Clarke, the Engineers' commanding officer, had a point when he wrote afterwards: 'You couldn't blame the birds for not leaving. There was no other place to go.'

SPACE AGE

1957–72

With the last of the Americans gone, the population fell back to about 180, and it seemed for a while as though the island would relapse into its former somnolence. A large programme of restoration and repairs was put in hand, but, as in the days of the Marines, there was so much to do that the depleted work force had to plough slowly through a mountain of jobs.

Yet, although the United States contingent had departed, the Americans had by no means lost interest in the island, and in 1949 a rather cryptic questionnaire arrived for Cable and Wireless's General Manager to fill in. Who owns the top of Green Mountain? it asked. What use is being made of the top? Could a flat area 300 feet in diameter be made on the top? Does a road go right to the summit? If so, can it take large trucks?

From these and other questions, it was clear that the Americans were contemplating some sort of radar or other tracking station. Long-range ballistic missiles were on the drawing-board, and, although space-flight was still an almost entirely theoretical exercise, it was already appreciated that rockets or spacecraft launched from the east coast of America would pass over Ascension before they reached any other land.

No further approach was made, however, until 1954. By then American rockets had become so powerful that the range down which they were tested had to be extended into the South Atlantic, and Ascension was chosen as the site for one of the stations which would track and observe the end of the missiles' flight. In June 1956 an agreement was signed between the British and American Governments, and later the same year advance parties arrived to survey the island. The runway of the airfield was repaired, and a new American base began to sprout – not on the site of the war-time camp, but nearer the sea and closer to Georgetown. The place was christened Miracle Mile, the name given it during the war when the first strip of tarmac road ever seen on Ascension was laid there in record time. From the levelled tops of some of the rust-red ash-cones, from Cross Hill, Cat Hill and South Gannet Hill, the gleaming white dishes of radar aerials began to poke skywards.

'Station 12' of the Eastern Test Range was opened in 1957; its original function was to track missiles fired from Cape Canaveral (now Cape Kennedy), 5560 miles away to the north-west, and in particular to monitor the final stages of their flight. The most frequent early missile was Atlas – eighty feet long, ten in diameter, and weighing 100 tons at lift-off. Since it arrived at about 17,000 m.p.h., its reentry into the atmosphere made a spectacular impact. In his diary for 22 January 1960 Richard Aria, a Cable and Wireless technician, described how he witnessed one such nocturnal reentry:

We gazed skywards over Red Hill. Nothing. Half an hour later – nothing. I noticed the Great Bear, which is upside-down here, then gazed seawards.

Suddenly there were two brilliant green flashes high up over Red Hill. This was it. The missile streamed earthwards, changing into the most brilliant colours, illuminating the whole island – yellow first, then red, orange, green. Down, down it fell until it disintegrated. Red hot pieces of fuselage rained down, and the now-incandescent ceramic nose-cone, glowing white, fell sea-wards changing colour as it went. Bright red, red, dull red, then nothing but silence.

We thought it was all over. I sat there absolutely transfixed for a full minute, when there was a long, low rumble, then a deafening explosion, then more rumbles, which went on for a full minute and a half. Then the silence was broken by an American saying: 'Get a load of that, you —— Russians.'

Since then repeated improvements and modification of equip-ment have continuously extended the test-range's capabilities, and now it keeps electronic eyes on all kinds of satellites in earth orbit. Physically the most obvious addition was the installation, in 1960–61, of the T.T.R. (Target Tracking Radar) at Pyramid point, near Comfortless Cove: the white, spherical dome of the aerial shows up from miles afield, and looks like a huge golf ball sitting abandoned among the wild black lava on the coast.

Thus, in a modest way, Ascension entered the space age. But as the Mercury and Gemini programmes gathered momentum (one-man and two-man capsules orbiting the earth), the island's attention was focused for the moment on a new project of its own – the establishment of a £4 million radio relay.

After carrying out preliminary transmission tests during 1963 from a caravan in English Bay, the British Broadcasting Corporation went ahead with its plans for building a major relay station on the island. Ascension, standing almost exactly half-way between Africa and the bulge of South America, is ideally placed for sending radio programmes into the two continents: transmitters can beam on to Africa until night falls there, and then the aerials are switched to reverse bearings so that they can beam evening broadcasts into South America.

In setting-up the B.B.C.'s installations, the Ministry of Public Building and Works faced almost exactly the same problems as had beset the Americans when they arrived to carve out the airstrip in 1942: they had to land an immense bulk of stores (in this case 25,000 tons) on the one cramped pier; they had to recruit from outside sources, and then import, their entire work force; and – since the island's resources were already stretched to the limit – they had to bring with them all their own food and create their own water supply.

A start was made in 1964, when an advance party landed. Some of the workmen were recruited in St Helena, but the majority came from the West Indies, principally Barbados, Grenada and St Lucia. At peak strength the force reached a total of 500 men; they lived in a tented camp at English Bay, and, together with some hundred British technical staff and supervisors, ate some seventy-two tons of food a month. Since most of them were fond of curry and spices,

some outlandish stores-demands found their way back to London:
one order for 200 lbs of garlic, for instance, cleared the entire stocks
in Covent Garden. One quartermaster, with misguided enthusiasm, ordered a large number of cases of Angostura bitters,
believing they were spices.

The project itself presented formidable problems. A hundred
thousand tons of rock had to be cleared away in order to level the
main site at English Bay, and there the principal buildings went
up – the transmitting and receiving stations, and a large new power
station which was to supply the whole British community not only
with electricity but also with fresh water, the waste heat from its
generators being harnessed to distil sea water.

Yet the English Bay complex, extensive as it was, formed only
part of the Ministry's task. Quite apart from it (and from two
separate aerial farms, one for transmitting and one for receiving),
they had to create an entire new village in which to house the radio
men and their families. The site chosen was at Muriel Avenue,
almost in the middle of the island; but the village was called by the
older and more evocative name of Two Boats, just nearby. A
cluster of bungalows, made mainly from prefabricated, termite-
proof sections, and gaily coloured orange and blue, gradually
emerged from the scrub and clinker, to be followed eventually by
a shop, bakery, laundry, clubhouse, swimming bath and school.
Twenty miles of new roads, eight miles of water-mains and twelve
miles of electric cables were needed to complete the project.

By 1966 the first full-scale broadcasting tests were being carried
out, and today the Atlantic Relay Station is on the air for some
twenty-two hours a day, carrying the B.B.C. world service in
English, the African service in Hausa, the French Language service
for French-speaking parts of Africa, and the Latin American service
in Spanish and Portuguese. Many of the programmes are relayed
directly from London, but others are broadcast from tape-
recordings flown out to the island, and considerable skill is needed to
weave the various sources together without leaving perceptible gaps.

The arrival of the B.B.C. finally put paid to Cable and Wireless's
long-standing informal reign on Ascension. In 1964 the Colonial

Office in London appointed a full-time Administrator to co-ordinate all the separate interests on the island, and San, the old Mountain hospital, was brought back into service as the official residence.

With the population swollen to 1400, and the administrative problems of running the island so enormously increased, some such move was clearly inevitable. Nevertheless to old Cable hands it was a disaster, for it meant the end of so many of the things they had cherished – not least the almost complete freedom from rules and the *cachet* of serving in, and more or less owning, a place of which most people had never even heard.

Meanwhile, however, the importance of Cable and Wireless's own role on Ascension was being enormously increased by the construction of two more space stations, one built under the auspices of the United States National Aeronautics and Space Administration (NASA), and the other *for* NASA by Cable and Wireless in conjunction with Marconi.

During the Mercury and Gemini space programmes NASA had used an effective but conventional system of communications for keeping track of its orbiting capsules, relying mainly on high-frequency radio and coaxial cables. For the far more ambitious Apollo programme, however, an altogether better and more reliable system was needed. The answer lay in microwave communication through satellites in synchronous earth orbit – that is, satellites parked in space 22,300 miles above the Equator, where they revolve round the earth's axis at the same speed as the earth itself, and therefore hover above the same spot indefinitely.

In July 1965 NASA proposed to Cable and Wireless that the company should establish and run an earth station on Ascension. Its function would be to pass data back and forth between the NASA tracking station, also to be built on the island, and Andover, in Maine, via a satellite in orbit over the Atlantic. Both stations were urgently needed as part of the chain that would support the Apollo moon programme.

NASA gave Cable and Wireless a definite order for an earth station costing £1.1 million in October 1965, with the proviso that seven voice or data channels would be ready for use within eleven months. Cable and Wireless appointed Marconi as its electrical engineering contractors, and the two firms began work at once.

From the start the project was conducted with the thoroughness of a military operation, and progress was continuously monitored by computer so that possible delays could be pin-pointed and forestalled. A site for the earth station was chosen on Donkey Plain, a level, rocky wilderness surrounded by a bowl of hills which effectively screen the place from all the other electronic chatter on the island. But it was decided that, rather than merely send out the parts, the whole station should be built and tested at Rivenhall, in England, before being dismantled and shipped to Ascension.

As soon as possible, Cable and Wireless began the civil engineering needed on the island – the construction of air-conditioned buildings at the site, a separate power-house, concrete foundations for the 42-foot dish aerial, and, a mile away, the building for the bore-sight which would be used for testing the aerial and checking its alignment.

Round-the-clock work was adopted both on Ascension and at Rivenhall. The aerial was erected during July 1966 and tested over a six-week period (during which, incidentally, it was inspected by the Duke of Edinburgh, who had visited Ascension for a day during 1957); being found satisfactory, it was then dismantled and carefully packed into crates, each part labelled to facilitate speedy re-building on the site.

The specially-chartered MV *Flut* left Felixstowe on 23 July and forty installation engineers followed by air. Allowing for the time taken by the voyage, they knew they would have only seven weeks to install and commission the station.

By 6 August the vessel was off Georgetown. Twenty-four hours later unloading had been completed. The ten-ton aerial frame, two transmitter cabins, control consoles and endless cases of test gear were hauled up to Donkey Plain, and the assembly of the huge jig-saw began. By the end of August the station was substantially complete, and on 9 September, amid intense excitement, it began to pick up and lock on to the beacon signal from the Early Bird Atlantic satellite.

On 19 September – two days before the deadline – the Ascension earth station was ready for service. Early tests were complicated by the fact that the Intelsat II Atlantic satellite, which should have been in synchronous orbit overhead, had gone berserk and was racing round the earth in a huge elliptical orbit, so that it was available for only short periods each time it went past. All the same, on 11 November 1966 Cable and Wireless in London received a triumphant telex message from Ascension: FIRST STATION WITH SOLID LOCK ON INTELSAT II WITH CLEAR SPEECH WITH ANDOVER.

The last station in the Apollo network to be given the go-ahead, Ascension was the first into action, and it was officially opened in February 1967 by Mr Henry Eggers, the company's Managing Director.

Meanwhile the NASA tracking station had gone up with equal speed high on the Devil's Ashpit, towards the south-east corner of the island. There two separate thirty-foot aerials were built, one specifically for the Apollo missions, and one for tracking deep-space probes. As with the Eastern Test Range, the equipment has since been continuously up-dated; but between them the Devil's Ashpit and Donkey Plain played an indispensable part in the exploration of the moon.

Every Apollo flight depended for its safety and success on the performance of NASA's global communications system. Wherever the spacecraft might be, and whichever way the earth might be facing, it was essential that commands and messages should pass instantly between the capsule and Mission Control in Houston, Texas. Ascension formed one vital link in the communication chain, and Cable and Wireless's earth station performed faultlessly during every Apollo mission.

SEA CREATURES

It is nine o'clock, two hours after dark. The night air is hot and soft. At one's back the conical humps of the extinct volcanoes poke up black against the brilliant stars; in front the sea glitters restlessly under the moon. The sand of the beach glows white, and as each long wave comes in it explodes with a crash into a mass of sparkling, grey-white foam that boils its energy away and sucks back with a hiss down the steeply-sloping shelf.

Another roller booms and dies, and another. Sparks of phosphorescence dart in shoals about the surf. Then, as the undertow roars back, a black lump is left on the gleaming, slicked-down sand at the water's edge. Was there a rock there before?

More waves break over it, alternately hiding it and leaving it exposed. Then at last the lump moves, and resolves itself into a turtle, which lowers its head to the sand and stays motionless for a whole minute, as though checking to make certain that its great journey has brought it to the proper shore.

Overhead satellites in earth orbit are passing at 17,000 miles per hour. From the tops of the volcanic hills the radar aerials lock on to them and track them across the sky until they go down over the eastern horizon. Every few minutes, with a *click* and a *tock*, an antenna turns back westward to greet some new arrival as it comes up over the rim of the world. But here on the beach one of the most primitive creatures on earth, a creature that has hardly evolved in twenty million years, is dragging her bulky body up the sand at half a mile an hour, to bury her eggs and then slip back into the sea. She will never set eyes on her eggs or see her young, but that does not deter her. A hundred years hence she may still be coming to this same moonlit beach to propagate her kind in this primeval way.

Up she comes – a sea monster four feet long and weighing five hundred pounds. Heaving that weight up the beach, she leaves a track like that of a small caterpillar tractor: having plodded clear of the tide-line, she hunts out a patch of sand just damp enough for her liking, and then, with her front flippers, she begins to dig.

Each stroke sends a spurt of sand flying yards behind her. She works in bursts – three or four strokes, then a pause, and occasionally a deep, rasping breath. By turning a little every minute or two, she gradually works herself down until she is in a pit six feet across and eighteen inches deep. Tears well out over her leathery cheeks to rinse her eyes clear of the flying sand.

The excavation of the body pit takes some twenty minutes. Then comes a long pause. For five or even ten minutes the turtle lies motionless, with the moon glittering on her domed, segmented shell. There is something infinitely ancient about the rhythm of her nesting: the bursts of energy, the slow, heavy movements, the long, inert waits.

At last she stirs again, and with her hind flippers starts to dig the egg-pit. Since she is now working behind and underneath her tail, she cannot see what she is doing. She does not even try to look round, but with wonderfully accurate and delicate movements scoops out a small cylindrical hole about a foot wide and nine inches deep.

Down goes each leathery flipper in turn, quivering as it gently feels and tests the shape of the cavity. Then it digs with a quick circular sweep and comes up cupped like a hand, carrying a load of sand. Back on the rim of the hole, it flicks the load out sideways, and down goes the opposite flipper.

If the sand is too dry, the walls of the egg-pit collapse. The turtle soon senses what has happened, and although she may persevere through one or two falls, she will decamp altogether if they persist, and start somewhere else.

When the pit is at last ready, there comes another pause. Then the turtle places her hind flippers neatly together, waits once more, and begins to lay. The eggs are white and round, rather smaller than those of a chicken, with a tough but pliable shell. They come out in clutches, three, four or even five at a time, until a heap of 100 or 150 fills the little pit. By now the turtle is oblivious of her surroundings. Early on, when she has just left the sea, she is easily disturbed by noise or alien movement; but by the time she is laying one can walk round her, talk, shine torches, take flashlight photographs and even sit on her, and she will carry on regardless.

Her final task is to bury the clutch, which she does by sweeping sand over it with her front flippers until not only the egg-pit but the body-pit as well has been filled in. As she works, she gradually pulls herself forward, so that the depression which finally remains is several feet from the nest, and the exact position of the eggs is concealed. Again, there are frequent pauses, and much wheezing and grunting. Finally she lumbers down the beach again and lets a wave carry her back into the ocean.

Chelonia mydas, the giant green turtle, is easily the most mysterious of the creatures that frequent Ascension. I have left detailed description of its habits to the end, for only in the past few years have men begun to understand its curious behaviour.

Virtually all that the Marines knew about the turtles was that they appeared obligingly every December, and began coming ashore to nest. Where they went between nesting seasons, nobody knew. As a gesture towards conservation the garrison generally observed the rule that turtles must be allowed to finish laying before being turned; but few people realised that every turtle, given the chance, would make three or four different nests in a single season – and so ignorance prevented thousands of eggs from being laid.

It is hardly surprising that the annual depredations brought about a slow but ultimately drastic reduction in the number of turtles caught. From the record bag of 1500 in 1829, the total fell to 160 in 1867 and only 122 in 1868. The decline brought an anxious note from the Lords Commissioners of the Admiralty asking how output could be increased, and, on the island, an order laying down that

Ships arriving at Ascension during the Turtle Season or

remaining there during any part of the season are never to salute nor are they to exercise their great guns with powder in the neighbourhood of the island, as it is supposed that the decrease in the annual yield of Turtle recently experienced is partly attributable to the noise caused thereby.

Restrictions on firing stayed in force throughout the naval occupation, and Clause XVIII of the Port Regulations of 1923 still reads: 'No person shall fire or cause to be fired any Firearms within the Territorial Waters or on Land of the Island during the Turtle Season.'

Alas, the prohibitions proved futile: the Admiralty never discovered any means of increasing the harvest, and it was not until 1960 – long after large-scale turtle-turning had ceased on Ascension - that any real progress was made towards solving the mysteries of *chelonia*'s life.

In that year Harold Hirth, a biologist from the University of Florida, began a programme of tagging which has proved conclusively that the turtles which nest on Ascension return between breeding seasons to the coast of Brazil, some 1400 miles away to the west. Fascinating though it was, this new information raised almost more problems than it solved. The most tantalising question – still not satisfactorily answered – is how the turtles find their way to Ascension at all. Their target is about seven miles wide; but to them, as they set out from Brazil, it is no more than a microscopic, invisible dot way out in an immensity of ocean.

In his book *The Turtle* Dr Archie Carr, the world's leading authority on the subject, discusses several possible methods of navigation, among them dead reckoning, celestial observation, and the use of the earth's natural magnetism and of the Coriolis Force, whereby birds and mammals may, in theory, be able to tell whether they are moving northwards or southwards. But the explanation which he most favours is that the turtles can taste or smell some chemical emanation which the island gives off: having been imprinted with it at birth, the first time they took to the water (just as salmon are thought to be imprinted with the taste of the river in which they were hatched), they naturally follow it back to its source.

As Dr Carr points out, the idea seems far-fetched, to say the least. How can the taste given off by one relatively small lump of rock still be present in appreciable strength after 1400 miles of dilution? The factor most in favour of the idea is that the South Equatorial Current flows steadily, throughout the year, straight from Ascension to Brazil, and so could in theory carry the elusive scent. But even if it does, a turtle must have amazingly delicate powers of discrimination to be able to decide, from hour to hour, whether the taste is growing stronger or weaker, or staying the same, and whether, therefore, it is travelling in the right or wrong direction.

In an attempt to discover the turtles' secret Dr Carr has made numerous experiments in Brazil, in the Caribbean and on Ascension, attaching balloons and miniature radios to their shells, and fitting them up with telemetry floats which send back data about speed, course, and position to listening-posts on land. So far, however, the tests have produced no conclusive evidence.

However they manage to steer, the turtles set off, every second or third year, on their great migration. Once they have left Brazil, they must live entirely off their own body-fat, for there is nothing for them to eat within hundreds of miles of Ascension: nowhere near the island is there shallow water of the kind in which turtles habitually feed.

Once they reach their destination, they cruise up and down off-shore, mating and awaiting a suitable moment to land. But here another mystery arises: the eggs which the turtle is about to lay are already fertilised and fully formed inside her, so that the present mating must be for her *next* season's production, in two or three years' time, or even the one after that.

The males scarcely ever venture ashore, but apparently cruise out to sea for months at a time, while the nesting season lasts. The females, always coming in at night, are often dashed against the rocks that guard the entrances to the nesting beaches, and many arrive with their shells cracked or torn. Tagging has shown that for their second and third nests many return to the same beach, and that the average interval between successive visits is about fourteen days. During the intervals the females presumably cruise up and down some distance out to sea, like the males: the water is usually too rough for them to stay close inshore with any safety. At last, after making three or four landings and laying perhaps 500 eggs altogether, they launch themselves for the last time and allow the current to carry them off, back the way they have come.

The performance of the babies is in some ways even more extraordinary. After an incubation period of some sixty days they hatch from the eggs and erupt out of the sand. Then, by a process not yet fully understood, they decide where the sea is and set off towards it, even though it may be out of their sight and several hundred yards away.

On Ascension there is at least one record of baby turtles emerging from the sand and marching straight for a power house at the back of the beach, apparently attracted by the noise of the generator; and the sound and smell of the sea may well play a part in the orientation process. But several different experiments have strongly suggested that the most important influence is light, and that the light coming from over the sea, being slightly bluer and greener than light from anywhere else, draws the turtles towards it.

Only about half the eggs laid hatch, and of the babies that do emerge the vast majority are eaten by predatory birds or fish. The mortality rate is phenomenal, but not exactly known, for – another mystery – no sooner are the turtles born than they disappear for a year or more.

At birth they weigh only two or three ounces, and their shells are only a couple of inches across. Those that are not eaten launch out (it is presumed) into the open sea and let themselves be carried by the current away towards Brazil. At this stage of their lives their diet is almost certainly animal (later they become vegetarians); but what they eat is unknown, for no food is available anywhere near Ascension.

Much about the green turtles, then, is still obscure. But an ambitious venture started on Grand Cayman Island in the Caribbean in 1966 may well produce answers to some of the questions. There, a firm called Mariculture has established the first-ever turtle farm, the aim being to produce turtles for the world market by careful husbandry rather than by the indiscriminate slaughter that has prevailed hitherto. Though primarily commercial, the experiment should prove of considerable value to conservation, for the company's hope is that, by turning-out a regular supply of turtle-products, they will take the pressure off the wild population and reduce the depredations made on it by poachers.

It is too early to know whether the experiment will succeed. But the initial results have been encouraging. From a batch of 15,000 eggs flown from Ascension in 1969, the firm obtained a hatch-rate of over eighty per cent, and from the hatchlings a survival rate (so far) of over fifty per cent – an immense improvement over anything normally achieved in the wild.

For the moment Ascension's turtle colony seems safe. Dr Carr estimates its numbers as possibly 10,000 strong, of which perhaps 3000 visit the island in a single year. In the old days every one was in some danger of being turned and eaten. Today the worst fate that can befall them is the indignity of having tags put into their leathery flippers or telemetry floats attached to their nerveless shells – and either, surely, is better than being shipped upside-down all the way to England and being made into soup for those still more unfeeling brutes, the Lords of the Admiralty.

Ascension's sea-birds, though less inscrutable, are even more attractive. They too have survived all the rigours of the human occupation, and although most of them have been driven by the wild cats to seek sanctuary on Boatswain Bird Island or the offshore stacks that are cut off from the mainland, they remain one of the island's most striking features.

The only detailed study made of the sea birds was carried out by members of the British Ornithologists' Union, who spent about eighteen months on Ascension between October 1957 and May 1959. Their leader, Bernard Stonehouse, gave an entertaining general account of the expedition in his book *Wideawake Island*; but this, unfortunately, soon went out of print, and his colleagues' specialised reports on the various species have appeared only in the journal *Ibis*.

As the early travellers' accounts all make clear, the plains of Ascension were once inhabited by immense numbers of birds, and even in their archaic descriptions one can recognise many of today's species. Van Linschoten's birds 'of the bignesse of young Geese', that 'came by thousands flying about our ships' in 1589 must have been boobies, and many of those that Peter Mundy saw in 1656 are clearly identifiable. The 'smalle sortt, very white, of the shape and bignesse of a white turtle dove' were fairy terns; the 'sortt called hewers, because they ly hovering over the water to descry their prey, as our country hewers in the West stand on the hills to discern the pilchard' were frigates or man-of-war birds – 'long-winged, cloven-footed, forcke-tayled. They soare exceeding high and steddy.' The gulls 'like mangas de veludo (velvett sleeves), their bodies white, the tops of their wings blacke' were obviously wideawake or sooty terns.

Besides these, however, Mundy found one strange anomaly. Some of his party ascended the Mountain and returned with

halfe a dozen of a strange kind of fowle, much bigger than our sterlings ore stares: collour gray or dappled, white and blacke feathers intermixed, eies red like rubies, wings very imperfitt, such as wherewith they cannott raise themselves from the ground. They were taken running, in which they are exceeding swift, helping themselves a little with their wings (as it is said of the estridge), shortt billed, cloven footed, thatt can neither fly nor swymme. It was more than ordinary dainety meatt, relishing like a roasting pigge.

In view of Mundy's general accuracy, Stonehouse accepted that this description was probably a good one, and that the birds – though they could have been young wideawakes – were probably some kind of flightless rail. How they reached Ascension is a mystery that will probably never be solved. But a small black flightless rail still exists on Inaccessible Island (part of the Tristan da Cunha group), and during the B.O.U.'s time on Ascension its members discovered the skull of a rail at the bottom on a fumarole. Also, the expedition came across a juvenile moorhen which had evidently been forced down by exhaustion during a long migration. Thus it seems possible that rails once flew to Ascension, lived there so long that they lost the power of flight, and still existed in the seventeenth century, even though there has been no record of any since.

The rats which came ashore from wrecks must have made some inroads into the sea-bird population, but when the British garrison arrived in 1815 huge colonies still occupied the western plains. During the next fifty years, however, the outward spread of wild cats from the settlement gradually drove them off. In 1836 Lieutenant George Bedford surveyed the island and on his chart marked six separate 'fairs', or breeding grounds – three of wide-awakes, one of boobies, and two of 'gannets' (presumably also boobies); but by about 1860 all the species except the wideawakes had departed to the safety of Boatswain Bird Island and the offshore stacks.

Today great white patches of guano, splashed and streaked over the rocks, are all that remain of the booby and gannet fairs. But on the south-west corner of the island immense numbers of wide-awakes (*Sterna fuscata*) still nest on the bare, rocky ground. The B.O.U. expedition estimated their total at 750,000, and attributed their successful defiance of the cats to the fact that they leave the island altogether for several months out of every ten-month breeding cycle. Whereas the other birds are present all the time, and therefore exposed to continuous predation, the wideawakes, by disappearing out to sea, leave the cats without their main food supply for three months at a time, so that starvation regularly depletes the predators numbers.

Even so, the wideawakes' survival is astonishing, for the naval garrison repeatedly robbed them of colossal quantities of eggs. Captain Brandreth, who organised the island's water supply in the

1830s, reported that in one week 120,000 eggs were collected, and that the collecting season lasted between one and two months. The Marines devised a simple method of ensuring that all the eggs they took were fresh: they cleared an area of ground and marked it out into squares with string or tape, and then, returning next day, could be sure that all the eggs within the marked areas were new. Sometimes each square was marked with a board bearing the owner's name, and during the early 1900s it became fashionable to be photographed in the middle of the fairs, surrounded by birds and (if possible) holding several.

Compared with the gargantuan human consumption, the feline depredations seem to have been relatively small. The B.O.U. team estimated that the number of chicks taken by cats was between 10,000 and 20,000 every season, and concluded that this was not a serious threat to the species' survival.

Now that the cats have been much reduced by poisoning, and the humans take scarcely any eggs, there must be a good chance that the number of wideawakes will pick up again. Even at their present strength they are an amazing sight – thousands upon thousands of black-and-white blobs dotted over the clinker as far as the eye can see, each no more than a couple of feet from the next, and all neatly aligned in the direction of the trade wind. Although most will not allow themselves to be handled, the majority take little notice of an intruder, hovering (if they take off at all) close overhead and screeching, but not pressing home any attack. In flight they are as graceful as large swallows, and the noise of them calling as they head for the fairs at night on their seasonal return from the ocean is not easily forgotten.

After the wideawakes, Ascension's next most numerous species is the black noddy (*Anous tenuirostris*), of which some 75,000 were thought to be on or around the island at the time of the B.O.U. survey. Yet, although of considerable interest to ornithologists, the noddies are a dull proposition for casual observers, for they live on the remote cliffs and appear only as slim, dark shadows flitting about the coast.

Far more attractive is the wideawakes' relative, the fairy tern

(*Gygis alba*). Snowy white all over, except for its black beak, eyes and feet, it is so delicately built that its wings are translucent, the bones showing dark against the sky as though in an X-ray. The fairy terns (some 2000 altogether) also nest on inaccessible cliffs, but they possess a charming curiosity which makes them familiar to Ascension's clinker-crawlers: anyone who walks to Letter Box is liable to have several of them keeping him company for much of the way, fluttering along no more than a yard or two from his head.

No such charm can be ascribed to the boobies – relatives of the gannet which live up to their name by wearing on their faces a look of exceptional foolishness perpetually tinged by anxiety. Of the three kinds present the most common are the white or masked boobies (*Sula dactylatra*), estimated by the B.O.U. to number 9000. Brown boobies (*Sula leucogaster*) numbered some 2000, and the red-footed boobies (*Sula sula*) only thirty.

Since the boobies generally fish out of sight of land, and scarcely nest on the main island, they are not much in evidence except when they speed along the coast flying fast and straight. Their main stronghold is Boatswain Bird Island, and after some fifteen months of intermittent observation there members of the B.O.U. produced fascinating records of their behaviour. Many of the boobies' ritual postures – sky-pointing, head-wagging, bowing, bill-touching and bill-hiding among them - were thoroughly analysed and interpreted for the first time. It seems strange that birds with such a highly developed social code should be so feckless over the vital business of reproduction. The B.O.U. team found that they became attached to the bare patches of rock on which they nested, rather than to their eggs, and that if an egg rolled off one pair's particular territory further than a bill's length, they would ignore it.

By far the largest of the birds are the frigates, or men-of-war (*Fregata aquila*), a species peculiar to Ascension. Mainly black, with forked tail, huge span, and angular, bent-back wings, they are somehow reminiscent of pterodactyls, and their gaunt silhouettes invest Ascension's skies with a trace of prehistoric magic.

They, too, are well established on Boatswain Bird Island, the colony numbering some 2,000 birds. The males, which sport a huge, brilliant red pouch beneath their beaks, have an elaborate courtship ritual, here described by Bernard Stonehouse:

> Lone males on their sites respond violently to females passing overhead. As the female hovers or sweeps past, the male leans on his tail with body almost upright, beak pointing vertically into the air and wings fully extended along the ground. With gular sac fully inflated he throbs rhythmically and shakes from side to side, vibrating his wings and clapping his beak noisily. . . . Landed, the female bobs her head repeatedly in front of the male, pressing forward into his chest or axilla and becoming enfolded in his wings. The two clap beaks, shuffle and circle on the nest site, pick up and drop nesting material and lunge with their beaks at neighbours.

Not all the frigate's habits are so friendly. One of the least sociable is cannibalism: Dr Stonehouse found that adult birds gobbled up any chicks other than their own, and that 'smaller chicks were invariably eaten by neighbours or interlopers if exposed even for a few seconds'. The frigates also harass the wretched boobies mercilessly, forcing them to drop fish which they have just caught, and themselves swooping on the spat-out food so fast that they catch it before it hits the water.

Even the delicate-looking tropic or boatswain birds (*genus Phaethon*) were revealed by the B.O.U.'s close study to be exceptionally ferocious. Two species nest on the island named after them, and on the cliffs of the main island: the red-billed (some 1000 birds) and the yellow-billed (about 2000). Since they neither stand nor walk easily, they tend to nest in holes and on ledges of cliffs, where they can fly straight in and out; and, as Dr Stonehouse recorded, possession of nesting-sites was bitterly disputed:

> The birds fought silently with beaks interlocked and wings spread, holding their positions, one inside the cavity, the other on the edge, for half an hour or more without movement. Many appeared subsequently with long gashes on head and neck, and

two adults were known to have been killed during fights over nest-sites.

This pugnacity combined with other factors to produce a high mortality rate among the chicks:

Some may have fallen accidentally from their nests or may have starved to death after the loss of both parents, but the majority which disappeared without trace are likely to have been killed by other tropic birds of either species in search of nest-sites. Of the large chicks which failed to survive, most were killed by invading birds; several which survived attack were bloodstained and wounded about the head and neck.

One of the puzzles which the B.O.U. expedition could not fully solve was that of the breeding cycles. Although some of the birds appeared to breed in the same season of each year (among them the white boobies and fairy terns), others bred at *less* than annual intervals, and so in different seasons of successive years (wideawakes, brown boobies, and black noddies), while the tropic birds bred all the year round. Since all the birds live on fish, and since there is a considerable overlap in the kinds of fish eaten, it is hard to see why the various species show such a variety of breeding cycles.

Now that the numbers of cats are being reduced on the main island, it remains to be seen whether the birds will re-colonise some of the places which they used a century ago. The great increase in the human population may prove a deterrent, but the wideawakes are living proof of what can be achieved by simply sitting tight.

Even if there is no mass return, the birds will always be an integral part of the Ascension scene. Whether or not the wideawakes are in, there are generally boobies skimming along the waves off Georgetown and frigates wheeling endlessly above the pierhead. On a reasonably still day, from anywhere on the eastern heights the raucous clamour rising from Boatswain Bird Island is clearly audible.

The sea birds, I believe, are part of the unique essence of Ascension, part of the image which people who have visited the island carry with them for the rest of their lives. No one, having known them, can forget the birds, any more than they can forget the ceaseless, hot bustle of the trade winds, the rust-red cones taking fire in the evening as the sun goes down into the Atlantic, and the turtles coming stealthily ashore under the brilliant moon.

THE PRESENT

It was inevitable that the build-up of activity would considerably change the face of the island. At the start of the space age the pier-head was enlarged. The runway of the airfield was lengthened to take big jets, and a new road, double-tracked and smoothly asphalted, was made from Command Hill, via Grazing Valley, to the NASA site 1750 feet up on the Devil's Ashpit. This – quite apart from its practical utility – meant that the hike to Letter Box could be accomplished in a couple of hours, instead of being a major, all-day expedition. Needless to say, the change mortified the old-timers who heard about it: in *their* day before the advent of cars, they had to set out before dawn and climb five miles and 2000 feet to the Mountain Settlement before they were in business at all. Then it was another six miles to Letter Box, six back to the Mountain, and five more home.

On Green Mountain itself the space age has brought greater efficiency, but no fundamental change. The present manager of the farm, Peter Critchley, took it over in 1957, and thus, with his wife Grace, has been on the island far longer than anyone else now there. A West Country farmer and former R.A.F. pilot, he responded to the challenge of agriculture on Ascension with at least as great energy, and rather greater skill, than any of his predecessors.

Although the job has many frustrations (not least the drought and the constant debilitating wind), it has its compensations, too – among them the fact that it is unique. Every normal farmer's aim is to increase production as much as he can, but Mr Critchley has to be more subtle than that. There is no point in growing a surplus of anything, since to export food would be ridiculously expensive.

Rather, he has to gear production as accurately as possible to meet the island's demand.

To this end, he has a dairy herd of about forty-five cows and followers, twenty breeding sows and some 2000 sheep. Even with the help of miniature crawler tractors, only about twenty acres of land can be cultivated (the rest is too steep); but large greenhouses in the Home Garden, new water-tanks and an irrigation system have brought about a substantial increase in vegetable production. The animals, too, have improved spectacularly, thanks mainly to the introduction of new blood. In-breeding had reduced the average number of piglets in a litter to two or three, but with the arrival of a new boar from England the average jumped to fourteen or fifteen. The dairy herd has been revived by the importation of Red Poll and Friesian bulls (among them the aptly named Mercury and Apollo), and a series of foreign rams has put new life into the sheep flock.

Until 1967 Cable and Wireless ran the farm entirely to suit themselves, subsidising it as necessary for the benefit of their staff. For the past few years, however, the subsidy has been shared by all the British organisations that now use the island. Several times it has been suggested that the farm, which is bound always to be uneconomic, should be closed down; but Cable and Wireless have always firmly resisted the idea, believing that the psychological advantages of the enterprise are at least as great as the physical advantages of the fresh food it produces.

If the farm were abandoned, the top of the Mountain would soon succumb to jungle. The paths would become choked, and the smooth, steep pastures would be invaded by scrub. Today – as throughout the period of human habitation – one of the main pleasures is to escape from the heat and dust of the plains into the cool, green world above. Families regularly go aloft to stay in one of the spare farm cottages, to walk and picnic in the wind; and if this recreation became impossible, it seems certain that the morale of the plain-dwellers would be undermined.

The Marines' century of agricultural labour is thus far from wasted, and their buildings still stand in the Mountain Settlement as solid as on the day they were finished. The original Mountain Barracks, now a dairy, still bears the regiment's crest, handsomely carved in stone, and the new Mountain Barracks (now known as the Red Lion) houses the St Helenians who work on the farm. The Critchleys live in Garden Cottage (mercifully modernised), which sits like an eyrie on the ledge and commands a stunning view of the extinct craters and lava flows, laid out as though on a relief map 2000 feet below.

The Marines' animal legacy is also still much in evidence. Large flocks of mynahs swoop chattering about the Mountain. Rabbits scuttle about the guava bushes, especially in Cricket Valley, and an occasional red-legged partridge jumps suddenly from the thickets of prickly pear or off the bare cinders. The rats and cats have been largely suppressed by efficient poisoning, but the donkeys – in spite of occasional round-ups and humane executions – are a considerable nuisance, since they eat much of the food that the sheep would otherwise get, kick the caps off water pipes, wander on to the runway of the airfield and at night infiltrate right into Georgetown, where they forage among the dustbins. One of Mr Critchley's more ambitious ideas is to get rid of the donkeys altogether and import in their place some suitable species of gazelle, which, besides browsing the otherwise useless scrub, would provide valuable fresh meat and keep away from the inhabited areas.

In the past few years a second considerable oasis of greenery has been established on the island, in and around the new village of Two Boats. Its main architect was David Stokes, the Ministry of Public Building and Works' first Grounds Maintenance Officer on Ascension.

By sheer ingenuity and persistence, he overcame the almost impossible handicaps of drought, heat, wind, excessive salinity and lack of soil to establish a thriving nursery beside the road to Georgetown. A hundred years before, John Bell had used butter firkins for striking out cuttings; Stokes used beer and Pepsi Cola cans. He had topsoil brought down from the Mountain, as well as hundreds of bamboo stems for windbreaks. For irrigation, he harnessed the effluent from Two Boats' sewage system. Modern sprays dealt with the insects that had so harassed the naval gardeners, but the donkeys still have to be kept at bay by means of conventional fences. Today hundreds of the shrubs that Stokes coaxed so carefully into life grace the new village; another small part of the volcano has been tamed. Down the hill at One Boat, a new 18-hole golf course has put the original one to shame.

Down in Georgetown enough of the original buildings survive to give a strong flavour of the past. The old stone houses in Scandal Terrace and Teapot Alley have been replaced by modern bungalows, and a new house stands on the site of Bate's cottage. But the Marine Barracks (now the Exiles' Club), the hospital, the church and the cavernous great naval store all speak loud and clear of the Royal Marines. The pierhead is still the only place on which cargo from ships can be landed, and human visitors from the sea must still negotiate the slippery Tartar Stairs, which have not changed in a century and a half.

In September 1966 Doug Rogers, one of the American contingent on the island, persuaded Major Anthony Beyts, the Acting Administrator, to call a meeting of all the people interested in forming an historical society. It so happened that Sir John Field, Governor of St Helena, was visiting Ascension at the time; he came to the meeting, agreed to become patron of the Society, and gave permission for Fort Hayes to be used as a museum. Today the Fort contains some interesting documents and a valuable collection of geological specimens. Its assortment of curious objects includes a wooden coffin discovered by F. E. Duncan, one of the St Helenian old-timers, in the lava behind Comfortless Cove, some cannon balls, bottles dating from the early 1800s onwards, an absolutely splendid Victorian fire engine, and the femur of a bulldog or bull-terrier – doubtless one of the Navy's pack of vermin dogs. Excavation of the Marines' rubbish dumps has become a popular pastime, and a huge number of bottles has been unearthed. From the size and nature of the deposits, it seems that the shepherds who lived at Palmer's were troubled by a prodigious thirst, and that the guano-hunters at English Bay subsisted almost entirely on tinned fish washed down by gin.

One of the most satisfactory features of the present century has been the unbroken association between Ascension and St Helena. 'The Saints' are a delightful people – courteous, easy-going and with a ready sense of humour. Their devious ancestry – part European, part African, part Indian – shows in their colour, which varies through every shade from black to off-white; and they talk a unique patois in which echoes of Africa are oddly but attractively married with bits of Cockney and the broad vowels of the British West Country. Many have outstanding records of long service on Ascension, and their presence is an integral part of the island scene.

Throughout all vicissitudes, Ascension has preserved intact its attraction to philatelists. Such was the hunger for the Coronation issue of 1937, for instance, that 30,000 envelopes descended on the island, each with a request for three stamps to be stuck on and post-marked. Alas, in spite of Trojan work in the little post office, only 2835 could be handled on the day of issue and in the early hours of the next morning. One of the envelopes eventually made history of a kind, for it took thirty years to reach its destination, arriving at the home of Mr George Rodell, in Hertfordshire, in December 1967.

Today the appetite for Ascension's stamps is unabated. When a Union Castle liner calls, it is not uncommon for £300 worth to be sold on board in the space of a few hours, and the island's philatelic turnover for a single year amounts to some £20,000. Ascension may be ruined, in that it has space stations, roads, driving regulations, two small supermarkets and a dentist; but stamp collectors obviously don't care.

How long the object of their fascination will remain in its present state is a matter of some dispute among geologists. According to Dr J. D. Bell, a member of the Oxford geological expedition which surveyed the island in 1964, the volcano could erupt again at any moment, with or without warning. Recent events certainly lend weight to this theory: the past ten years have brought a number of eruptions up and down the peaks of the Mid-Atlantic Ridge, from Surtsey (an entirely new island off Iceland) in the north, through the Canaries to Tristan da Cunha (which blew up in 1965) and

Bouvet Island in the South. By the law of averages (if such a thing exists), Ascension's turn could well come soon.

The reports of the Oxford expedition suggest that although parts of Ascension may be as many as one-and-a-half million years old, some of the newest lava flows may have solidified not more than a few hundred years ago. Thus the experts have by no means killed the tradition (passed on by Captain Slocum among others) that the island was still warm when men first set foot on it.

Although much is known about Ascension, much remains to be discovered. In June 1970 Storrs Olson, an American naturalist, visited the island to look for bones of rails, of the kind reported by Bernard Stonehouse a dozen years before. He found so many that he was able to reconstruct an almost complete skeleton of a bird that proved new to science. During the same visit he noticed some tiny phosphorescent shrimps in a brine pool on Shelley Beach, near Mars Bay; they, too, proved unique – a species previously unknown, whose nearest relatives occur only in caves in Cuba.

How did flightless rails reach Ascension? How did the minute shrimps get there? There are still many secrets to be unravelled on and around the lump of useless cinder, the abomination of desolation, which no one but the British could be bothered to take in hand.

SOURCES

BOOKS

Africa Pilot, Part II. H.M. Stationery Office, 1922.

ALBUQUERQUE, ALFONSO D', *Commentaries, Vol 1.* Translated from the Portuguese edition of 1774 by W. de Gray Birch, Hakluyt Society, 1875.

ALLEN, LT. WILLIAM, R.N., *Picturesque Views in the Island of Ascension,* London, 1835.

AVEZAC-MACAYA, M.A.P. D', *Iles d'Afrique,* L'Univers Pittoresque, Paris, 1848.

BAGLEHOLE, K. C., *A Century of Service,* Bournehall Press, 1969.

Barlow's Journal, 1659–1703, Transcribed by B. Lubbock, London, 1934.

BARROS, JOAO DE, *Da Asia,* Vol. 1, first published 1552.

BEAULIEU, AUGUSTIN DE, *Expedition to the East Indies, 1619–22,* account in 'A Complete Collection of Voyages and Travels' by John Harris, London, 1744.

BOUGAINVILLE, LOUIS, DE, *A Voyage Round the World,* 1766–69, London, 1772.

BOXER, C. R., *The Portuguese Seaborne Empire, 1414–1825,* Hutchinson, 1969.

CARR, ARCHIE, *The Turtle,* Cassell, 1968. (First published in America by Doubleday under the title *So Excellent a Fishe.*)

CARSON, RACHEL, *The Sea Around Us,* Staples Press, 1951.

CHURCHILL, A. and J., *A Collection of Voyages and Travels,* London, 1752.

COOK, JAMES, *Cook's Voyages,* first published 1777.

COX, JOHN GEORGE, *Cox and the Juju Coast,* Ellison & Co., 1968.

CRAVEN, W. F. and CATE, J. L., (Editors) *The United States Army Airforces in World War II,* Vols 1, 2 and 7.

DAMPIER, WILLIAM, (ed. John Masefield), *Voyage to New Holland 1699–1701*, E. Grant Richards, 1906.

DARWIN, CHARLES, *Geological Observations on the Volcanic Islands visited during the Voyage of H.M.S. Beagle*, London, 1844.

DARWIN, CHARLES, *Diary of the Voyage of H.M.S. Beagle*, ed. N. Barlow, London, 1933.

DE LA CAILLE, ABBE, *Journal Historique du Voyage fait au Cap de Bonne-Espérance*, Paris, 1763.

ELLIS, A. B., *West African Islands*, Chapman & Hall, 1885.

ELWOOD, MRS. A. K., *Narrative of a Journey Overland from England to India 1825–28*, London, 1830.

FORD, E. H., *The History and Postage Stamps of Ascension Island*, privately published, 1933.

FORSTER, GEORGE, *A Voyage Round the World in H.M. Sloop Resolution*, London, 1777.

GERBAULT, ALAIN, *In Quest of the Sun*, Hodder & Stoughton, 1930.

GILL, MRS. DAVID, *Six Months in Ascension*, John Murray, 1878.

GOES, DAMIAN DE, *Cronica do Rei D. Manuel*. Vols 1 and 2, first published 1566–67.

GRAVES, CHARLES, *The Thin Red Lines*, Standard Art Book Co., 1946.

GREEN, LAWRENCE G., *Islands Time Forgot*, Putnam, 1962.

HARDY, ALISTER, *Great Waters*, Collins, 1967.

HISCOCK, ERIC, *Around the World in Wanderer III*.

HOLMAN, JAMES, *A Voyage Round the World*, Vol. 1, London, 1834.

LATROBE, C. I., *Journal of a Visit to South Africa*, London, 1821.

LEONARD, JOHN, *The Postage Stamps of Ascension*, Harris, 1958.

LESSON, P., *Voyage autour du Monde, 1822–25*, Paris, 1839.

LUCAS, SIR CHARLES, *The Empire at War*, Vol. 4, Oxford, 1925.

MUNDY, G. C., *Journal of a Tour in India*, John Murray, 1833.

MUNDY, PETER, *The Travels of Peter Mundy*, Vol. 5, 1650–67, Hakluyt Society, 1936.

NAVARRETE, FRIAR DOMINGO, ed. J. S. Cummins, *Travels and Controversies, 1618–86*, Vol. 2, Cambridge University Press, 1962.

OSBECK, PETER, *A Voyage to China and the East Indies*, London, 1771.

OSORIO DA FONSECA, JERONIMO, trans. J. Gibbs, *The History of the Portugese*, Book 2, London, 1752.

OVINGTON, J., *A Voyage to Suratt in the Year 1689*, London, 1696.

PACKER, JOHN E., *Ascension Island – a Concise Handbook*, privately printed, 1968.

RAMUSIO, G. B., *Raccolta di Viaggi*, Venice, 1563.

ROSKILL, S. W., *The War at Sea 1939–45*, Vols 2 and H.M.3, Stationery Office, 1960.

SLOCUM, JOSHUA, *Sailing Alone Around the World*, first published 1900.

STONEHOUSE, BERNARD, *Wideawake Island*, Hutchinson, 1960.

STRUYS, JAN, trans. J. Morison, *The Voyages of Jan Struys*, London, 1684.

THOMSON, C. WYVILLE, *The Atlantic: A Preliminary Account of the Voyage of H.M.S. Challenger*, Vol. 2, 1877.

THOMSON, C. WYVILLE, *The Challenger Expedition*, Vol. 1, London, 1884.

VAN LINSCHOTEN, JOHN HUYGHEN, from the Old English translation of 1598, *Voyage to the East Indies*, Hakluyt Society, 1885.

WARD, W. E. F., *The Royal Navy and the Slavers*, Allen & Unwin, 1969.

WATTS, C. C., *In Mid-Atlantic*, S.P.C.K., 1936.

WEBSTER, W. H. B., *Voyage of the Chanticleer, 1828–30*, London, 1834.

WILD, FRANK, *Shackleton's Last Voyage*, Cassell, 1923.

MAGAZINES AND PERIODICALS

African Islands – Ascension Island. Treaty Series No. 77, Cmnd 867, H.M.S.O., 1959.

ASHMOLE, N. P., 'The Black Noddy *(Anous tenuirostris)* on Ascension Island', *Ibis* 103b (1962).

ASHMOLE, N. P., 'The Biology of the Wideawake or Sooty Tern *(Sterna fuscata)* on Ascension Island', *Ibis* 103b (1962).

ATKINS, F. B., *et. al.* 'Oxford Expedition to Ascension Island', *Nature* Vol. *204* (1964).

ATKINS, F. B., *et al.*, 'Eruption Mechanisms on Ascension Island', *Proc. Geol. Soc.* London No. 1626, p. 145 (1965).

ATKINS, F. B., *et al.*, 'The Occurrence of Obsidian and other Natural Glass on Ascension Island', *Proc. Geol. Soc.* London No. 1641, p. 171 (1967).

BAINES, T., 'The Island of Ascension', *The Leisure Hour* (1867).

BARNARD, CAPT. F. L., *Observations on Ascension*, Eyre & Spottiswoode 1864.

BEE, A. G., 'Farewell to Ascension', *Blackwoods* (April 1952).

BRANDRETH, H. R. and POWER, MRS. C., 'Communications on the Island of Ascension', *Royal Geographical Journal*, Vol. 5 (1835).

CARR, A. (with KOCH, A. L. and EHRENFELD, D. W.), 'The Problem of Open-Sea Navigation: the Migration of the Green Turtle to Ascension Island', *Journal of Theoretical Biology*, Vol. 22 No. 1 (1969).

CARR, A., 'The Navigation of the Green Turtle', *Scientific American*, Vol. 212 (1962).

CHAPIN, J. P., 'Wideawake Fair Invaded', *Natural History* (September 1946).

CHAPIN, J. P., 'The Calendar of Wideawake Fair', *The Auk*, Vol. 74 (1954).

CHAPIN, J. P., 'The Wideawake Calendar 1953–58', *The Auk*, Vol. 76 (1959).

CLARKE, LT. COL. FREDERICK J., 'Ascension Island, an Engineering Victory', *National Geographical Magazine* (May 1944).

CULLEN, J. M., 'The Pecking Response of Young Wideawake Terns (*Sterna fuscata*)', *Ibis* 103b (1962).

CUNNINGHAME, J., 'A Catalogue of Shells etc. Gathered at the Island of Ascension', *Transactions of the Royal Society*, Vol. 21 (1696).

DALY, R. A., 'The Geology of Ascension Island', *Proceedings of the American Academy of Arts and Sciences*, Vol. 60 (1924).

DORWARD, D. F., 'Comparative Biology of the White Booby and Brown Booby (Sula) at Ascension', *Ibis* 103b (1962).

DORWARD, D. F., 'Behaviour of Boobies (*Sula*)', *Ibis* 103b (1962).

DORWARD, D. F., 'The Fairy Tern (*Gygis alba*) on Ascension Island', *Ibis* 103b (1962).

DUFFEY, E., 'The Terrestrial Ecology of Ascension Island', *Journal of Applied Ecology*, Vol. 1 (1964).

GIFFORD, C. E., 'Recollections of a Naval Secretary', *Chambers Journal*, Vol. 10 (1920).

HEAWOOD, E., 'Correspondence on the Island of St Matthew', *Nature* (22 September 1928).

KINNEAR, N. B., 'Zoological Notes from the Voyage of Peter Mundy in 1655–56', *Proceedings of the Linnean Society, London*, Vol. 2 (1935).

LORD, W. B., 'Ascension Island', *Nautical Magazine*, Vol. LXX No. 6 (June 1901).

MCLACHLAN, R., 'Destructive Insects in the Island of Ascension', *Entomologists' Monthly Magazine*, No. 15 (1878).

Mission Field, The, Vol. VI, London, 1861.

MORRIS, DEBORAH, 'Ascension', *Blackwoods No. 1796* (1965).

SIMMONS, G. F., 'Sinbads of Science', *National Geographical Magazine*, Vol. 52 (1927).

STONEHOUSE, B., 'Ascension Island and the British Ornithologists' Union Centenary Expedition, 1957–59', *Ibis* 103b (1962).

STONEHOUSE, B., 'The Tropic Birds (*Phaethon*) of Ascension Island', *Ibis* 103b (1962).

STONEHOUSE, B. and S., 'The Frigate Bird (*Fregate aquila*) of Ascension Island', *Ibis* 103b (1962).

STONEHOUSE, B., 'Ascension Island', *The Geographical Magazine*, Vol. 33 No. 4 (August 1960).

TATCHELL STUDLEY, J., 'Turtle Catching and Fishing at Ascension', *Badminton Magazine* (1898).

YARHAM, E. R., 'Ascension Island – a South Atlantic Airport', *Trident*, Vol. 6, No. 59 (March 1944).

Zodiac, Vol. XVI, No. 185 (December 1923). Ascension Number.

UNPUBLISHED

The main unpublished source is the Admiralty archives in the Public Record Office. Although many documents relating to Ascension were destroyed (as Major Ford discovered during his researches between the wars), thousands still repose there. I do not claim to have found by any means all of them.

There are also a number of naval documents on the island, and some on St Helena, many of them copies of those in London. The library at Kew Gardens has one volume of correspondence about Ascension.

Other sources include:

Bartlett's Book
Private letters
The journals of: William Davies (1798);
William Roberts (Commandant in 1816);
Thomas Dwyer (Commandant 1843–44);
Thomas Saumarez (1861);
R. H. Morgan (Commandant 1904–1908).

COMMANDING OFFICERS

1816–1922

The names of the officially-appointed commandants are inscribed on turtle-shells hanging on the walls of the Exiles' Club in Georgetown. The list below also includes those officers who filled the post temporarily.

18 March 1816	William Roberts, Flag Lt., R.N. (invalided)
26 August 1817	Lt. J. Thorn, R.N.
11 September 1819	Lt. R. Campbell, R.N.
21 March 1823	Lt.-Col. E. Nicolls, R.M.
3 November 1828	Capt. W. Bate, R.M. (died)
15 April 1838	Capt. H. Evans, R.M.
25 January 1839	Capt. R. S. Tinklar, R.M. (died)
14 September 1840	Lt. J. Wade, R.M.
7 December 1840	Lt. W. Lee, R.M.
27 April 1841	Capt. H. Bennett, R.M. (died)
9 December 1841	Lt. W. Lee, R.M.
26 July 1842	Capt. T. P. Dwyer, R.M.
18 April 1844	Lt. T. C. C. Moore, R.M.
18 May 1844	Capt. J. Fraser, R.M.A.
11 October 1844	Cdr. A. Morrell, R.N.
18 January 1847	Capt. F. Hutton, R.N.
14 October 1851	Capt. W. H. Kitchen, R.N.
1 June 1855	Capt. G. A. Seymour, R.N.
13 March 1858	Capt. W. F. Burnett, R.N. (invalided)
5 July 1861	Capt. F. L. Barnard, R.N.
5 March 1864	Lt. F. Hammond, R.N.
15 June 1864	Capt. G. G. Bickford, R.N.
25 September 1866	Capt. H. W. Hunt-Grubbe, R.N.
3 March 1867	Capt. A. Wilmshurst, R.N.
16 November 1868	Cdr. J. G. Mead, R.N.

4 May 1869	Lt. R. W. Evans, R.N.
1 October 1869	Cdr. E. F. Kirby, R.N.
15 October 1872	Cdr. J. B. Creagh, R.N.
19 January 1874	Capt. J. W. East, R.N.
8 February 1877	Capt. H. B. Phillimore, R.N.
12 December 1878	Capt. A. G. Roe, R.N.
10 September 1882	Capt. C. Parsons, R.N.
10 October 1886	Capt. R. H. Napier, R.N.
16 June 1890	Capt. R. Evans, R.N.
31 May 1893	Capt. J. G. Jones, R.N.
27 May 1896	Capt. J. E. Blaxland, R.N.
15 July 1899	Capt. C. N. A. Pochard, R.N.
13 May 1902	Capt. R. K. McAlpine, R.N.
14 March 1905	Capt. R. H. Morgan, R.M.
29 April 1908	Capt. J. Dustan, R.M.
27 April 1910	Capt. G. Carpenter, R.M.
21 April 1913	Capt. H. C. Benett, R.M.
8 June 1919	Major H. G. Grant, R.M.
15 October 1920	Major C. A. Tennyson, R.M.

Island paid off – 31 October 1922

INDEX